Lefèvre was born **George Edwin Henry** Lefèvre on January 23, 1870 in Colón, Colombia (now the Republic of Panama).[1] He was the son of Emilia Luísa María Santiago de la Ossa, sister of Jerónimo and María de la Ossa de Amador, and Henry Lefèvre (1841–1899).Henry was born in Jersey, in the Channel Islands and emigrated to the United States in his youth.For many years, Henry was the general agent of the Pacific Steamship Company American for Panama. Their son, Edwin, bore duel citizenship and was sent to the United States when he was a boy. He completed his education at Lehigh University, where he received training as a mining engineer. At the age of nineteen, however, he began his career as a journalist and eventually, became a stockbroker, as well. Following his father's death, Edwin inherited some wealth and became an independent investor. While living in Hartsdale, New York, a collection of Edwin Lefèvre's short stories were published (1901) under the title, Wall Street Stories. This was followed by several novels about money and finance, until 1908, when Lefèvre and his wife, Martha, and their children moved to a country estate in East Dorset, Vermont. In 1909, he was appointed ambassador to Spain and Italy by his native country, Panama. Lefèvre did work as a broker on Wall Street and was the financial writer for the New York Sun newspaper. He later returned to his home in Vermont where he resumed his literary work, providing short stories for magazines such as, The Saturday Evening Post, and writing novels

REMINISCENCES OF A STOCK OPERATOR

EDWIN LEFEVRE

SASA Publishing (OPC) Pvt. Ltd.
Andhra Pradesh

Reminiscences of a stock operator
Edwin Lefevre

Re-Published in 2024
Published by

SASA Publishing (OPC) Private Limited
Address is No.8-1, Neelithotti Kandriga,
Satyavedu - 517 588, Chitoor District,
Andhra Pradesh.
Tel.:9441595078
Email Id: sasapublishing@outlook.com

ISBN: 978-93-48584-72-4

Contents

Chapter I

I went to work when I was just out of grammar school. I got a job as quotation-board boy in a stockbrokerage office. I was quick at figures. At school I did three years of arithmetic in one. I was particularly good at mental arithmetic. As quotation-board boy I posted the numbers on the big board in the customers' room. One of the customers usually sat by the ticker and called out the prices. They couldn't come too fast for me. I have always remembered figures. No trouble at all.

There were plenty of other employees in that office. Of course I made friends with the other fellows, but the work I did, if the market was active, kept me too busy from ten a.m. to three p.m. to let me do much talking. I don't care for it, anyhow, during business hours.

But a busy market did not keep me from thinking about the work. Those quotations did not represent prices of stocks to me, so many dollars per share. They were numbers. Of course, they meant something. They were always changing. It was all I had to be interested in the changes. Why did they change? I didn't know. I didn't care. I didn't think about that. I simply saw that they changed. That was all I had to think about five hours every day and two on Saturdays: that they were always changing.

That is how I first came to be interested in the behaviour of prices. I had a very good memory for figures. I could remember in detail how the prices had acted on the previous day, just before they went up or down. My fondness for mental arithmetic came in very handy.

I noticed that in advances as well as declines, stock prices were apt to show certain habits, so to speak. There was no end of parallel cases and these made precedents to guide me. I was only fourteen, but after I had taken hundreds of observations in my mind I found myself testing their accuracy, comparing the behaviour of stocks to-day with other days. It was not long before I was anticipating movements in prices. My only guide, as I say, was their past performances. I carried the "dope sheets" in my mind. I looked for stock prices to run on form. I had "clocked" them. You know what I mean.

You can spot, for instance, where the buying is only a trifle better than the selling. A battle goes on in the stock market and the tape is your telescope. You can depend upon it seven out of ten cases.

Another lesson I learned early is that there is nothing new in Wall Street. There can't be because speculation is as old as the hills. Whatever happens in the stock market to-day has happened before and will happen again. I've never forgotten that. I suppose I really manage to remember when and how it happened. The fact that I remember that way is my way of capitalizing experience.

I got so interested in my game and so anxious to anticipate advances and declines in all the active stocks that I got a little book. I put down my observations in it. It was not a record of imaginary transactions such as so many people keep merely to make or lose millions of dollars without getting the swelled head or going to the poorhouse. It was rather a sort of record of my hits and misses, and next to the determination of probable movements I was most interested in verifying whether I had observed accurately; in other words, whether I was right.

Say that after studying every fluctuation of the day in an active stock I would conclude that it was behaving as it always did before it broke eight or ten points. Well, I would jot down the stock and the price on Monday, and remembering past performances I would write down what it ought to do on Tuesday and Wednesday. Later I would check up with actual transcriptions from the tape.

That is how I first came to take an interest in the message of the tape. The fluctuations were from the first associated in my mind with upward or downward movements. Of course there is always a reason for fluctuations, but the tape does not concern itself with the why and wherefore. It doesn't go into explanations. I didn't ask the tape why when I was fourteen, and I don't ask it to-day, at forty. The reason for what a certain stock does to-day may not be known for two or three days, or weeks, or months. But what the dickens does that matter? Your business with the tape is now not tomorrow. The reason can wait. But you must act instantly or be left. Time and again I see this happen. You'll remember that Hollow Tube went down three points the other day while the rest of the market rallied sharply. That was the fact. On the following Monday you saw that the directors passed the dividend. That was the reason. They knew what they were going to do, and even if they didn't sell the stock themselves they at least didn't buy it There was no inside buying; no reason why it should not break.

Well, I kept up my little memorandum book perhaps six months. Instead of leaving for home the moment I was through with my work, I'd jot down the figures I wanted and would study the changes, always looking for the repetitions and parallelisms of behaviour learning to read the tape, although I was not aware of it at the time.

One day one of the office boys he was older than I came to me where I was eating my lunch and asked me on the quiet if I had any money.

"Why do you want to know?" I said.

"Well," he said, "I've got a dandy tip on Burlington. I'm going to play it if I can get somebody to go in with me."

"How do you mean, play it?" I asked. To me the only people who played or could play tips were the customers old jiggers with oodles of dough. Why, it cost hundreds, even thousands of dollars, to get into the game. It was like owning your private carriage and having a coachman who wore a silk hat.

"That's what I mean; play it!" he said. "How much you got?"

"How much you need?"

"Well, I can trade in five shares by putting up $5." "How are you going to play it?"

"I'm going to buy all the Burlington the bucket shop will let me carry with the money I give him for margin," he said. "It's going up sure. It's like picking up money. We'll double ours in a jiffy."

"Hold on!" I said to him, and pulled out my little dope book.

I wasn't interested in doubling my money, but in his saying that Burlington was going up. If it was, my note-book ought to show it. I looked. Sure enough, Burlington, according to my figuring, was acting as it usually did before it went up. I had never bought or sold anything in my life, and I never gambled with the other boys. But all I could see was that this was a grand chance to test the accuracy of my work, of my hobby. It struck me at once that if my dope didn't work in practice there was nothing in the theory of it to interest anybody. So I gave him all I had, and with our pooled resources he went to one of the nearby bucket shops and bought some Burlington. Two days later we cashed in. I made a profit of $3.12.

After that first trade, I got to speculating on my own hook in the bucket shops. I'd go during my lunch hour and buy or sell it never made any difference to me. I was playing a system and not a favorite stock or backing opinions. All I knew was the arithmetic of it. As a matter of fact, mine was the ideal way to operate in a bucket shop, where all that a trader does is to bet on fluctuations as they are printed by the ticker on the tape.

It was not long before I was taking much more money out of the bucket shops than I was pulling down from my job in the brokerage office. So I gave up my position. My folks objected, but they couldn't say much when they saw what I was making. I was only a kid and office-boy wages were not very high. I did mighty well on my own hook.

I was fifteen when I had my first thousand and laid the cash in front of my mother all made in the bucket shops in a few months, besides what I had taken home. My mother carried on something awful. She wanted me to put it away in the savings bank out of reach of temptation. She said it was more money than she ever heard any boy of fifteen had made, starting with nothing. She didn't quite believe it was real money. She used to worry and fret about it. But I didn't think of anything except that I could keep on proving my figuring was right. That's all the fun there is being right by using your head. If I was right when I tested my convictions with ten shares I would be ten times more right if I traded in a hundred shares. That is all that having more margin meant to me I was right more emphatically. More courage? No! No difference! If all I have is ten dollars and I risk it, I am much braver than when I risk a million, if I have another million salted away.

Anyhow, at fifteen I was making a good living out of the stock market. I began in the smaller bucket shops, where the man who traded in twenty shares at a clip was suspected of being John W. Gates in disguise or J. P. Morgan traveling incognito. Bucket shops in those days seldom lay down on their customers. They didn't have to. There were other ways of parting customers from their money, even when they guessed right. The business was tremendously profitable. When it was conducted legitimately I mean straight, as far as the bucket shop went the fluctuations took care of the shoestrings. It doesn't take much of a reaction to wipe out a margin of only three quarters of a point. Also, no welsher could ever get back in the game. Wouldn't have any trade.

I didn't have a following. I kept my business to myself. It' was a one-man business, anyhow. It was my head, wasn't it? Prices either were going the way I doped them out, without any help from friends or partners, or they were going the other way, and nobody could stop them out of kindness to me. I couldn't see where I needed to tell my business to anybody else. I've got friends, of course, but my business has always been the same a one-man affair. That is why I have always Played a lone hand.

As it was, it didn't take long for the bucket shops to get sore on me for beating them. I'd walk in and plank down my margin, but they'd look at it without making a move to grab it. They'd tell me there was nothing doing. That was the time they got to calling me the Boy Plunger. I had to be changing brokers all the time, going from one bucket shop to another. It got so that I had to give a fictitious name. I'd begin light, only fifteen or twenty shares. At times, when they got suspicious, I'd lose on purpose at first and then sting them proper. Of course after a little while they'd find me too expensive and they'd tell me to take myself and my business elsewhere and not interfere with the owners' dividends.

Once, when the big concern I'd been trading with for months shut down on me I made up my mind to take a little more of their money away from them. That bucket shop had branches all over the city, in hotel lobbies, and in near-by towns. I went to one of the hotel branches and asked the manager a few questions and finally got to trading. But as soon as I played an active stock my especial way he began to get messages from the head office asking who it was that was operating. The manager told me what they asked him and I told him my name was Edward Robinson, of Cambridge. He telephoned the glad news to the big chief. But the other end wanted to know what I looked like. When the manager told me that I said to him, "Tell him I am a short fat man with dark hair and a bushy beard!" But he described me instead, and then he listened and his face got red and he hung up and told me to beat it.

"What did they say to you?" I asked him politely.

"They said, 'You blankety-blank fool, didn't we tell you to take no business from Larry Livingston? And you deliberately let him trim us out of $700!" He didn't say what else they told him.

I tried the other branches one after another, but they all got to know me, and my money wasn't any good in any of their offices. I couldn't even go in to look at the quotations without some of the clerks making cracks at me. I tried to get them to let me trade at long intervals by dividing my visits among them all. But that didn't work.

Finally there was only one left to me and that was the biggest and richest of all the Cosmopolitan Stock Brokerage Company.

The Cosmopolitan was rated as A-1 and did an enormous business. It had branches in every manufacturing town in New England. They took my trading all right, and I bought and sold stocks and made and lost money for months, but in the end it happened with them as usual. They didn't refuse my business point-blank, as the small concerns had. Oh, not because it wasn't sportsmanship, but because they knew it would give them a black eye to publish the news that they wouldn't take a fellow's business just because that fellow happened to make a little money. But they did the next worse thing that is, they made me put up a three-point margin and compelled me to pay a premium at first of a half point, then a point, and finally, a point and a half. Some handicap, that! How? Easy! Suppose Steel was selling at 90 and you bought it. Your ticket read, normally: "Bot ten Steel at 90-1/8." If you put up a point margin it meant that if it broke 89-1/4 you were wiped out automatically. In a bucket shop the customer is not importuned for more margin or put to the painful necessity of telling his broker to sell for anything he can get.

But when the Cosmopolitan tacked on that premium they were hitting below the belt. It meant that if the price was 90 when I bought, instead of making my ticket: "Bot Steel at 90-l/8," it read: "Bot Steel at 91-1/8." Why, that stock could advance a point and a quarter after I bought it and I'd still be losing money if I closed the trade. And by also insisting that I put up a three-point margin at the very start they reduced my trading capacity by two thirds. Still, that was the only bucket shop that would take my business at all, and I had to accept their terms or quit trading.

Of course I had my ups and downs, but was a winner on balance. However, the Cosmopolitan people were not satisfied with the awful handicap they had tacked on me, which should have been enough to beat anybody. They tried to double-cross me. They didn't get me. I escaped because of one of my hunches.

The Cosmopolitan, as I said, was my last resort. It was the richest bucket shop in New England, and as a rule they put no limit on a trade. I think I was the heaviest individual trader they had that is, of the steady, every-day customers. They had a fine office and the largest and completest quotation board I have ever seen anywhere. It ran along the whole length of the big room and every imaginable thing was quoted. I mean stocks dealt in on the New York and Boston Stock Exchanges, cotton, wheat, provisions, metals everything that was bought and sold in New York, Chicago, Boston and Liverpool.

You know how they traded in bucket shops. You gave your money to a clerk and told him what you wished to buy or sell. He looked at the tape or the quotation board and took the price from there the last one, of course. He also put down the time on the ticket so that it almost read like a regular broker's report that is, that they had bought or sold for you so many shares of such a stock at such a price at such a time on such a day and how much money they received from you. When you wished to close your trade you went to the clerk the same or another, it depended on the shop and you told him. He took the last price or if the stock had not been active he waited for the next quotation that came out on the tape. He wrote that price and the time on your ticket, O.K.'d it and gave it back to you, and then you went to the cashier and got whatever cash it called for. Of course, when the market went against you and the price went beyond the limit set by your margin, your trade automatically closed itself and your ticket became one more scrap of paper.

In the humbler bucket shops, where people were allowed to trade in as little as five shares, the tickets were little slips different colors for buying and selling and at times, as for instance in boiling bull markets, the shops would be hard hit because all the customers were bulls and happened to be right. Then the bucket shop would deduct both buying and selling commissions and if you bought a stock at 20 the ticket would read 20-1/4. You thus had only 3/4 of a point's run for your money.

But the Cosmopolitan was the finest in New England. It had thousands of patrons and I really think I was the only man they were afraid of. Neither the killing premium nor the three-point margin they made me put up reduced my trading much. I kept on buying and selling as much as they'd let me. I sometimes had a line of 5000 shares.

Well, on the day the thing happened that I am going to tell

you, I was short thirty-five hundred shares of Sugar. I had seven big pink tickets for five hundred shares each. The Cosmopolitan used big slips with a blank space on them where they could write down additional margin. Of course, the -bucket shops never ask for more margin. The thinner the shoestring the better for them, for their profit lies in your being wiped. In the smaller shops if you wanted to margin your trade still further they'd make out a new ticket, so they could charge you the buying commission and only give you a run of 3/4 of a point on each point's decline, for they figured the selling commission also exactly as if it were a new trade.

Well, this day I remember I had up over $10,000 in margins.

I was only twenty when I first accumulated ten thousand dollars in cash. And you ought to have heard my mother. You'd have thought that ten thousand dollars in cash was more than anybody carried around except old John D., and she used to tell me to be satisfied and go into some regular business. I had a hard time convincing her that I was not gambling, but making money by figuring. But all she could see was that ten thousand dollars was a lot of money and all I could see was more margin.

I had put out my 3509 shares of Sugar at 105-1/4. There was another fellow in the room, Henry Williams, who was short 2500 shares. I used to sit by the ticker and call out the quotations for the board boy. The price behaved as I thought it would. It promptly went down a couple of points and paused a little to get its breath before taking another dip. The general market was pretty soft and everything looked promising. Then all of a sudden I didn't like the way Sugar was doing its hesitating. I began to feel uncomfortable. I thought I ought to get out of the market. Then it sold at

103 that was low for the day but instead of feeling more confident I felt more uncertain. I knew something was wrong somewhere, but I couldn't spot it exactly. But if something was coming and I didn't know where from, I couldn't be on my guard against it. That being the case I'd better be out of the market.

You know, I don't do things blindly. I don't like to. I never did. Even as a kid I had to know why I should do certain things. But this time I had no definite reason to give to myself, and yet I was so uncomfortable that I couldn't stand it. I called to a fellow I knew, Dave Wyman, and said to him : "Dave, you take my place here. I want you to do something for me. Wait a little before you call out the next price of Sugar, will you?"

He said he would, and I got up and gave him my place by the ticker so he could call out the prices for the boy. I took my seven Sugar tickets out of my pocket and walked over to the counter, to where the clerk was who marked the tickets when you closed your trades. But I didn't really know why I should get out of the market, so I just stood there, leaning against the counter, my tickets in my hand so that the clerk couldn't see them. Pretty soon I heard the clicking of a telegraph instrument and I saw Tom Burnham, the clerk, turn his head quickly and listen. Then I felt that something crooked was hatching, and I decided not to wait any longer. Just then Dave Wyman by the ticker, began: "Su-" and quick as a flash I slapped my tickets on the counter in front of the clerk and yelled, "Close Sugar!" before Dave had finished calling the price. So, of course, the house had to close my Sugar at the last quotation. What Dave called turned out to be 103 again.

According to my dope Sugar should have broken 103 by now.

The engine wasn't hitting right. I had the feeling that there was a trap in the neighborhood. At all events, the telegraph instrument was now going like mad and I noticed that Tom Burnham, the clerk, had left my tickets unmarked where I laid them, and was listening to the clicking as if he were waiting for something. So I yelled at him: "Hey, Tom, what in hell are you waiting for? Mark the price on these tickets 103! Get a gait on!"

Everybody in the room heard me and began to look toward us and ask what was the trouble, for, you see, while the Cosmopolitan had never laid down, there was no telling, and a run on a bucket shop can start like a run on a bank. If one customer gets suspicious the others follow suit. So Tom looked sulky, but came over and marked my tickets "Closed at 103" and shoved the seven of them over toward me. He sure had a sour face.

Say, the distance from Tom's place to the cashier's cage "wasn't over eight feet. But I hadn't got to the cashier to get my money when Dave Wyman by the ticker yelled excitedly: "Gosh! Sugar, 108!" But it was too late; so I just laughed and called over to Tom, "It didn't work that time, did it, old boy?"

Of course, it was a put-up job. Henry Williams and I together were short six thousand shares of Sugar. That bucket shop had my margin and Henry's, and there may have been a lot of other Sugar shorts in the office; possibly eight or ten thousand shares in all. Suppose they had $20,000 in Sugar margins. That was enough to pay the shop to thimblerig the market on the New York Stock Exchange and wipe us out. In the old days whenever a bucket shop found itself loaded with too many bulls on a certain stock it was a common practice to get some broker to wash down the price of that particular stock far enough to wipe out all the customers that were long of it. This seldom cost the bucket shop more than a couple of points on a few hundred shares, and they made thousands of dollars.

That was what the Cosmopolitan did to get me and Henry Williams and the other Sugar shorts. Their brokers in New York ran up the price to 108. Of course it fell right back, but Henry and a lot of others were wiped out. Whenever there was an unexplained sharp drop which was followed by instant recovery, the newspapers in those days used to call it a bucket-shop drive.

And the funniest thing was that not later than ten days after the Cosmopolitan people tried to double-cross me a New York operator did them out of over seventy thousand dollars. This man, who was quite a market factor in his day and a member of the New York Stock Exchange, made a great name for himself as a bear during the Bryan panic of '96. He was forever running up against Stock Exchange rules that kept him from carrying out some of his plans at the expense of his fellow members. One day he figured that there would be no complaints from either the Exchange or the police authorities if he took from the bucket shops of the land some of their ill-gotten gains. In the instance I speak of he sent thirty-five men to act as customers. They went to the main office and to the bigger branches. On a certain day at a fixed hour the agents all bought as much of a certain stock as the managers would let them. They had instructions to sneak out at a certain profit. Of course what he did was to distribute bull tips on that stock among his cronies and then he went in to the floor of the Stock Exchange and bid up the price, helped by the room traders, who thought he was a good sport

Being careful to pick out the right stock for that work, there was no trouble in putting up the price three or four points. His agents at the bucket shops cashed in as prearranged.

A fellow told me the originator cleaned up seventy thousand dollars net, and his agents made their expenses and then pay besides. He played that game several times all over the country, punishing the bigger bucket shops of New York, Boston, Philadelphia, Chicago, Cincinnati and St. Louis. One of his favorite stocks was Western Union, because it was so easy to move a semi active stock like that a few points up en-down. His agents bought it at a certain figure, sold at two points profit, went short and took three points more. By the way, I read the other day that that man died, poor and obscure. If he had died in 1896 he would have got at least a column on the first page of every New York paper. As it was he got two lines on the fifth.

Chapter II

Between the discovery that the Cosmopolitan Stock Brokerage Company was ready to beat me by foul means if the killing handicap of a three-point margin and a point-and-a- half premium didn't do it, and hints that they didn't want my business anyhow, I soon made up my mind to go to New York, where I could trade in the office of some member of the New York Stock Exchange. I didn't want any Boston branch, where the quotations had to be telegraphed. I wanted to be close to the original source. I came to New York at the age of 21, bringing with me all I had, twenty-five hundred dollars.

I told you I had ten thousand dollars when I was twenty, and my margin on that Sugar deal was over ten thousand. But I didn't always win. My plan of trading was sound enough and won oftener than it lost. If I had stuck to it I'd have been right perhaps as often as seven out of ten times. In fact, I always made money when I was sure I was right before I began. What beat me was not having brains enough to stick to my own game that is, to play the market only when I was satisfied that precedents favored my play. There is a time for all things, but I didn't know it. And that is precisely what beats so many men in Wall Street who are very far from being in the main sucker class. There is the plain fool, who does the wrong thing at all times everywhere, but there is the Wall Street fool, who thinks he must trade all the time. No man can always have adequate reasons for buying or selling stocks daily or sufficient knowledge to make his play an intelligent play.

I proved it Whenever I read the tape by the light of experience I made money, but when I made a plain fool play I had to lose. I was no exception, was I? There was the huge quotation board staring me in the face, and the ticker going on, and people trading and watching their tickets turn" into cash or into waste paper. Of course I let the craving for excitement get the better of my judgment. In a bucket shop where your margin is a shoestring you don't play for long pulls. You are wiped too easily and quickly. The desire for constant action irrespective of underlying conditions is responsible for many losses in Wall Street even among the professionals, who feel that they must take home some money every day, as though they were working for regular wages. I was only a kid, remember. I did not know then what I learned later, what made me fifteen years later, wait two long weeks and see a stock on which I was very bullish go up thirty points before I felt that it was safe to buy it. I was broke and was trying to get back, and I couldn't afford to play recklessly. I had to be right, and so I waited. That was in 1915. It's a long story. I'll tell it later in its proper place. Now let's go on from where after years of practice at beating them I let the bucket shops take away most of my winnings.

And with my eyes wide open, to boot! And it wasn't the only period of my life when I did it, either. A stock operator has to fight a lot of expensive enemies within himself. Anyhow, I came to New York with twenty-five hundred dollars. There were no bucket shops here that a fellow could trust. The Stock Exchange and the police between them had succeeded in closing them up pretty tight. Besides, I wanted to find a place where the only limit to my trading would be the size of my stake. I didn't have much of one, but I didn't expect it to stay little forever. The main thing at the start was to find a place where I wouldn't have to worry about getting a square deal. So I went to a New York Stock Exchange house that had a branch at home where I knew some of the clerks. They have long since gone out of business. I wasn't there long, didn't like one of the partners, and then I went to A. R. Fullerton & Co. Somebody must have told them about my early experiences, because it was not long before they all got to calling me the Boy Trader. I've always looked young. It was a handicap in some ways but it compelled me to fight for my own because so many tried to take advantage of my youth. The chaps at the bucket shops seeing what a kid I was, always thought I was a fool for luck and that that was the only reason why I beat them so often.

Well, it wasn't six months before I was broke. I was a pretty active trader and had a sort of reputation as a winner. I guess my commissions amounted to something. I ran up my account quite a little, but, of course, in the end I lost. I played carefully; but I had to lose. I'll tell you the reason: it was my remarkable success in the bucket shops!

I could beat the game my way only in a bucket shop; where I was betting on fluctuations. My tape reading had to do with that exclusively. When I bought the price was there on the quotation board, right in front of me. Even before I bought I knew exactly the price I'd have to pay for my stock. And I always could sell on the instant. I could scalp successfully, because I could move like lightning. I could follow up my luck or cut my loss in a second. Sometimes, for instance, I was certain a stock would move at least a point. Well, I didn't have to hog it, I could put up a point margin and double my money in a jiffy; or I'd take half a point. On one or two hundred shares a day, that wouldn't be bad at the end of the month, what?

The practical trouble with that arrangement, of course, was

that even if the bucket shop had the resources to stand a big steady loss, they wouldn't do it. They wouldn't have a customer around the place who had the bad taste to win all the time.

At all events, what was a perfect system for trading in bucket shops didn't work in Fullerton's office. There I was actually buying and selling stocks. The price of Sugar on the tape might be 105 and I could see a three-point drop coming. As a matter of fact, at the very moment the ticker was printing 105 on the tape the real price on the floor of the Exchange might be 104 or 103. By the time my order to sell a thousand shares got to Fullerton's floor man to execute, the price might be still lower. I couldn't tell at what price I had put out my thousand shares until I got a report from the clerk. When I surely would have made three thousand on the same transaction in a bucket shop I might not make a cent in a Stock Exchange house. Of course, I have taken an extreme case, but the fact remains that in A. R. Fullerton's office the tape always talked ancient history to me, as far as my system of trading went, and I didn't realise it.

And then, too, if my order was fairly big my own sale would tend further to depress the price. In the bucket shop I didn't have to figure on the effect of my own trading. I lost in New York because the game was altogether different. It was not that I now was playing it legitimately that made me lose, but that I was playing it ignorantly. I have been told that I am a good reader of the tape. But reading the tape like an expert did not save me. I might have made out a great deal better if I had been on the floor myself, a room trader. In a particular crowd perhaps I might have adapted my system to the conditions immediately before me. But, of course, if I had got to operating on such a scale as I do now, for instance, the system would have equally failed me, on account of the effect of my own trading on prices.

In short, I did not know the game of stock speculation. I knew a part of it, a rather important part, which has been very valuable to me at all times. But if with all I had I still lost, what chance does the green outsider have of winning, or, rather, of cashing in?

It didn't take me long to realise that there was something wrong with my play, but I couldn't spot the exact trouble. There were times when my system worked beautifully, and then, all of a sudden, nothing but one swat after another. I was only twenty-two, remember; not that I was so stuck on myself that I didn't want to know just where I was at fault, but that at that age nobody knows much of anything.

The people in the office were very nice to me. I couldn't plunge as I wanted to because of their margin requirements, but old A. R. Fullerton and the rest of the firm were so kind to me that after six months of active trading I not only lost all I had brought and all that I had made there but I even owed the firm a few hundreds.

There I was, a mere kid, who had never before been away from home, flat broke; but I knew there wasn't anything wrong with me; only with my play. I don't know whether I make myself plain, but I never lose my temper over the stock market. I never argue with the tape. Getting sore at the market doesn't get you anywhere.

I was so anxious to resume trading that I didn't lose a minute, but went to old man Fullerton and said to him, "Say, A. R., lend me five hundred dollars."

"What for?" says he. "I've got to have some money."

"What for?" he says again.

"For margin, of course," I said.

"Five hundred dollars?" he said, and frowned. "You know they'd expect you to keep up a 10 per cent margin, and that means one thousand dollars on one hundred shares. Much better to give you a credit-"

"No," I said, "I don't want a credit here. I already owe the firm something. What I want is for you to lend me five hundred dollars so I can go out and get a roll and come back."

"How are you going to do it?" asked old A. R. "I'll go and trade in a bucket shop," I told him.

"Trade here," he said.

"No," I said. "I'm not sure yet I can beat the game in this office, but I am sure I can take money out of the bucket shops. I know that game. I have a notion that I know just where I went wrong here."

He let me have it, and I went out of that office where the Boy Terror of the Bucket Shops, as they called him, had lost his pile. I couldn't go back home because the shops there would not take my business. New York was out of the question; there weren't any doing business at that time. They tell me that in the go's Broad Street and New Street were full of them. But there weren't any when I needed them in my business. So after some thinking I decided to go to St. Louis. I had heard of two concerns there that did an enormous business all through the Middle West. Their profits must have been huge. They had branch offices in dozens of towns. In fact I had been told that there were no concerns in the East to compare with them for volume of business. They ran openly and the best people traded there without any qualms. A fellow even told me that the owner of one of the concerns was a vice-president of the Chamber of Commerce but that couldn't have been in St. Louis. At any rate, that is where I went with my five hundred dollars to bring back a stake to use as margin in the office of A. R. Fullerton & Co., members of the New York Stock Exchange.

When I got to St. Louis I went to the hotel, washed up and went out to find the bucket shops. One was the J. G. Dolan Company, and the other was H. S. Teller & Co. I knew I could beat them. I was going to play dead safe carefully and conservatively. My one fear was that somebody might recognise me and give me away, because the bucket shops all over the country had heard of the Boy Trader. They are like gambling houses and get all the gossip of the professionals. Dolan was nearer than Teller, and I went there first. I was hoping I might be allowed to do business a few days before they told me to take my trade somewhere else. I walked in. It was a whopping big place and there must have been at least a couple of hundred people there staring at the quotations. I was glad, because in such a crowd I stood a better chance of being unnoticed. I stood and watched the board and looked them over carefully until I picked out the stock for my initial play.

I looked around and saw the order-clerk at the window where you put down your money and get your ticket. He was looking at me so I walked up to him and asked, "Is this where you trade in cotton and wheat?"

"Yes, sonny," says he.

"Can I buy stocks too?"

"You can if you have the cash," he said.

"Oh, I got that all right, all right," I said like a boasting boy.

"You have, have you?" he says with a smile.

"How much stock can I buy for one hundred dollars?" I asked, peeved-like. "One hundred; if you got the hundred."

"I got the hundred. Yes; and two hundred too!" I told him. "Oh, my!" he said.

"Just you buy me two hundred shares," I said sharply.

"Two hundred what?" he asked, serious now. It was business.

I looked at the board again as if to guess wisely and told him, "Two hundred Omaha." "All right!" he said. He took my money, counted it and wrote out the ticket.

"What's your name?" he asked me, and I answered, "Horace Kent."

He gave me the ticket and I went away and sat down among the customers to wait for the roll to grow.

I got quick action and I traded several times that day. On

the next day too. In two days I made twenty-eight hundred dollars, and I was hoping they'd let me finish the week out. At the rate I was going, that wouldn't be so bad. Then I'd tackle the other shop, and if I had similar luck there I'd go back to New York with a wad I could do something with.

On the morning of the third day, when I went to the window, bashful-like, to buy five hundred B. R. T. the clerk said to me, "Say, Mr. Kent, the boss wants to see you."

I knew the game was up. But I asked him, "What does he want to see me about?"

"I don't know." "Where is he?"

"In his private office. Go in that way." And he pointed to a door. I went in. Dolan was sitting at his desk. He swung around and said, "Sit down, Livingston."

He pointed to a chair. My last hope vanished. I don't know how he discovered who I was; perhaps from the hotel register.

"What do you want to see me about?" I asked him.

"Listen, kid. I ain't got nothin' again yeh, see? Nothin' at all. See?" "No, I don't see," I said.

He got up from his swivel chair. He was a whopping big guy. He said to me, "Just come over here, Livingston, will yeh?" and he walked to the door. He opened it and then he pointed to the customers in the big room. "D'yeh see them?" he asked.

"See what?"

"Them guys. Take a look at 'em, kid. There's three hundred of 'em! Three hundred suckers! They feed me and my family. See? Three hundred suckers! Then yeh come in, and in two days yeh cop more than I get out of the three hundred in two weeks. That ain't business, kid not for me! I ain't got nothin' agin yeh. Yer welcome to what ye've got. But yeh don't get any more. There ain't any here for yeh!"

"Why, I…"

"That's all. I seen yeh come in day before yesterday, and I didn't like yer looks. On the level, I didn't. I spotted yeh for a ringer. I called in that jackass there" he pointed to the guilty clerk "and asked what you'd done; and when he told me I said to him: 'I don't like that guy's looks. He's a ringer!' And that piece of cheese says: 'Ringer my eye, boss! His name is Horace Kent, and he's a rah-rah boy playing at being used to long pants. He's all right!' Well, I let him have his way. That blankety-blank cost me twenty-eight hundred dollars. I don't grudge it yeh, my boy. But the safe is locked for yeh."

"Look here " I began.

"You look here, Livingston," he said. "I've heard all about yeh. I make my money coppering suckers' bets, and yeh don't belong here. I aim to be a sport and yer welcome to what yeh pried off'n us. But more of that would make me a sucker, now that I know who yeh are. So toddle along, sonny!"

I left Dolan's place with my twenty-eight hundred dollars' profit. Teller's place was in the same block. I had found out that Teller was a very rich man who also ran up a lot of pool rooms. I decided to go to his bucket shop. I wondered whether it would be wise to start moderately and work up to a thousand shares or to begin with a plunge, on the theory that I might not be able to trade more than one day. They get wise mighty quick when they're losing and I did want to buy one thousand B. R. T. I was sure I could take four or five points out of it. But if they got suspicious or if too many customers were long of that stock they might not let me trade at all. I thought perhaps I'd better scatter my trades at first and begin small.

It wasn't as big a place as Dolan's, but the fixtures were nicer and evidently the crowd was of a better class. This suited me down to the ground and I decided to buy my one thousand B. R. T. So I stepped up to the proper window and said to the clerk, "I'd like to buy some B. R. T. What's the limit?"

> "There's no limit," said the clerk. "You can buy all you please if you've got the money."

"Buy fifteen hundred shares," I says, and took my roll from my pocket while the clerk starts to write the ticket.

Then I saw a red-headed man just shove that clerk away from the counter. He leaned across and said to me, 'Say, Livingston, you go back to Dolan's. We don't want your business."

> "Wait until I get my ticket," I said. "I just bought a little B. R. T."

"You get no ticket here," he said. By this time other clerks had got behind him and were looking at me. "Don't ever come here to trade. We don't take your business. Understand?"

There was no sense in getting mad or trying to argue, so I

went back to the hotel, paid my bill and took the first train back to New York. It was tough. I wanted to take back some real money and that Teller wouldn't let me make even one trade.

I got back to New York, paid Fullerton his five hundred, and started trading again with the St. Louis money. I had good and bad spells, but I was doing better than breaking even. After all, I didn't have much to unlearn; only to grasp the one fact that there was more to the game of stock speculation than I had considered before I went to Fullerton's office to trade. I was like one of those puzzle fans, doing the crossword puzzles in the Sunday supplement. He isn't satisfied until he gets it. Well, I certainly wanted to find the solution to my puzzle. I thought I was done with trading in bucket shops. But I was mistaken.

About a couple of months after I got back to New York an old jigger came into Fullerton's office. He knew A. R. Somebody said they'd once owned a string of race horses together. It was plain he'd seen better days. I was introduced to old McDevitt. He was telling the crowd about a bunch of Western racetrack crooks who had just pulled off some skin game out in St. Louis. The head devil, he said, was a poolroom owner by the name of Teller.

"What Teller?" I asked him. "Hi Teller; H. S. Teller."

"I know that bird," I said. "He's no good," said McDevitt.

"He's worse than that," I said, "and I have a little matter to settle with him." "Meaning how?"

"The only way I can hit any of these short sports is through their pocketbook. I can't touch him in St. Louis just now, but some day I will." And I told McDevitt my grievance.

"Well," says old Mac, "he tried to connect here in New York and couldn't make it, so he's opened a place in Hoboken. The word's gone out that there is no limit to the play and that the house roll has got the Rock of Gibraltar faded to the shadow of a bantam flea."

"What sort of a place?" I thought he meant pool room.
"Bucket shop," said McDevitt.

"Are you sure it's open?"

"Yes; I've seen several fellows who've told me about it."

"That's only hearsay," I said. "Can you find out positively if it's running, and also how heavy they'll really let a man trade?"

"Sure, sonny," said McDevitt. "I'll go myself to-morrow morning, and come back here and tell you."

He did. It seems Teller was already doing a big business and would take all he could get. This was on a Friday. The market had been going up all that week this was twenty years ago, remember and it was a cinch the bank statement on Saturday would show a big decrease in the surplus reserve. That would give the conventional excuse to the big room traders to jump on the market and try to shake out some of the weak commission-house accounts. There would be the usual reactions in the last half hour of the trading, particularly in stocks in which the public had been the most active. Those, of course, also would be the very stocks that

Teller's customers would be most heavily long of, and the shop might be glad to see some short selling in them. There is nothing so nice as catching the suckers both ways; and nothing so easy with one-point margins.

That Saturday morning I chased over to Hoboken to the Teller place. They had fitted up a big customers' room with a dandy quotation board and a full force of clerks and a special policeman in gray. There were about twenty-five customers.

I got talking to the manager. He asked me what he could do for me and I told him nothing; that a fellow could make much more money at the track on account of the odds and the freedom to bet your whole roll and stand to win thousands in minutes instead of piking for chicken feed in stocks and having to wait days, perhaps. He began to tell me how much safer the stock-market game was, and how much some of their customers made you'd have sworn it was a regular broker who actually bought and sold your stocks on the Exchange and how if a man only traded heavy he could make enough to satisfy anybody. He must have thought I was headed for some pool room and he wanted a whack at my roll before the ponies nibbled it away, for he said I ought to hurry up as the market closed at twelve o'clock on Saturdays. That would leave me free to devote the entire afternoon to other pursuits. I might have a bigger roll to carry to the track with toe if I picked the right stocks.

I looked as if I didn't believe him, and he kept on buzzing me. I was watching the clock. At n 115 I said, "All right," and I began to give him selling orders in various stocks. I put up two thousand dollars in cash, and he was very glad to get it. He told me he thought I'd make a lot of money and hoped I'd come in often.

It happened just as I figured. The traders hammered the stocks in which they figured they would uncover the most stops, and, sure enough, prices slid off. I closed out my trades just before the rally of the last five minutes on the usual traders' covering.

There was fifty-one hundred dollars coming to me. I went to cash in.

"I am glad I dropped in," I said to the manager, and gave him my tickets.

"Say," he says to me, "I can't give you all of it. I wasn't looking for such a run. I'll have it here for you Monday morning, sure as blazes."

"All right. But first I'll take all you have in the house," I said.

"You've got to let me pay off the little fellows," he said. "I'll give you back what you put up, and anything that's left. Wait till I cash the other tickets." So I waited while he paid off the other winners. Oh, I knew my money was safe. Teller wouldn't welsh with the office doing such a good business. And if he did, what else could I do better than to take all he had then and there? I got my own two thousand dollars and about eight hundred dollars besides, which was all he had in the office. I told him I'd be there Monday morning. He swore the money would be waiting for me.

I got to Hoboken a little before twelve on Monday. I saw a fellow talking to the manager that I had seen in the St. Louis office the day Teller told me to go back to Dolan. I knew at once that the manager had telegraphed to the home office and they'd sent up one of their men to investigate the story.

Crooks don't trust anybody.

"I came for the balance of my money," I said to the manager.

"Is this the man?" asked the St. Louis chap.

"Yes," said the manager, and took a bunch of yellow backs from his pocket.

"Hold on!" said the St. Louis fellow to him and then turns to me, "Say, Livingston, didn't we tell you we didn't want your business?"

"Give me my money first," I said to the manager, and he forked over two thousands, four five-hundreds and three hundreds.

"What did you say?" I said to St. Louis.

"We told you we didn't want you to trade in our place."
"Yes," I said; "that's why I came."
"Well, don't come any more. Keep away!" he snarled at me.

The private policeman in gray came over, casual-like. St. Louis shook his fist at the manager and yelled: "You ought to've known better, you poor boob, than to let this guy get into you. He's Livingston. You had your orders."

"Listen, you," I said to the St. Louis man. "This isn't St. Louis. You can't pull off any trick here, like your boss did with Belfast Boy."

"You keep away from this office! You can't trade here!" he

yells.

"If I can't trade here nobody else is going to," I told him. "You can't get away with that sort of stuff here."

Well, St. Louis changed his tune at once.

"Look here, old boy," he said, all fussed up, "do us a favor. Be reasonable! You know we can't stand this every day. The old man's going to hit the ceiling when he hears who it was. Have a heart, Livingston!"

"I'll go easy," I promised.

"Listen to reason, won't you? For the love of Pete, keep away! Give us a chance to get a good start. We're new here. Will you?"

"I don't want any of this high-and-mighty business the next time I come," I said, and left him talking to the manager at the rate of a million a minute. I'd got some money out of them for the way they treated me in St. Louis. There wasn't any sense in my getting hot or trying to close them up. I went back to Fullerton's office and told McDevitt what had happened. Then I told him that if it was agreeable to him I'd like to have him go to Teller's place and begin trading in twenty or thirty share lots, to get them used to him. Then, the moment I saw a good chance to clean up big, I'd telephone him and he could plunge.

I gave McDevitt a thousand dollars and he went to Hoboken and did as I told him. He got to be one of the regulars. Then one day when I thought I saw a break impending I slipped Mac the word and he sold all they'd let him. I cleared twenty-eight hundred dollars that day, after giving Mac his rake-off and paying expenses, and I suspect Mac put down a little bet of his own besides. Less than a month after that, Teller closed his Hoboken branch. The police got busy. And, anyhow, it didn't pay, though I only traded there twice. We ran into a crazy bull market when stocks didn't react enough to wipe out even the one-point margins, and, of course, all the customers were bulls and winning and pyramiding. No end of bucket shops busted all over the country.

Their game has changed. Trading in the old-fashioned bucket shop had some decided advantages over speculating in a reputable broker's office. For one thing, the automatic closing out of your trade when the margin reached the exhaustion point was the best kind of stop-loss order. You couldn't get stung for more than you had put up, and there was no danger of rotten execution of orders, and so on. In New York the shops never were as liberal with their patrons as I've heard they were in the West. Here they used to limit the possible profit on certain stocks of the football order to two points. Sugar and Tennessee Coal and Iron were among these. No matter if they moved ten points in ten minutes you could only make two on one ticket. They figured that otherwise the customer was getting too big odds; he stood to lose one dollar and to make ten. And then there were times when all the shops, including the biggest, refused to take orders on certain stocks. In 1900, on the day before Election Day, when it was a foregone conclusion that McKinley would win, not a shop in the land let its customers buy stocks. The election odds were 3 to i on McKinley. By buying stocks on Monday you stood to make from three to six points or more. A man could bet on Bryan and buy stocks and make sure money. The bucket shops refused orders that day.

If it hadn't been for their refusing to take my business I never would have stopped trading in them. And then I never would have learned that there was much more to the game of stock speculation than to play for fluctuations of a few points.

Chapter III

It takes a man a long time to learn all the lessons of all his mistakes. They say there are two sides to everything. But there is only one side to the stock market; and it is not the bull side or the bear side, but the right side. It took me longer to get that general principle fixed firmly in my mind than it did most of the more technical phases of the game of stock speculation.

I have heard of people who amuse themselves conducting imaginary operations in the stock market to prove with imaginary dollars how right they are. Sometimes these ghost gamblers make millions. It is very easy to be a plunger that way. It is like the old story of the man who was going to fight a duel the next day.

His second asked him, “Are you a good shot?”

“Well,” said the duelist, “I can snap the stem of a wineglass at twenty paces,” and he looked modest.

“That’s all very well,” said the unimpressed second. “But can you snap the stem of the wineglass while the wineglass is pointing a loaded pistol straight at your heart?”

With me I must back my opinions with my money. My losses have taught me that I must not begin to advance until I am sure I shall not have to retreat. But if I cannot advance I do not move at all. I do not mean by this that a man should not limit his losses when he is wrong. He should. But that should not breed indecision. All my life I have made mistakes, but in losing money I have gained experience and accumulated a lot of valuable don'ts. I have been flat broke several times, but my loss has never been a total loss. Otherwise, I wouldn't be here now. I always knew I would have another chance and that I would not make the same mistake a second time. I believed in myself.

A man must believe in himself and his judgment if he expects to make a living at this game. That is why I don't believe in tips. If I buy stocks on Smith's tip I must sell those same stocks on Smith's tip. I am depending on him. Suppose Smith is away on a holiday when the selling time comes around? No, sir, nobody can make big money on what someone else tells him to do. I know from experience that nobody can give me a tip or a series of tips that will make more money for me than my own judgment. It took me five years to learn to play the game intelligently enough to make big money when I was right.

I didn't have as many interesting experiences as you might imagine. I mean, the process of learning how to speculate does not seem very dramatic at this distance. I went broke several times, and that is never pleasant, but the way I lost money is the way everybody loses money who loses money in Wall Street. Speculation is a hard and trying business, and a speculator must be on the job all the time or he'll soon have no job to be on.

My task, as I should have known after my early reverses at Fullerton's, was very simple: To look at speculation from another angle. But I didn't know that there was much more to the game than I could possibly learn in the bucket shops. There I thought I was beating the game when in reality I was only beating the shop. At the same time the tape- reading ability that trading in bucket shops developed in me and the training of my memory have been extremely valuable. Both of these things came easy to me. I owe my early success as a trader to them and not to brains or knowledge, because my mind was untrained and my ignorance was colossal. The game taught me the game. And it didn't spare the rod while teaching.

I remember my very first day in New York. I told you how the bucket shops, by refusing to take my business, drove me to seek a reputable commission house. One of the boys in the office where I got my first job was working for Harding Brothers, members of the New York Stock Exchange. I arrived in this city in the morning, and before one o'clock that same day I had opened an account with the firm and was ready to trade.

I didn't explain to you how natural it was for me to trade there exactly as I had done in the bucket shops, where all I did was to bet on fluctuations and catch small but sure changes in prices. Nobody offered to point out the essential differences or set me right. If somebody had told me my method would not work I nevertheless would have tried it out to make sure for myself, for when I am wrong only one thing convinces me of it, and that is, to lose money. And I am only right when I make money. That is speculating.

They were having some pretty lively times those days and the market was very active. That always cheers up a fellow. I felt at home right away. There was the old familiar quotation board in front of me, talking a language that I had learned before I was fifteen years old. There was a boy doing exactly the same thing I used to do in the first office I ever worked in. There were the customers same old bunch looking at the board or standing by the ticket calling out the prices and talking about the market. The machinery was to all appearances the same machinery that I was used to. The atmosphere was the atmosphere I had breathed since I had made my first stock-market money $3.12 in Burlington. The same kind of ticker and the same kind of traders, therefore the same kind of game. And remember, I was only twenty-two. I suppose I thought I knew the game from A to Z. Why shouldn't I?

I watched the board and saw something that looked good to me. It was behaving right. I bought a hundred at 84. I got out at 85 in less than a half hour. Then I saw something else I liked, and I did the same thing; took three-quarters of a point net within a very short time. I began well, didn't I?

Now mark this: On that, my first day as a customer of a reputable Stock Exchange house, and only two hours of it at that, I traded in eleven hundred shares of stock, jumping in and out. And the net result of the day's operations was that I lost exactly eleven hundred dollars. That is to say, on my first attempt, nearly one-half of my stake went up the flue. And remember, some of the trades showed me a profit. But I quit eleven hundred dollars minus for the day.

It didn't worry me, because I couldn't see where there was anything wrong with me. My moves, also, were right enough, and if I had been trading in the old Cosmopolitan shop I'd have broken better than even. That the machine wasn't as it ought to be, my eleven hundred vanished dollars plainly told me. But as long as the machinist was all right there was no need to stew. Ignorance at twenty-two isn't a structural defect.

After a few days I said to myself, "I can't trade this way

here. The ticker doesn't help as it should!" But I let it go at that without getting down to bed rock. I kept it up, having good days and bad days, until I was cleaned out. I went to old Fullerton and got him to stake me to five hundred dollars. And I came back from St. Louis, as I told you, with money I took out of the bucket shops there a game I could always beat.

I played more carefully and did better for a while. As soon as I was in easy circumstances I began to live pretty well. I made friends and had a good time. I was not quite twenty-three, remember; all alone in New York with easy money in my pockets and the belief in my heart that I was beginning to understand the new machine.

I was making allowances for the actual execution of my orders on the floor of the Exchange, and moving more cautiously. But I was still sticking to the tape that is, I was still ignoring general principles; and as long as I did that I could not spot the exact trouble with my game.

We ran into the big boom of 1901 and I made a great deal of money that is, for a boy. You remember those times? The prosperity of the country was unprecedented. We not only ran into an era of industrial consolidations and combinations of capital that beat anything we had had up to that time, but the public went stock mad. In previous flush times, I have heard, Wall Street used to brag of two-hundred-and-fifty-thousand-share days, when securities of a par value of twenty-five million dollars changed hands. But in 1901 we had a three-million-share day. Everybody was making money. The steel crowd came to town, a horde of millionaires with no more regard for money than drunken sailors. The only game that satisfied them was the stock market. We had some of the biggest high rollers the Street ever saw: John W. Gates, of 'Bet-you-a-million' fame, and his friends, like John A. Drake, Loyal Smith, and the rest; the Reid-Leeds-Moore crowd, who sold part of their Steel holdings and with the proceeds bought in the open market the actual majority of the stock of the great Rock Island system; and Schwab and Frick and Phipps and the Pittsburgh coterie; to say nothing of scores of men who were lost in the shuffle but would have been called great plungers at any other time. A fellow could buy and sell all the stock there was. Keene made a market for the U. S. Steel shares. A broker sold one hundred thousand shares in a few minutes. A wonderful time! And there were some wonderful winnings. And no taxes to pay on stock sales! And no day of reckoning in sight.

Of course, after a while, I heard a lot of calamity howling and the old stagers said everybody except themselves had gone crazy. But everybody except themselves was making money. I knew, of course, there must be a limit to the advances and an end to the crazy buying of A. O. T. Any Old Thing and I got bearish. But every time I sold I lost money, and if it hadn't been that I ran darn quick I'd have lost a heap more. I looked for a break, but I was playing safe making money when I bought and chipping it out when I sold short so that I wasn't profiting by the boom as much as you'd think when you consider how heavily I used to trade, even as a boy.

There was one stock that I wasn't short of, and that was Northern Pacific. My tape reading came in handy. I thought most stocks had been bought to a standstill, but Little Nipper behaved as if it were going still higher. We know now that both the common and the preferred were being steadily absorbed by the Kuhn-Loeb-Harriman combination. Well, I was long a thousand shares of Northern Pacific common, and held it against the advice of everybody in the office. When it got to about 110 I had thirty points profit, and I grabbed it. It made my balance at my brokers' nearly fifty thousand dollars, the greatest amount of money I had been able to accumulate up to that time. It wasn't so bad for a chap who had lost every cent trading in that selfsame office a few months before.

If you remember, the Harriman crowd notified Morgan and Hill of their intention to be represented in the Burlington-Great Northern-Northern Pacific combination, and then the Morgan people at first instructed Keene to buy fifty thousand shares of N. P. to keep the control in their possession. I have heard that Keene told Robert Bacon to make the order one hundred and fifty thousand shares and the bankers did. At all events, Keene sent one of his brokers, Eddie Norton, into the N. P. crowd and he bought one hundred thousand shares of the stock. This was followed by another order, I think, of fifty thousand shares additional, and the famous corner followed. After the market closed on May 8, 1901, the whole world knew that a battle of financial giants was on. No two such combinations of capital had ever opposed each other in this country. Harriman against Morgan; an irresistible force meeting an immovable object.

There I was on the morning of May ninth with nearly fifty thousand dollars in cash and no stocks. As I told you, I had been very bearish for some days, and here was my chance at last. I knew what would happen an awful break and then some wonderful bargains. There would be a quick recovery and big profits for those who had picked up the bargains. It didn't take a Sherlock Holmes to figure this out. We were going to have an opportunity to catch them coming and going, not only for big money but for sure money.

Everything happened as I had foreseen. I was dead right and I lost every cent I had! I was wiped out by something that was unusual. If the unusual never happened there would be no difference in people and then there wouldn't be any fun in life. The game would become merely a matter of addition and subtraction. It would make of us a race of bookkeepers with plodding minds. It's the guessing that develops a man's brain power. Just consider what you have to do to guess right.

The market fairly boiled, as I had expected. The transactions were enormous and the fluctuations unprecedented in extent. I put in a lot of selling orders at the market. When I saw the opening prices I had a fit, the breaks were so awful. My brokers were on the job. They were as competent and conscientious as any; but by the time they executed my orders the stocks had broken twenty points more. The tape was way behind the market and reports were slow in coming in by reason of the awful rush of business. When I found out that the stocks I had ordered sold when the tape said the price was, say, 100 and they got mine off at 80, making a total decline of thirty or forty points from the previous night's close, it seemed to me that I was putting out shorts at a level that made the stocks I sold the very bargains I had planned to buy. The market was not going to drop right through to China. So I decided instantly to cover my shorts and go long.

My brokers bought; not at the level that had made me turn, but at the prices prevailing in the Stock Exchange when their floor man got my orders. They paid an average of fifteen points more than I had figured on. A loss of thirty-five points in one day was more than anybody could stand.

The ticker beat me by lagging so far behind the market. I was accustomed to regarding the tape as the best little friend I had because I bet according to what it told me. But this time the tape double-crossed me. The divergence between the printed and the actual prices undid me. It was the sublimation of my previous unsuccess, the selfsame thing that had beaten me before. It seems so obvious now that tape reading is not enough, irrespective of the brokers' execution, that I wonder why I didn't then see both my trouble and the remedy for it.

I did worse than not see it; I kept on trading, in and out, regardless of the execution. You see, I never could trade with a limit. I must take my chances with the market. That is what I am trying to beat the market, not the particular price. When I think I should sell, I sell. When I think stocks will go up, I buy. My adherence to that general principle of speculation saved me. To have traded at limited prices simply would have been my old bucket-shop method inefficiently adapted for use in a reputable commission broker's office. I would never have learned to know what stock speculation is, but would have kept on betting on what a limited experience told me was a sure thing.

Whenever I did try to limit the prices in order to minimize the disadvantages of trading at the market when the ticker lagged, I simply found that the market got away from me. This happened so often that I stopped trying. I can't tell you how it came to take me so many years to learn that instead of placing piking bets on what the next few quotations were going to be, my game was to anticipate what was going to happen in a big way.

After my May ninth mishap I plugged along, using a modified but still defective method. If I hadn't made money some of the time I might have acquired market wisdom quicker. But I was making enough to enable me to live well. I liked friends and a good time. I was living down the Jersey Coast that summer, like hundreds of prosperous Wall Street men. My winnings were not quite enough to offset both my losses and my living expenses.

I didn't keep on trading the way I did through stubbornness. I simply wasn't able to state my own problem to myself, and, of course, it was utterly hopeless to try to solve it. I harp on this topic so much to show what I had to go through before I got to where I could really make money. My old shotgun and BB shot could not do the work of a high- power repeating rifle against big game.

Early that fall I not only was cleaned out again but I was so sick of the game I could no longer beat that I decided to leave New York and try something else some other place. I had been trading since my fourteenth year. I had made my first thousand dollars when I was a kid of fifteen, and my first *en thousand before I was twenty-one. I had made and lost a ten-thousand-dollar stake more than once. In New York I had made thousands and lost them. I got up to fifty thousand dollars and two days later that went. I had no other business and knew no other game. After several years I was back where I began. No worse, for I had acquired habits and a style of living that required money; though that part didn't bother me as much as being wrong so consistently.

Chapter IV

Well, I went home. But the moment I was back I knew that I had but one mission in life and that was to get a stake and go back to Wall Street. That was the only place in the country where I could trade heavily. Some day, when my game was all right, I'd need such a place. When a man is right he wants to get all that is coming to him for being right.

I didn't have much hope, but, of course, I tried to get into the bucket shops again. There were fewer of them and some of them were run by strangers. Those who remembered me wouldn't give me a chance to show them whether I had gone back as a trader or not. I told them the truth, that I had lost in New York whatever I had made at home; that I didn't know as much as I used to think I did; and that there was no reason why it should not now be good business for them to let me trade with them. But they wouldn't. And the new places were unreliable. Their owners thought twenty shares was as much as a gentleman ought to buy if he had any reason to suspect he was going to guess right.

I needed the money and the bigger shops were taking in plenty of it from their regular customers. I got a friend of mine to go into a certain office and trade. I just sauntered in to look them over. I again tried to coax the order clerk to accept a small order, even if it was only fifty shares. Of course he said no. I had rigged up a code with this friend so that he would buy or sell when and what I told him. But that only made me chicken feed. Then the office began to grumble about taking my friend's orders. Finally one day he tried to sell a hundred St. Paul and they shut down on him.

We learned afterward that one of the customers saw us talking together outside and went in and told the office, and when my friend went up to the order clerk to sell that hundred St. Paul the guy said:

"We're not taking any selling orders in St. Paul, not from you." "Why, what's the matter, Joe?" asked my friend.

"Nothing doing, that's all," answered Joe.

"Isn't that money any good? Look it over. It's all there." And my friend passed over the hundred my hundred in tens. He tried to look indignant and I was looking unconcerned; but most of the other customers were getting close to the combatants, as they always did when there was loud talking or the slightest semblance of a scrap between the shop and any customer. They wanted to get a line on the merits of the case in order to get a line on the solvency of the concern.

The clerk, Joe, who was a sort of assistant manager, came out from behind his cage, walked up to my friend, looked at him and then looked at me.

"It's funny," he said slowly "it's damned funny that you never do a single thing here when your friend Livingston isn't around. You just sit and look at the board by the hour. Never a peep. But after he comes in you get busy all of a sudden. Maybe you are acting for yourself; but not in this office any more. We don't fall for Livingston tipping you off."

Well, that stopped my board money. But I had made a few

hundred more than I had spent and I wondered how I could" use them, for the need of making enough money to go back to New York with was more urgent than ever. I felt that I would do better the next time. I had had time to think calmly of some of my foolish plays; and then, one can see the whole better when one sees it from a little distance. The immediate problem was to make the new stake.

One day I was in a hotel lobby, talking to some fellows I knew, who were pretty steady traders. Everybody was talking stock market. I made the remark that nobody could beat the game on account of the rotten execution he got from his brokers, especially when he traded at the market, as I did.

A fellow piped up and asked me what particular brokers I meant.

I said, "The best in the land," and he asked who might they be. I could see he wasn't going to believe I ever dealt with first-class houses.

But I said, "I mean, any member of the New York Stock Exchange. It isn't that they are crooked or careless, but when a man gives an order to buy at the market he never knows what that stock is going to cost him until he gets a report from the brokers. There are more moves of one or two points than of ten or fifteen. But the outside trader can't catch the small rises or drops because of the execution. I'd rather trade in a bucket shop any day in the week, if they'd only let a fellow trade big."

The man who had spoken to me I had never seen before. His name was Roberts. He seemed very friendly disposed. He took me aside and asked me if I had ever traded in any of the other exchanges, and I said no. He said he knew some houses that were members of the Cotton Exchange and the Produce Exchange and the smaller stock exchanges. These firms were very careful and paid special attention to the execution. He said that they had confidential connections with the biggest and smartest houses on the New York Stock Exchange and through their personal pull and by guaranteeing a business of hundreds of thousands of shares a month they got much better service than an individual customer could get.

"They really cater to the small customer," he said. "They make a specialty of out-of- town business and they take just as much pains with a ten-share order as they do with one for ten thousand. They are very competent and honest."

"Yes. But if they pay the Stock Exchange house the regular eighth commission, where do they come in?"

"Well, they are supposed to pay the eighth. But you know!" He winked at me.

"Yes," I said. "But the one thing a Stock Exchange firm will not do is to split commissions. The governors wou'i rather a member committed murder, arson and bigamy than to do business for outsiders for less than a kosher eighth. The very life of the Stock Exchange depends upon their not violating that one rule."

He must have seen that I had talked with Stock Exchange people, for he said, "Listen! Every now and then one of those pious Stock Exchange houses is suspended for a year for violating that rule, isn't it? There are ways and ways of rebating so nobody can squeal." He probably saw unbelief in my face, for he went on: "And besides, on certain kind of business we I mean, these wire houses charge a thirty-second extra, in addition to the eighth commission. They are very nice about it. They never charge the extra commission except in unusual cases, and then only if the customer has an inactive account. It wouldn't pay them, you know, otherwise. They aren't in business exclusively for their health."

By that time I knew he was touting for some phony brokers.

"Do you know any reliable house of that kind?" I asked him.

"I know the biggest brokerage firm in the United States," he said. "I trade there myself. They have branches in seventy-eight cities in the United States and Canada. They do an enormous business. And they couldn't very well do it year in and year out if they weren't strictly on the level, could they?"

"Certainly not," I agreed. "Do they trade in the same stocks that are dealt in on the New York Stock Exchange?"

"Of course; and on the curb and on any other exchange in this country, or Europe. They deal in wheat, cotton, provisions ; anything you want. They have correspondents everywhere and memberships in all the exchanges, either in their own name or on the quiet."

I knew by that time, but I thought I'd lead him on.

"Yes," I said, "but that does not alter the fact that the orders have to be executed by somebody, and nobody living can guarantee how the market will be or how close the ticker's prices are to the actual prices on the floor of the Exchange. By the time a man gets the quotation here and he hands in an order and it's telegraphed to New York, some valuable time has gone. I might better go back to New York and lose my money there in respectable company."

"I don't know anything about losing money; our customers don't acquire that habit. They make money. We take care of that."

"Your customers?"

"Well, 1 take an interest in the firm, and if I can turn some business their way I do so because they've always treated me white and I've made a good deal of money through them. If you wish I'll introduce you to the manager."

"What's the name of the firm?" I asked him.

He told me. I had heard about them. They ran ads in all the papers, calling attention to the great profits made by those customers who followed their inside information on active stocks. That was the firm's great specialty. They were not a regular bucket shop, but bucketeers, alleged brokers who bucketed their orders but nevertheless went through an elaborate camouflage to convince the world that they were regular brokers engaged in a legitimate business. They were one of the oldest of that class of firms.

They were the prototype at that time of the same sort of brokers that went broke this year by the dozen. The general principles and methods were the same, though the particular devices for fleecing the public differed somewhat, certain details having been changed when the old tricks became too well known.

These people used to send out tips to buy or sell a certain stock hundreds of telegrams advising the instant purchase of a certain stock and hundreds recommending other customers to sell the same stock, on the old racing-tipster plan. Then orders to buy and sell would come in. The firm would buy and sell, say, a thousand of that stock through a reputable Stock Exchange firm and get a regular report on it. This report they would show to any doubting Thomas who was impolite enough to speak about bucketing customers' orders.

They also used to form discretionary pools in the office and as a great favor allowed their customers to authorize them, in writing, to trade with the customer's money and in the customer's name, as they in their judgment deemed best. That way the most cantankerous customer had no legal redress when his money disappeared. They'd bull a stock, on paper, and put the customers in and then they'd execute one of the old- fashioned bucket-shop drives and wipe out hundreds of shoestring margins. They did not spare anyone, women, schoolteachers and old men being their best bet.

"I'm sore on all brokers," I told the tout. "I'll have to think this over," and I left him so he wouldn't talk any more to me.

I inquired about this firm. I learned that they had hundreds of customers and although there were the usual stories I did not find any case of a customer not getting his money from them if he won any. The difficulty was in finding anybody who had ever won in that office; but I did. Things seemed to be going their way just then, and that meant that they probably would not welsh if a trade went against them. Of course most concerns of that kind eventually go broke. There are times when there are regular epidemics of bucketeering bankruptcies, like the old-fashioned runs on several banks after one of them goes up. The customers of the others get frightened and they run to take their money out. But there are plenty of retired bucket-shop keepers in this country.

Well, I heard nothing alarming about the tout's firm except that they were on the make, first, last and all the time, and that they were not always truthful. Their specialty was trimming suckers who wanted to get rich quick. But they always asked their customers' permission, in writing, to take their rolls away from them.

One chap I met did tell me a story about seeing six hundred telegrams go out one day advising customers to get aboard a certain stock and six "hundred telegrams to other customers strongly urging them to sell that same stock, at once.

"Yes, I know the trick," I said to the chap who was telling me.

"Yes," he said. "But the next day they sent telegrams to the same people advising them to close out their interest in everything and buy or sell another stock. I asked the senior partner, who was in the office, 'Why do you do that? The first part I understand. Some of your customers are bound to make money on paper for a while, even if they and the others eventually lose. But by sending out telegrams like this you simply kill them all. What's the big idea?"

"Well, he said, the customers are bound to lose their money anyhow, no matter what they buy, or how or where or when. When they lose their money I lose the customers. Well, I might as well get as much of their money as I can and then look for a new crop."

Well, I admit frankly that I wasn't concerned with the business ethics of the firm. I told you I felt sore on the Teller concern and how it tickled me to get even with them. But I didn't have any such feeling about this firm. They might be crooks or they might not be as black as they were painted. I did not propose to let them do any trading for me, or follow their tips or believe their lies. My one concern was with getting together a stake and returning to New York to trade in fair amounts in an office where you did not have to be afraid the police would raid the joint, as they did the bucket shops, or see the postal authorities swoop down and tie up your money so that you'd be lucky to get eight cents on the dollar a year and a half later.

Anyhow, I made up my mind that I would see what trading advantages of this firm offered over what you might call the legitimate brokers. I didn't have much money to put up as margin, and firms that bucketed orders were naturally much more liberal in that respect, so that a few hundred dollars went much further in their offices.

I went down to their place and had a talk with the manager himself. When he found out that I was an old trader and had formerly had accounts in New York with Stock Exchange houses and that I had lost all I took with me he stopped promising to make a million a minute for me if I let them invest my savings. He figured that I was a permanent sucker, the ticker-hound kind that always plays and always loses; a steady- income provider for brokers, whether they were the kind that bucket your orders or modestly content themselves with the commissions.

I just told the manager that what I was looking for was decent execution, because I always traded at the market and I didn't want to get reports that showed a difference of a half or a whole point from the ticker price.

He assured me on his word of honor that they would do whatever I thought was right. They wanted my business because they wanted to show me what high-class brokering was. They had in their employ the best talent in the business. In fact, they were famous for their execution. If there was any difference between the ticker price and the report it was always in favor of the customer, though of course they didn't guarantee that. If I opened an account with them I could buy and sell at the price which came over the wire, they were so confident of their brokers.

Naturally that meant that I could trade there to all intents and purposes as though I were in a bucket shop that is, they'd let me trade at the next quotation. I didn't want to appear too anxious, so I shook my head and told him I guessed I wouldn't open an account that day, but I'd let him know. He urged me strongly to begin right away as it was a good market to make money in. It was for them; a dull market with prices seesawing slightly, just the kind to get customers in and then wipe them out with a sharp drive in the tipped stock. I had some trouble in getting away.

I had given him my name and address, and that very same day I began to get prepaid telegrams and letters urging me to get aboard of some stock or other in which they said they knew an inside pool was operating for a fifty-point rise.

I was busy going around and finding out all I could about several other brokerage concerns of the same bucketing kind. It seemed to me that if I could be sure of getting my winnings out of their clutches the only way of my getting together some real money was to trade in these near bucket-shops.

When I had learned all I could I opened accounts with three firms. I had taken a small office and had direct wires run to the three brokers.

I traded in a small way so they wouldn't get frightened off at the very start. I made money on balance and they were not slow in telling me that they expected real business from customers who had direct wires to their offices. They did not hanker for pikers. They figured that the more I did the more I'd lose, and the more quickly I was wiped out the more they'd make. It was a sound enough theory when you consider that these people necessarily dealt with averages and the average customer was never long-lived, financially speaking. A busted customer can't trade. A half-crippled customer can whine and insinuate things and make trouble of one or another kind that hurts business.

I also established a connection with a local firm that had a direct wire to its New York correspondent, who were also members of the New York Stock Exchange. I had a stock ticker put in and I began to trade conservatively. As I told you, it was pretty much like trading in bucket shops, only it was a little slower.

It was a game that I could beat, and I did. I never got it down to such a fine point that I could win ten times out of ten; but I won on balance, taking it week in and week out. I was again living pretty well, but always saving something, to increase the stake that I was to take back to Wall Street. I got a couple of wires into two more of these bucketing brokerage houses, making five in all and, of course, my good firm.

There were times when my plans went wrong and my stocks did not run true to form, but did the opposite of what they should have done if they had kept up their regard for precedent. But they did not hit me very hard they couldn't, with my shoestring margins. My relations with my brokers were friendly enough. Their accounts and records did not always agree with mine, and the differences uniformly happened to be against me. Curious coincidence not! But I fought for my own and usually had my way in the end. They always had the hope of getting away from me what I had taken from them. They regarded my winnings as temporary loans, I think.

They really were not sporty, being in the business to make money by hook or by crook instead of being content with the house percentage. Since suckers always lose money when they gamble in stocks they never really speculate you'd think these fellows would run what you might call a legitimate illegitimate business. But they didn't. "Copper your customers and grow rich" is an old and true adage, but they did not seem ever to have heard of it and didn't stop at plain bucketing., Several times they tried to double-cross me with the old tricks. They caught me a couple of times because I wasn't looking. They always did that when I had taken no more than my usual line. I accused them of being short sports or worse, but they denied it and it ended by -my going back to trading as usual. The beauty of doing business with a crook is that he always forgives you for catching-him, so long as you don't stop doing business with him. It's all right as far as he is concerned. He is willing to meet you more than halfway. Magnanimous souls!

Well, I made up my mind that I couldn't afford to have the

normal rate of increase of my stake impaired by crooks' tricks, so I decided to teach them a lesson. I picked out some stock that after having been a speculative favorite had become inactive. Water-logged. If I had taken one that never had been active they would have suspected my play. I gave out buying orders on this stock to my five bucketeering brokers. When the orders were taken and they were waiting for the next quotation to come out on the tape I sent in an order through my Stock Exchange house to sell a hundred shares of that particular stock at the market. I urgently asked for quick action. Well, you can imagine what happened when the selling order got to the floor of the Exchange; a dull inactive stock that a commission house with out-of-town connections wanted to sell in a hurry. Somebody got cheap stock. But the transaction as it would be printed on the tape was the price that I would pay on my five buying orders. I was long on balance four hundred shares of that stock at a low figure. The wire house asked me what I'd heard, and I said I had a tip on it. Just before the close of the market I sent an order to my reputable house to buy back that hundred shares, and not waste any time; that I didn't want to be short under any circumstances; and I didn't care what they paid. So they wired to New York and the order to buy that hundred quick resulted in a sharp advance. I of course had put in selling orders for the five hundred shares that my friends had bucketed. It worked very satisfactorily.

Still, they didn't mend their ways, and so I worked that trick on them several times. I did not dare punish them as severely as they deserved, seldom more than a point or two on a hundred shares. But it helped to swell my little hoard that I was saving for my next Wall Street venture. I sometimes varied the process by selling some stock short, without overdoing it. I was satisfied with my six or eight hundred clear for each crack.

One day the stunt worked so well that it went far beyond all calculations for a ten-point swing. I wasn't looking for it. As a matter of fact it so happened that I had two hundred shares instead of my usual hundred at one broker's, though only a hundred in the four other shops. That was too much of a good thing for them. They were sore as pups about it and they began to say things over the wires. So I went and saw the manager, the same man who had been so anxious to get my account, and so forgiving every time I caught him trying to put something over on me. He talked pretty big for a man in his position.

"That was a fictitious market for that stock, and we won't pay you a damned cent!" he swore.

"It wasn't a fictitious market when you accepted my order to buy. You let me in then, all right, and now you've got to let me out. You can't get around that for fairness, can you?"

"Yes, I can!" he yelled. "I can prove that somebody put up a job." "Who put up a job?" I asked.
"Somebody!"

"Who did they put it up on?" I asked.

"Some friends of yours were in it as sure as pop," he said.

But I told him, "You know very well that I play a lone hand. Everybody in this town knows that. They've known it ever since I started trading in stocks. Now I want to give you some friendly advice: you just send and get that money for me. I don't want to be disagreeable. Just do what I tell you."

"I won't pay it. It was a rigged-up transaction," he yelled.

I got tired of his talk. So I told him: "You'll pay it to me right now and here."

Well, he blustered a little more and accused me flatly of being the guilty thimblerigger; but he finally forked over the cash. The others were not so rambunctious. In one office the manager had been studying these inactive-stock plays of mine and when he got my order he actually bought the stock for me and then some for himself in the Little Board, and he made some money. These fellows didn't mind being sued by customers on charges of fraud, as they generally had a good technical legal defense ready. But they were afraid I'd attach the furniture the money in the bank I couldn't because they took care not to have any funds exposed to that danger. It would not hurt them to be known as pretty sharp, but to get a reputation for welshing was fatal. For a customer to lose money at his broker's is no rare event. But for a customer to make money and then not get it is the worst crime on the speculators' statute books.

I got my money from all; but that ten-point jump put an end to the pleasing pastime of skinning skinners. They were on the lookout for the little trick that they themselves had used to defraud hundreds of poor customers. I went back to my regular trading; but the market wasn't always right for my system that is, limited as I was by the size of the orders they would take, I couldn't make a killing.

I had been at it over a year, during which I used every device that I could think of to make money trading in those wire houses. I had lived very comfortably, bought an automobile and didn't limit myself about my expenses. I had to make a stake, but I also had to live while I was doing it. If my position on the market was right I couldn't spend as much as I made, so that I'd always be saving some. If I was wrong I didn't make any money and therefore couldn't spend. As I said, I had saved up a fair-sized roll, and there wasn't so much money to be made in the five wire houses; so I decided to return to New York.

I had my own automobile and I invited a friend of mine who also was a trader to motor to New York with me. He accepted and we started. We stopped at New Haven for dinner. At the hotel I met an old trading acquaintance, and among other things he told me there was a shop in town that had a wire and was doing a pretty good business.

We left the hotel on our way to New York, but I drove by the street where the bucket shop was to see what the outside looked like. We found it and couldn't resist the temptation to stop and have a look at the inside. It wasn't very sumptuous, but the old blackboard was there, and the customers, and the game was on.

The manager was a chap who looked as if he had been an actor or a stump speaker. He was very impressive. He'd say good morning as though he had discovered the morning's goodness after ten years of searching for it with a microscope and was making you a present of the discovery as well as of the sky, the sun and the firm's bank roll. He saw us come up in the sporty-looking automobile, and as both of us were young and careless I don't suppose I looked twenty he naturally concluded we were a couple of Yale boys. I didn't tell him we weren't. He didn't give me a chance, but began delivering a speech. He was very glad to see us. Would we have a comfortable seat? The market, we would find, was philanthropically inclined that morning; in fact, clamoring to increase the supply of collegiate pocket money, of which no intelligent undergraduate ever had a sufficiency since the dawn of historic time. But here and now, by the beneficence of the ticker, a small initial investment would return thousands. More pocket money than anybody could spend was what the stock market yearned to yield.

Well, I thought it would be a pity not to do as the nice man of the bucket shop was so anxious to have us do, so I told him I would do as he wished, because I had heard that lots of people made lots of money in the stock market.

I began to trade, very conservatively, but increasing the line as I won. My friend followed me.

We stayed overnight in New Haven and the next morning found us at the hospitable shop at five minutes to ten. The orator was glad to see us, thinking his turn would cony day. But I cleaned up within a few dollars of fifteen hundred. The next morning when we dropped in on the great orator, and handed him an order to sell five hundred Sugar he hesitated, but finally accepted it in silence! The stock broke over a point and I closed out and gave him the ticket. There was exactly five hundred dollars coming to me in profits, and my five hundred dollar margin. He took twenty fifties from the safe, counted them three times very slowly, then he counted them again in front of me. It looked as if his fingers were sweating mucilage the way the notes seemed to stick to him, but finally he handed the money to me. He folded his arms, bit his lower lip, kept it bit, and stared at the top of a window behind me.

I told him I'd like to sell two hundred Steel. But he never

stirred. He didn't hear me. I repeated my wish, only I made it three hundred shares. He turned his head. I waited for the speech. But all he did was to look at me. Then he smacked his lips and swallowed as if he was going to start an attack on fifty years of political misrule by the unspeakable grafters of the opposition.

Finally he waved his hand toward the yellow-backs in my hand and said, "Take away that bauble!"

"Take away what?" I said. I hadn't quite understood what he was driving at. "Where are you going, student?" He spoke very impressively.

"New York," I told him.

"That's right," he said, nodding about twenty times. "That is ex-actly right. You are going away from here all right, because now I know two things two, student! I know what you are not, and I know what you are. Yes! Yes! Yes!"

"Is that so?" I said very politely.

"Yes. You two " He paused; and then he stopped being in Congress and snarled: "You two are the biggest sharks in the United States of America! Students? Ye-eh! You must be Freshmen! Ye-eh!"

We left him talking to himself. He probably didn't mind the money so much. No professional gambler does. It's all in the game and the luck's bound to turn. It was his being fooled in us that hurt his pride.

That is how I came back to Wall Street for a third attempt. I had been studying, of course, trying to locate the exact trouble with my system that had been responsible for my defeats in A. R. Fullerton & Co.'s office. I was twenty when I made my first ten thousand, and I lost that. But I knew how and why because I traded out of season all the time; because when I couldn't play according to my system, which was based on study and experience, I went in and gambled. I hoped to win, instead of knowing that I ought to win on form. When I was about twenty-two I ran up my stake to fifty thousand dollars; I lost it on May ninth. But I knew exactly why and how. It was the laggard tape and the unprecedented violence of the movements that awful day. But I didn't know why I had lost after my return from St. Louis or after the May ninth panic. I had theories that is, remedies for some of the faults that I thought I found in my play. But I needed actual practice.

There is nothing like losing all you have in the world for teaching you what not to do. And when you know what not to do in order not to lose money, you begin to learn what to do in order to win. Did you get that? You begin to learn!

Chapter V

The average ticker hound or, as they used to call him, tape-worm goes wrong, I suspect, as much from over-specialization as from anything else. It means a highly expensive inelasticity. After all, the game of speculation isn't all mathematics or set rules, however rigid the main laws may be. Even in my tape reading something enters that is more than mere arithmetic. There is what I call the behavior of a stock, actions that enable you to judge whether or not it is going to proceed in accordance with the precedents that your observation has noted. If a stock doesn't act right don't touch it; because, being unable to tell precisely what is wrong, you cannot tell which way it is going. No diagnosis, no prognosis. No prognosis, no profit.

It is a very old thing, this of noting the behavior of a stock and studying its past performances. When I first came to New York there was a broker's office where a Frenchman used to talk about his chart. At first I thought he was a sort of pet freak kept by the firm because they were good-natured. Then I learned that he was a persuasive and most impressive talker. He said that the only thing that didn't lie because it simply couldn't was mathematics. By means of his curves he could forecast market movements. Also he could analyse them, and tell, for instance, why Keene did the right thing in his famous Atchison preferred bull manipulation, and later why he went wrong in his Southern Pacific pool. At various times one or another of the professional traders tried the Frenchman's system and then went back to their old unscientific methods of making a living. Their hit-or-miss system was cheaper, they said. I heard that the Frenchman said Keene admitted that the chart was 100 per cent right but claimed that the method was too slow for practical use in an active market.

Then there was one office where a chart of the daily movement of prices was kept. It showed at a glance just what each stock had done for months. By comparing individual curves with the general market curve and keeping in mind certain rules the customers could tell whether the stock on which they got an unscientific tip to buy was fairly entitled to a rise. They used the chart as a sort of complementary tipster. To-day there are scores of commission houses where you find trading charts. They come ready-made from the offices of statistical experts and include not only stocks but commodities.

"I should say that a chart helps those who can read it or rather who can assimilate what they read. The average chart reader, however, is apt to become obsessed with the notion that the dips and peaks and primary and secondary movements are all there is to stock speculation. If he pushes his confidence to its logical limit he is bound to go broke. There is an extremely able man, a former partner of a well-known Stock Exchange house, who is really a trained mathematician. He is a graduate of a famous technical school. He devised charts based upon a very careful and minute study of the behaviour of prices in many markets stocks, bonds, grain, cotton, money, and so on. He went back years and years and traced the correlations and seasonal movements oh, everything. He used his charts in his stock trading for years. What he really did was to take advantage of some highly intelligent averaging. They tell me he won regularly until the World War knocked all precedents into a cocked hat. I heard that he and his large following lost millions before they desisted.

But not even a world war can keep the stock market from being a bull market when conditions are bullish, or a bear market when conditions are bearish. And all a man needs to know to make money is to appraise conditions.

I didn't mean to get off the track like that, but I can't help it when I think of my first few years in Wall Street. I know now what I did not know then, and I think of the mistakes of my ignorance because those are the very mistakes that the average stock speculator makes year in and year out.

After I got back to New York to try for the third time to beat the market in a Stock Exchange house I traded quite actively. I didn't expect to do as well as I did in the bucket shops, but I thought that after a while I would do much better because I would be able to swing a much heavier line. Yet, I can see now that my main trouble was my failure to grasp the vital difference between stock gambling and stock speculation. Still, by reason of my seven years' experience in reading the tape and a certain natural aptitude for the game, my stake was earning not indeed a fortune but a very high rate of interest. I won and lost as before, but I was winning on balance. The more I made the more I spent. This is the usual experience with most men. No, not necessarily with easy- money pickers, but with every human being who is not a slave of the hoarding instinct.

Some men, like old Russell Sage, have the money-making and the money-hoarding instinct equally well developed, and of course they die disgustingly rich.

The game of beating the market exclusively interested me from ten to three every day, and after three, the game of living my life. Don't misunderstand me. I never allowed pleasure to interfere with business. When I lost it was because I was wrong and not because I was suffering from dissipation or excesses. There never were any shattered nerves or rum-shaken limbs to spoil my game. I couldn't afford anything that kept me from feeling physically and mentally fit. Even now I am usually in bed by ten. As a young man I never kept late hours, because I could not do business properly on insufficient sleep. I was doing better than breaking even and that is why I didn't think there was any need to deprive myself of the good things of life. The market was always there to supply them. I was acquiring the confidence that comes to a man from a professionally dispassionate attitude toward his own method of providing bread and butter for himself.

The first change I made in my play was in the matter of time. I couldn't wait for the sure thing to come along and then take a point or two out of it as I could in the bucket shops. I had to start much earlier if I wanted to catch the move in Fullerton's office. In other words, I had to study what was going to happen; to anticipate stock movements. That sounds asininely commonplace, but you know what I mean. It was the change in my own attitude toward the game that was of supreme importance to me. It taught me, little by little, the essential difference between betting on fluctuations and anticipating inevitable advances and declines, between gambling and speculating.

I had to go further back than an hour in my studies of the market which was something I never would have learned to do in the biggest bucket shop in the world. I interested myself in trade reports and railroad earnings and financial and commercial statistics. Of course I loved to trade heavily and they called me the Boy Plunger; but I also liked to study the moves. I never thought that anything was irksome if it helped me to trade more intelligently. Before I can solve a problem I must state it to myself. When I think I have found the solution I must prove I am right. I know of only one way to prove it; and that is, with my own money.

Slow as my progress seems now, I suppose I learned as fast as I possibly could, considering that I was making money on balance. If I had lost oftener perhaps it might have spurred me to more continuous study. I certainly would have had more mistakes to spot. But I am not sure of the exact value of losing, for if I had lost more I would have lacked the money to test out the improvements in my methods of trading.

Studying my winning plays in Fullerton's office I discovered that although I often was 100 per cent right on the market that is, in my diagnosis of conditions and general trend I was not making as much money as my market "tightness" entitled me to. Why wasn't I?

There was as much to learn from partial victory as from defeat.

For instance, I had been bullish from the very start of a bull market, and I had backed my opinion by buying stocks. An advance followed, as I had clearly foreseen. So far, all very well. But what else did I do? Why, I listened to the elder statesmen and curbed my youthful impetuousness. I made up my mind to be wise and play carefully, conservatively. Everybody knew that the way to do that was to take profits and buy back your stocks on reactions. And that is precisely what I did, or rather what I tried to do; for I often took profits and waited for a reaction that never came. And I saw my stock go kiting up ten points more and I sitting there with my four-point profit safe in my conservative pocket. They say you never grow poor taking profits. No, you don't. But neither do you grow rich taking a four-point profit in a bull market.

Where I should have made twenty thousand dollars I made two thousand. That was what my conservatism did for me. About the time I discovered what a small percentage of what I should have made I was getting I discovered something else, and that is that suckers differ among themselves according to the degree of experience.

The tyro knows nothing, and everybody, including himself, knows it. But the next, or second, grade thinks he knows a great deal and makes others feel that way too. He is the experienced sucker, who has studied not the market itself but a few remarks about the market made by a still higher grade of suckers. The second-grade sucker knows how to keep from losing his money in some of the ways that get the raw beginner. It is this semisucker rather than the 100 per cent article who is the real all-the-year-round support of the commission houses. He lasts about three and a half years on an average, as compared with a single season of from three to thirty weeks, which is the usual Wall Street life of a first offender. It is naturally the semisucker who is always quoting the famous trading aphorisms and the various rules of the game. He knows all the don'ts that ever fell from the oracular lips of the old stagers excepting the principal one, which is:

Don't be a sucker!

This semisucker is the type that thinks he has cut his wisdom teeth because he loves to buy on declines. He waits for them.

He measures his bargains by the number of points it has sold off from the top. In big bull markets the plain unadulterated sucker, utterly ignorant of rules and precedents, buys blindly because he hopes blindly. He makes most of the money until one of the healthy reactions takes it away from him at one fell swoop. But the Careful Mike sucker does what I did when I thought I was playing the game intelligently according to the intelligence of others. I knew I needed to change my bucket-shop methods and I thought I was solving my problem with any change, particularly one that assayed high gold values according to the experienced traders among the customers.

Most -let us call 'em customers -are alike. You find very few who can truthfully say that Wall Street doesn't owe them money. In Fullerton's there were the usual crowd. All grades! Well, there was one old chap who was not like the others. To begin with, he was a much older man. Another thing was that he never volunteered advice and never bragged of his winnings. He was a great hand for listening very attentively to the others. He did not seem very keen to get tips that is, he never asked the talkers what they'd heard or what they knew. But when somebody gave him one he always thanked the tipster very politely. Sometimes he thanked the tipster again when the tip turned out O.K. But if it went wrong he never whined, so that nobody could tell whether he followed it or let it slide by. It was a legend of the office that the old jigger was rich and could swing quite a line. But he wasn't donating much to the firm in the way of commissions; at least not that anyone could see. His name was Partridge, but they nicknamed him Turkey behind his back, because he was so thick-chested and had a habit of strutting about the various rooms, with the point of his chin resting on his breast.

The customers, who were all eager to be shoved and forced

into doing things so as to lay the blame for failure on others, used to go to old Partridge and tell him what some friend of a friend of an insider had advised them to do in a certain stock. They would tell him what they had not done with the tip so he would tell them what they ought to do. But whether the tip they had was to buy or to sell, the old chap's answer was always the same.

The customer would finish the tale of his perplexity and then ask: "What do you think I ought to do?"

Old Turkey would cock his head to one side, contemplate his fellow customer with a fatherly smile, and finally he would say very impressively, "You know, it's a bull market!"

Time and again I heard him say, "Well, this is a bull market, you know!" as though he were giving to you a priceless talisman wrapped up in a million-dollar accident- insurance policy. And of course I did not get his meaning.

One day a fellow named Elmer Harwood rushed into the office, wrote out an order and gave it to the clerk. Then he rushed over to where Mr. Partridge was listening politely to John Fanning's story of the time he overheard Keene give an order to one of his brokers and all that John made was a measly three points on a hundred shares and of course the stock had to go up twenty-four points in three days right after John sold out. It was at least the fourth time that John had told him that tale of woe, but old Turkey was smiling as sympathetically as if it was the first time he heard it.

Well, Elmer made for the old man and, without a word of apology to John Fanning, told Turkey, "Mr. Partridge, I have just sold my Climax Motors. My people say the market is entitled to a reaction and that I'll be able to buy it back cheaper. So you'd better do likewise. That is, if you've still got yours."

Elmer looked suspiciously at the man to whom he had given the original tip to buy. The amateur, or gratuitous, tipster always thinks he owns the receiver of his tip body and soul, even before he knows how the tip is going to turn out.

"Yes, Mr. Harwood, I still have it. Of course!" said Turkey gratefully. It was nice of Elmer to think of the old chap. "Well, now is the time to take your profit and get in again on the next dip," said Elmer, as if he had just made out the deposit slip for the old man. Failing to perceive enthusiastic gratitude in the beneficiary's face Elmer went on: "I have just sold every share I owned!"

From his voice and manner you would have conservatively estimated it at ten thousand shares. But Mr. Partridge shook his head regretfully and whined, "No! No! I can't do that!"

"What?" yelled Elmer.

"I simply can't!" said Mr. Partridge. He was in great trouble.

"Didn't I give you the tip to buy it?"

"You did, Mr. Harwood, and I am very grateful to you. Indeed, I am, sir. But "

"Hold on! Let me talk! And didn't that stock go op seven points in ten days? Didn't it?"

"It did, and I am much obliged to you, my dear boy. But

I couldn't think of selling that stock."

"You couldn't?" asked Elmer, beginning to look doubtful himself. It is a habit with most tip givers to be tip takers.

"No, I couldn't."

"Why not?" And Elmer drew nearer.

"Why, this is a bull market!" The old fellow said it as though he had given a long and detailed explanation.

"That's all right," said Elmer, looking angry because of his disappointment. "I know this is a bull market as well as you do. But you'd better slip them that stock of yours and buy it back on the reaction. You might as well reduce the cost to yourself."

"My dear boy," said old Partridge, in great distress "my dear boy, if I sold that stock now I'd lose my position; and then where would I be?"

Elmer Harwood threw up his hands, shook his head and walked over to me to get sympathy: "Can you beat it?" he asked me in a stage whisper. "I ask you 1"

I didn't say anything. So he went on: "I give him a tip on Climax Motors. He buys five hundred shares. He's got seven points' profit and I advise him to get out and buy 'em back on the reaction that's overdue even now. And what does he say when I tell him? He says that if he sells he'll lose his job. What do you know about that?"

"I beg your pardon, Mr. Harwood; I didn't say I'd lose my

job," cut in old Turkey. "I said I'd lose my position. And when you are as old as I am and you've been through as many booms and panics as I have, you'll know that to lose your position is something nobody can afford; not even John D. Rockefeller. I hope the stock reacts and that you will be able to repurchase your line at a substantial concession, sir. But I myself can only trade in accordance with the experience of many years. I paid a high price for it and I don't feel like throwing away a second tuition fee. But I am as much obliged to you as if I had the money in the bank. It's a bull market, you know." And he strutted away, leaving Elmer dazed.

What old Mr. Partridge said did not mean much to me until I began to think about my own numerous failures to make as much money as I ought to when I was so right on the general market. The more I studied the more I realized how wise that old chap was. He had evidently suffered from the same defect in his young days and knew his own human weaknesses. He would not lay himself open to a temptation that experience had taught him was hard to resist and had always proved expensive to him, as it was to me.

I think it was a long step forward in my trading education when I realized at last that when old Mr. Partridge kept on telling the other customers, "Well, you know this is a bull market!" he really meant to tell them that the big money was not in the individual fluctuations but in the main movements that is, not in reading the tape but in sizing up the entire market and its trend.

And right here let me say one thing: After spending many years in Wall Street and after making and losing millions of dollars I want to tell you this: It never was my thinking that made the big money for me. It always was my sitting. Got that? My sitting tight! It is no trick at all to be right on the market. You always find lots of early bulls in bull markets and early bears in bear markets. I've known many men who were right at exactly the right time, and began buying or selling stocks when prices were at the very level which should show the greatest profit. And their experience invariably matched mine that is, they made no real money out of it. Men who can both be right and sit tight are uncommon. I found it one of the hardest things to learn. But it is only after a stock operator has firmly grasped this that he can make big money. It is literally true that millions come easier to a trader after he knows how to trade than hundreds did in the days of his ignorance.

The reason is that a man may see straight and clearly and yet become impatient or doubtful when the market takes its time about doing as he figured it must do. That is why so many men in Wall Street, who are not at all in the sucker class, not even in the third grade, nevertheless lose money. The market does not beat them. They beat themselves, because though they have brains they cannot sit tight. Old Turkey was dead right in doing and saying what he did. He had not only the courage of his convictions but the intelligent patience to sit tight.

Disregarding the big swing and trying to jump in and out was fatal to me. Nobody can catch all the fluctuations. In a bull market your game is to buy and hold until you believe that the bull market is near its end. To do this you must study general conditions and not tips or special factors affecting individual stocks. Then get out of all your stocks; get out for keeps! Wait until you see or if you prefer, until you think you see the turn of the market; the beginning of a reversal of general conditions. You have to use your brains and your vision to do this; otherwise my advice would be as idiotic as to tell you to buy cheap and sell dear. One of the most helpful things that anybody can learn is to give up trying to catch the last eighth or the first. These two are the most expensive eighths in the world. They have cost stock traders, in the aggregate, enough millions of dollars to build a concrete highway across the continent.

Another thing I noticed in studying my plays in Fullerton's office after I began to trade less unintelligently was that my initial operations seldom showed me a loss. That naturally made me decide to start big. It gave me confidence in my own judgment before I allowed it to be vitiated by the advice of others or even by my own impatience at times. Without faith in his own judgment no man can go very far in this game. That is about all I have learned to study general conditions, to take a position and stick to it. I can wait without a twinge of impatience. I can see a setback without being shaken, knowing that it is only temporary. I have been short one hundred thousand shares and I have seen a big rally coming. I have figured and figured correctly that such a rally as I felt was inevitable, and even wholesome, would make a difference of one million dollars in my paper profits. And I nevertheless have stood pat and seen half my paper profit wiped out, without once considering the advisability of covering my shorts to put them out again on the rally. I knew that if I did I might lose my position and with it the certainty of a big killing. It is the big swing that makes the big money for you.

If I learned all this so slowly it was because I learned by my mistakes, and some time always elapses between making a mistake and realizing it, and more time between realizing it and exactly determining it. But at the same time I was faring pretty comfortably and was very young, so that I made up in other ways. Most of my winnings were still made in part through my tape reading because the kind of markets we were having lent themselves fairly well to my method. I was not losing either as often or as irritatingly as in the beginning of my New York experiences. It wasn't anything to be proud of, when you think that I had been broke three times in less than two years. And as I told you, being broke is a very efficient educational agency.

I was not increasing my stake very fast because I lived up to the handle all the time. I did not deprive myself of many of the things that a fellow of my age and tastes would want. I had my own automobile and I could not see any sense in skimping on living when I was taking it out of the market. The ticker only stopped Sundays and holidays, which was as it should be. Every time I found the reason for a loss or the why and how of another mistake, I added a brand-new Don't! to my schedule of assets. And the nicest way to capitalize my increasing assets was by not cutting down on my living expenses. Of course I had some amusing experiences and some that were not so amusing, but if I told them all in detail I'd never finish. As a matter of fact, the only incidents that I remember without special effort are those that taught me something of definite value to me in my trading; something that added to my store of knowledge of the game and of myself!

Chapter VI

In the spring of 1906 I was in Atlantic City for a short vacation. I was out of stocks and was thinking only of having a change of air and a nice rest. By the way, I had gone back to my first brokers, Harding Brothers, and my account had got to be pretty active. I could swing three or four thousand shares. That wasn't much more than I had done in the old Cosmopolitan shop when I was barely twenty years of age. But there was some difference between my one-point margin in the bucket shop and the margin required by brokers who actually bought or sold stocks for my account on the New York Stock Exchange.

You may remember the story I told you about that time when I was short thirty-five hundred Sugar in the Cosmopolitan and I had a hunch something was wrong and I'd better close the trade? Well, I have often had that curious feeling. As a rule, I yield to it. But at times I have pooh-poohed the idea and have told myself that it was simply asinine to follow any of these sudden blind impulses to reverse my position. I have ascribed my hunch to a state of nerves resulting from too many cigars or insufficient sleep or a torpid liver or something of that kind. When I have argued myself into disregarding my impulse and have stood pat I have always had cause to regret it. A dozen instances occur to me when I did not sell as per hunch, and the next day I'd go downtown and the market would be strong, or perhaps even advance, and I'd tell myself how silly it would have been to obey the blind impulse to sell. But on the following day there would be a pretty bad drop. Something had broken loose somewhere and I'd have made money by not being so wise and logical. The reason plainly was not physiological but psychological.

I want to tell you only about one of them because of what it did for me. It happened when I was having that little vacation in Atlantic City in the spring of 1906. I had a friend with me who also was a customer of Harding Brothers. I had no interest in the market one way or another and was enjoying my rest. I can always give up trading to play, unless of course it is an exceptionally active market in which my commitments are rather heavy. It was a bull market, as I remember it. The outlook was favorable for general business and the stock market had slowed down but the tone was firm and all indications pointed to higher prices.

One morning after we had breakfasted and had finished reading all the New York morning papers, and had got tired of watching the sea gulls picking up clams and flying up with them twenty feet in the air and dropping them on the hard wet sand to open them for their breakfast, my friend and I started up the Boardwalk. That was the most exciting thing we did in the daytime.

It was not noon yet, and we walked up slowly to kill time and breathe the salt air. Harding Brothers had a branch office on the Boardwalk and we used to drop in every morning and see how they'd opened. It was more force of habit than anything else, for I wasn't doing anything.

The market, we found, was strong and active. My friend, who was quite bullish, was carrying a moderate line purchased several points lower. He began to tell me what an obviously wise thing it was to hold stocks for much higher prices. I wasn't paying enough attention to him to take the trouble to agree with him. I was looking over the quotation board, noting the changes they were mostly advances until I came to Union Pacific. I got a feeling that I ought to sell it. I can't tell you more. I just felt like selling it. I asked myself why I should feel like that, and I couldn't find any reason whatever for going short of UP.

I stared at the last price on the board until I couldn't see any figures or any board or anything else, for that matter. All I knew was that I wanted to sell Union Pacific and I couldn't find out why I wanted to. I must have looked queer, for my friend, who was standing alongside of me, suddenly nudged me and asked, "Hey, what's the matter?"

"I don't know," I answered. "Going to sleep?" he said.

"No," I said. "I am not going to sleep. What I am going to do is to sell that stock." I had always made money following my hunches. I walked over to a table where there were some blank order pads. My friend followed me. I wrote out an order to sell a thousand Union Pacific at the market and handed it to the manager. He was smiling when I wrote it and when he took it. But when he read the order he stopped smiling and looked at me.

"Is this right?" he asked me. But I just looked at him and he rushed it over to the operator. "What are you doing?" asked my friend.

"I'm selling it!" I told him.

"Selling what?" he yelled at me. If he was a bull how could I be a bear? Something was wrong.

"A thousand UP," I said.

"Why?" he asked me in great excitement.

I shook my head, meaning I had no reason. But he must have thought I'd got a tip, because he took me by the arm and led me outside into the hall, where we could be out of sight and hearing of the other customers and rubbering chair-warmers.

"What did you hear?" he asked me. He was quite excited. UP. was one of his pets and he was bullish on it because of its earnings and its prospects. But he was willing to take a bear tip on it at second hand. "Nothing!" I said.

"You didn't?" He was skeptical and showed it plainly. "I didn't hear a thing."

"Then why in blazes are you selling?"

"I don't know," I told him. I spoke gospel truth. "Oh, come across, Larry," he said.

He knew it was my habit to know why I traded. I had sold a thousand shares of Union Pacific. I must have a very good reason to sell that much stock in the face of the strong market.

"I don't know," I repeated. "I just feel that something is going to happen." "What's going to happen?"

"I don't know. I can't give you any reason. All I know is that I want to sell that stock. And I'm going to let 'em have another thousand."

I walked back into the office and gave an order to sell a

second thousand. If I was right in selling the first thousand I ought to have out a little more.

"What could possibly happen?" persisted my friend, who couldn't make up his mind to follow my lead. If I'd told him that I had heard UP. was going down he'd have sold it without asking me from whom I'd heard it or why. "What could possibly happen?" he asked again.

"A million things could happen. But I can't promise you that any of them will. I can't give you any reasons and I can't tell fortunes," I told him.

"Then you're crazy," he said. "Stark crazy, selling that stock without rime or reason. You don't know why you want to sell it?"

"I don't know why I want to sell it. I only know I do want to," I said. "I want to, like everything." The urge was so strong that I sold another thousand.

That was too much for my friend. He grabbed me by the arm and said, "Here! Let's get out of this place before you sell the entire capital stock."

I had sold as much as I needed to satisfy my feeling, so I followed him without waiting for a report on the last two thousand shares. It was a pretty good jag of stock for me to sell even with the best of reasons. It seemed more than enough to be short of without any reason whatever, particularly when the entire market was so strong and there was nothing in sight to make anybody think of the bear side. But I remembered that on previous occasions when I had the same urge to sell and didn't do it I always had reasons to regret it.

I have told some of these stories to friends, and some of million. And Jim Fisk just looked at him and said, "Go ahead! Do! Sell it short and invite me to your funeral.' "

"Yes," I said; "and if that chap had sold it short, look at the killing he would have made! Sell some UP. yourself."

"Not I! I'm the kind that thrives best on not rowing against wind and tide."

On the following day, when fuller reports came in, the market began to slide off, but even then not as violently as it should. Knowing that nothing under the sun could stave off a substantial break I doubled up and sold five thousand shares. Oh, by that time it was plain to most people, and my brokers were willing enough. It wasn't reckless of them or of me, not the way I sized up the market. On the day following, the market began to go for fair. There was the dickens to pay. Of course I pushed my luck for all it was worth. I doubled up again and sold ten thousand shares more. It was the only play possible.

I wasn't thinking of anything except that I was right 100 per cent right and that this was a heaven-sent opportunity. It was up to me to take advantage of it. I sold more. Did I think that with such a big line of shorts out, it wouldn't take much of a rally to wipe out my paper profits and possibly my principal? I don't know whether I thought of that or not, but if I did it didn't carry much weight with me. I wasn't plunging recklessly. I was really playing conservatively. There was nothing that anybody could do to undo the earthquake, was there? They couldn't restore the crumpled

buildings overnight, free, gratis, for nothing, could they? AH the money in the world couldn't help much in the next few hours, could it?
I was not betting blindly. I wasn't a crazy bear. I wasn't drunk with success or thinking that because Frisco was pretty well wiped off the map the entire country was headed for the scrap heap. No, indeed! I didn't look for a panic. Well, the next day I cleaned up. I made two hundred and fifty thousand dollars. It was my biggest winnings up to that time. It was all made in a few days. The Street paid no attention to the earthquake the first day or two. They'll tell you that it was because the first despatches were not so alarming, but I think it was because it took so long to change the point of view of the public toward the securities markets. Even the professional traders for the most part were slow and shortsighted.

I have no explanation to give you, either scientific or childish. I am telling you what I did, and why, and what came of it. I was much less concerned with the mystery of the hunch than with the fact that I got a quarter of a million out of it. It meant that I could now swing a much bigger line than ever, if or when the time came for it.

That summer I went to Saratoga Springs. It was supposed to be a vacation for me, but I kept an eye on the market. To begin with, I wasn't so tired that it bothered me to think about it. And then, everybody I knew up there had or had had an active interest in it. We naturally talked about it. I have noticed that there is quite a difference between talking and trading. Some of these chaps remind you of the bold clerk who talks to his cantankerous employer as to a yellow dog when he tells you about it.

Harding Brothers had a branch office in Saratoga. Many of

their customers were there. But the real reason, I suppose, was the advertising value. Having a branch office in a resort is simply high-class billboard advertising. I used to drop in and sit around with the rest of the crowd. The manager was a very nice chap from the New York office who was there to give the glad hand to friends and strangers and, if possible, to get business. It was a wonderful place for tips all kinds of tips, horse-race, stock-market, and waiters'. The office knew I didn't take any, so the manager didn't come and whisper confidentially in my ear what he'd just got on the q. t. from the New York office. He simply passed over the telegrams, saying, "This is what they're sending out," or something of the kind.

Of course I watched the market. With me, to look at the quotation board and to read the signs is one process. My good friend Union Pacific, I noticed, looked like going up. The price was high, but the stock acted as if it were being accumulated. I watched it a couple of days without trading in it, and the more I watched it the more convinced I became that it was being bought on balance by somebody who was no piker, somebody who not only had a big bank roll but knew what was what. Very clever accumulation, I thought.

As soon as I was sure of this I naturally began to buy it, at about 160. It kept on acting all hunky, and so I kept on buying it, five hundred shares at a clip. The more I bought the stronger it got, without any spurt, and I was feeling very comfortable. I couldn't see any reason why that stock shouldn't go up a great deal more; not with what I read on the tape.

All of a sudden the manager came to me and said they'd got a message from New York they had a direct wire of course asking if I was in the office, and when they answered yes, another came saying: "Keep him there. Tell him Mr. Harding wants to speak to him."

I said I'd wait, and bought five hundred shares more of UP. I couldn't imagine what Harding could have to say to me. I didn't think it was anything about business. My margin was more than ample for what I was buying. Pretty soon the manager came and told me that Mr. Ed Harding wanted me on the long-distance telephone.

"Hello, Ed," I said.

But he said, "What the devil's the matter with you? Are you crazy?" "Are you?" I said.

"What are you doing?" he asked. "What do you mean?"

"Buying all that stock."

"Why, isn't my margin all right?"

"It isn't a case of margin, but of being a plain sucker." "I don't get you."

"Why are you buying all that Union Pacific?" "It's going up," I said.

"Going up, hell! Don't you know that the insiders are feeding it out to you? You're just about the easiest mark up there. You'd have more fun losing it on the ponies. Don't let them kid you."

"Nobody is kidding me," I told him. "I haven't talked to

a soul about it."

But he came back at me: "You can't expect a miracle to save you every time you plunge in that stock. Get out while you've still got a chance," he said. "It's a crime to be long of that stock at this level when these highbinders are shoveling it out by the ton."

"The tape says they're buying it," I insisted.

"Larry, I got heart disease when your orders began to come in. For the love of Mike, don't be a sucker. Get out! Right away. It's liable to bust wide open any minute. I've done my duty. Good-by!" And he hung up.

Ed Harding was a very clever chap, unusually well-informed and a real friend, disinterested and kindhearted. And what was even more, I knew he was in position to hear things. All I had to go by, in my purchases of UP., was my years of studying the behaviour of stocks and my perception of certain symptoms which experience had taught me usually accompanied a substantial rise. I don't know what happened to me, but I suppose I must have concluded that my tape reading told me the stock was being absorbed simply because very clever manipulation by the insiders made the tape tell a story that wasn't true. Possibly I was impressed by the pains Ed Harding took to stop me from making what he was so sure would be a colossal mistake on my part. Neither his brains nor his motives were to be questioned. Whatever it was that made me decide to follow his advice, I cannot tell you; but follow it, I did.

I sold out all my Union Pacific. Of course if it was unwise to be long of it it was equally unwise not to be short of it. So after I got rid of my long stock I sold four thousand shares short. I put out most of it around 162.

The next day the directors of the Union Pacific Company declared a 10 per cent dividend on the stock. At first nobody in Wall Street believed it. It was too much like the desperate maneuver of cornered gamblers. All the newspapers jumped on the directors. But while the Wall Street talent hesitated to act the market boiled over. Union Pacific led, and on huge transactions made a new high-record price. Some of the room traders made fortunes in an hour and I remember later hearing about a rather dull-witted specialist who made a mistake that put three hundred and fifty thousand dollars in his pocket. He sold his seat the following week and became a gentleman farmer the following month.

Of course I realised, the moment I heard the news of the declaration of that unprecedented 10 per cent dividend, that I got what I deserved for disregarding the voice of experience and listening to the voice of a tipster. My own convictions I had set aside for the suspicions of a friend, simply because he was disinterested and as a rule knew what he was doing.

As soon as I saw Union Pacific making new high records I said to myself, "This is no stock for me to be short of."

All I had in the world was up as margin in Harding's office. I was neither cheered nor made stubborn by the knowledge of that fact. What was plain was that I had read the tape accurately and that I had been a ninny to let Ed Harding shake my own resolution. There was no sense in recriminations, because I had no time to lose; and besides, what's done is done. So I gave an order to take in my shorts. The stock was around 165 when I sent in that order to buy in the four thousand UP. at the market. I had a three-point loss on it at that figure. Well, my brokers paid 172 and 174 for some of it before they were through. I found when I got my reports that Ed Harding's kindly intentioned interference cost me forty thousand dollars. A low price for a man to pay for not having the courage of his own convictions! It was a cheap lesson.

I wasn't worried, because the tape said still higher prices. It was an unusual move and there were no precedents for the action of the directors, but I did this time what I thought I ought to do. As soon as I had given the first order to buy four thousand shares to cover my shorts I decided to profit by what the tape indicated and so I went along. I bought four thousand shares and held that stock until the next morning. Then I got out. I not only made up the forty thousand dollars I had lost but about fifteen thousand besides. If Ed Harding hadn't tried to save me money I'd have made a killing. But he did me a very great service, for it was the lesson of that episode that, I firmly believe, completed my education as a trader.

It was not that all I needed to learn was not to lake tips but follow my own inclination. It was that I gained confidence in myself and I was able finally to shake off the old method of trading. That Saratoga experience was my last haphazard, hit-or-miss operation. From then on I began to think of basic conditions instead of individual stocks. I promoted myself to a higher grade in the hard school of speculation. It was a long and difficult step to take.

Chapter VII

I never hesitate to tell a man that I am bullish or bearish. But I do not tell people to buy or sell any particular stock. In a bear market all stocks go down and in a bull market they go up. I don't mean of course that in a bear market caused by a war, ammunition shares do not go up. I speak in a general sense. But the average man doesn't wish to be told that it is a bull or a bear market. What he desires is to be told specifically which particular stock to buy or sell. He wants to get something for nothing. He does not wish to work. He doesn't even wish to have to think. It is too much bother to have to count the money that he picks up from the ground.

Well, I wasn't that lazy, but I found it easier to think of individual stocks than of the general market and therefore of individual fluctuations rather than of general movements. I had to change and I did.

People don't seem to grasp easily the fundamentals of stock trading. I have often said that to buy on a rising market is the most comfortable way of buying stocks. Now, the point is not so much to buy as cheap as possible or go short at top prices, but to buy or sell at the right time. When I am bearish and I sell a stock, each sale must be at a lower level than the previous sale. When I am buying, the reverse is true. I must buy on a rising scale. I don't buy long stock on a scale down, I buy on a scale up.

Let us suppose, for example, that I am buying some stock.

I'll buy two thousand shares at no. If the stock goes up to ill after I buy it I am, at least temporarily, right in my operation, because it is a point higher; it shows me a profit. Well, because I am right I go in and buy another two thousand shares. If the market is still rising I buy a third lot of two thousand shares. Say the price goes to 114. I think it is enough for the time being. I now have a trading basis to work from. I am long six thousand shares at an average of in%, and the stock is selling at 114. I won't buy any more just then. I wait and see.

I figure that at some stage of the rise there is going to be a reaction. I want to see how the market takes care of itself after that reaction. It will probably react to where I got my third lot. Say that after going higher it falls back to H2J4, and then rallies. Well, just as it goes back to 113% I shoot an order to buy four thousand at the market of course. Well, if I get that fouf thousand at 113% I know something is wrong and I'll give a testing order that is, I'll sell one thousand shares to see how the market takes it. But suppose that of the order to buy the four thousand shares that I put in when the price was 113^4 I get two thousand at 114 and five hundred at 114^ and the rest on the way up so that for the last five hundred I pay 115^. Then I know I am right. It is the way I get the four thousand shares that tells me whether I am right in buying that particular stock at that particular time for of course I am working on the assumption that I have checked up general conditions pretty well and they are bullish. I never want to buy stocks too cheap or too easily.

I remember a story I heard about Deacon S. V. White when he was one of the big operators of the Street. He was a very fine old man, clever as they make them, and brave. He did some wonderful things in his day, from all I've heard.

It was in the old days when Sugar was one of the most

continuous purveyors of fireworks in the market.

H. O. Havemeyer, president of the company, was in the heyday of his power. I gather from talks with the old-timers that H. O. and his following had all the resources of cash and cleverness necessary to put through successfully any deal in their- own stock. They tell me that Havemeyer trimmed more small professional traders in that stock than any other insider in. any other stock. As a rule, the floor traders are more likely to thwart the insiders' game than help it.

One day a man who knew Deacon White rushed into the office all excited and said, "Deacon, you told me if I ever got any good information to come to you at once with it and if you used it you'd carry me for a few hundred shares." He paused for breath and for confirmation.

The deacon looked at him in that meditative way he had and said, "I don't know whether I ever told you exactly that or not, but I am willing to pay for information that I can use."

"Well, I've got it for you."

"Now, that's nice," said the deacon, so mildly that the man with the info swelled up and said,

"Yes, sir, deacon." Then he came closer so nobody else would hear and said, "H. O. Havemeyer is buying Sugar."

"Is he?" asked the deacon quite calmly.

It peeved the informant, who said impressively: "Yes, sir. Buying all he can get, deacon."

"My friend, are you sure?" asked old S. V.

"Deacon, I know it for a positive fact. The old inside gang are buying all they can lay their hands on. It's got something to do with the tariff and there's going to be a killing in the common. It will cross the preferred. And that means a sure thirty points for a starter."

"Do you really think so?" And the old man looked at him over the top of the old- fashioned silver-rimmed spectacles that he had put on to look at the tape.

"Do I think so? No, I don't think so; I know so. Absolutely! Why, deacon, when H. O. Havemeyer and his friends buy Sugar as they're doing now they're never satisfied with anything less than forty points net. I shouldn't be surprised to see the market get away from them any minute and shoot up before they've got their full lines. There ain't as much of it kicking around the brokers' offices as there was a month ago."

"He's buying Sugar, eh?" repeated the deacon absently.

"Buying it? Why, he's scooping it in as fast as he can without putting up the price on himself."

"So?" said the deacon. That was all. But it was enough to nettle the tipster, and he said, "Yes, sir-ree! And I call that very good information. Why, it's absolutely straight."

"Is it?"

"Yes; and it ought to be worth a whole lot. Are you going to use it?"

"Oh, yes. I'm going to use it."

"When?" asked the information bringer suspiciously.

"Right away." And the deacon called: -"Frank!" It was the first name of his shrewdest broker, who was then in the adjoining room.

"Yes, sir," said Frank.

"I wish you'd go over to the Board and sell ten thousand Sugar."

"Sell?" yelled the tipster. There was such suffering in his voice that Frank, who had started out at a run, halted in his tracks.

"Why, yes," said the deacon mildly.

"But I told you H. O. Havemeyer was buying it!"

"I know you did, my friend," said the deacon calmly; and turning to the broker: "Make haste, Frank!"

The broker rushed out to execute the order and the tipster turned red.

"I came in here," he said furiously, "with the best information I ever had. I brought it to you because I thought you were my friend, and square. I expected you to act on it." "I am acting on it," interrupted the deacon in a tranquillising voice. "But I told you H. O. and his gang were buying!"

"That's right. I heard you."

"Buying! Buying! I said buying!" shrieked the tipster.

"Yes, buying! That is what I understood you to say," the deacon assured him. He was standing by the ticker, looking at the tape. "But you are selling it."

"Yes; ten thousand shares." And the deacon nodded. "Selling it, of course."

He stopped talking to concentrate on the tape and the tipster approached to see what the deacon saw, for the old man was very foxy. While he was looking over the deacon's shoulder a clerk came in with a slip, obviously the report from Frank. The deacon barely glanced at it. He had seen on the tape "how his order had been executed.

It made him say to the clerk, "Tell him to sell another ten thousand Sugar." "Deacon, I swear to you that they really are buying the stock!"

"Did Mr. Havemeyer tell you?" asked the deacon quietly.

"Of course not! He never tells anybody anything. He would not bat an eyelid to help his best friend make a nickel. But I know this is true."

"Do not allow yourself to become excited, my friend." And the deacon held up a hand. He was looking at the tape. The tip-bringer said, bitterly:

"If I had known you were going to do the opposite of what I expected I'd never have wasted your time or mine. But I am not going to feel glad when you cover that stock at an awful loss. I'm sorry for you, deacon. Honest! If you'll excuse me I'll go elsewhere and act on my own information."

"I'm acting on it. I think I know a little about the market;

not as much, perhaps, as you and your friend H. O. Havemeyer, but still a little. What I am doing is what my experience tells me is the wise thing to do with the information you brought me. After a man has been in Wall Street as long as I have he is grateful for anybody who feels sorry for him. Remain calm, my friend."

The man just stared at the deacon, for whose judgment and nerve he had great respect.

Pretty soon the clerk came in again and handed a report to the deacon, who looked at it and said: "Now tell him to buy thirty thousand Sugar. Thirty thousand!"

The clerk hurried away and the tipster just grunted and looked at the old gray fox.

"My friend," the deacon explained kindly, "I did not doubt that you were telling me the truth as you saw it. But even if I had heard H. O. Havemeyer tell you himself, I still would have acted as I did. For there was only one way to find out if anybody was buying the stock in the way you said H. O. Havemeyer and his friends were buying it, and that was to do what I did. The first ten thousand shares went fairly easily. It was not quite conclusive. But the second ten thousand was absorbed by a market that did not stop rising. The way the twenty thousand shares were taken by somebody proved to me that somebody was in truth willing to take all the stock that was offered. It doesn't particularly matter at this point who that particular somebody may be. So I have covered my shorts and am long ten thousand shares, and I think that your information was good as far as it went."

"And how far does it go?" asked the tipster.

"You have five hundred shares in this office at the average price of the ten thousand shares," said the deacon. "Good day, my friend. Be calm the next time."

"Say, deacon," said the tipster, "won't you please sell mine when you sell yours? I don't know as much as I thought I did."

That's the theory. That is why I never buy stocks cheap. Of course I always try to buy effectively in such a way as to help my side of the market. When it comes to selling stocks, it is plain that nobody can sell unless somebody wants those stocks.

If you operate on a large scale you will have to bear that in mind all the time. A man studies conditions, plans his operations carefully and proceeds to act. He swings a pretty fair line and he accumulates a big profit on paper. Well, that man can't sell at will. You can't expect the market to absorb fifty thousand shares of one stock as easily as it does one hundred. He will have to wait until he has a market there to take it. There comes the time when he thinks the requisite buying power is there. When that opportunity comes he must seize it. As a rule he will have been waiting for it. He has to sell when he can, not when he wants to. To learn the time, he has to watch and test. It is no trick to tell when the market can take what you give it. But in starting a movement it is unwise to take on your full line unless you are convinced that conditions are exactly right. Remember that stocks are never too high for you to begin buying or too low to begin selling. But after the initial transaction, don't make a second unless the first shows you a profit. Wait and watch. That is where your tape reading conies in to enable you to decide as to the proper time for beginning. Much depends upon beginning at exactly the right time. It took me years to realize the importance of this. It also cost me some hundreds of thousands of dollars.

I don't mean to be understood as advising persistent pyramiding. A man can pyramid and make big money that he couldn't make if he didn't pyramid; of course. But what I meant to say was this: Suppose a man's line is five hundred shares of stock. I say that he ought not to buy it all at once ; not if he is speculating. If he is merely gambling the only advice I have to give him is, don't!

Suppose he buys his first hundred, and that promptly shows" him a loss. Why should he go to work and get more stock? He ought to see at once that he is in wrong; at least temporarily.

Chapter VIII

The Union Pacific incident in Saratoga in the summer of 1906 made me more independent than ever of tips and talk that is, of the opinions and surmises and suspicions of other people, however friendly or however able they might be personally. Events, not vanity, proved for me that I could read the tape more accurately than most of the people about me. I also was better equipped than the average customer of Harding Brothers in that I was utterly free from speculative prejudices. The bear side doesn't appeal to me any more than the bull side, or vice versa. My one steadfast prejudice is against being wrong.

Even as a lad I always got my own meanings out of such facts as I observed. It is the only way in which the meaning reaches me. I cannot get out of facts what somebody tells me to get. They are my facts, don't you see? If I believe some thing you can be sure it is because I simply must. When I am long of stocks it is because my reading of conditions has made me bullish. But you find many people, reputed to be intelligent, who are bullish because they have stocks. I do not allow my possessions or my prepossessions either to do any thinking for me. That is why I repeat that I never argue with the tape. To be angry at the market because it unexpectedly or even illogically goes against you is like getting mad at your lungs because you have pneumonia.

I had been gradually approaching the full realization of how much more than tape reading there was to stock speculation. Old man Partridge's insistence on the vital importance of being continuously bullish in a bull market doubtless made tny mind dwell on the need above all other things of determining the kind of market a man is trading in. I began to realize that the big money must necessarily be in the big swing. Whatever might seem to give a big swing its initial impulse, the fact is that its continuance is not the result of manipulation by pools or artifice by financiers, but depends upon basic conditions. And no matter who opposes it, the swing must inevitably run as far and as fast and as long as the impelling forces determine.

After Saratoga I began to see more clearly perhaps I should say more maturely that since the entire list moves in accordance with the main current there was not so much need as I had imagined to study individual plays or the behaviour of this or the other stock. Also, by thinking of the swing a man was not limited in his trading. He could buy or sell the entire list. In certain stocks a short line is dangerous after a man sells more than a certain percentage of the capital stock, the amount depending upon how, where and by whom the stock is held. But he could sell a million shares of the general list if he had the price without the danger of being squeezed. A great deal of money used to be made periodically by insiders in the old days out of the shorts and their carefully fostered fears of corners and squeezes.

Obviously the thing to do was to be bullish in a bull market and bearish in a bear market. Sounds silly, doesn't it? But I had to grasp that general principle firmly before I saw that to put it into practice really meant to anticipate probabilities. It took me a long time to learn to trade on those lines. But in justice to myself I must remind you that up to then I had never had a big enough stake to speculate that way. A big swing will mean big money if your line is big, and to be able to swing a big line you need a big balance at your broker's.

I always had or felt that I had to make my daily bread out of the stock market. It interfered with my efforts to increase the stake available for the more profitable but slower and therefore more immediately expensive method of trading on swings.

But now not only did my confidence in myself grow stronger but my brokers ceased to think of me as a sporadically lucky Boy Plunger. They had made a great deal out of me in commissions, but now I was in a fair way to become their star customer and as such to have a value beyond the actual volume of my trading. A customer who makes money is an asset to any broker's office.

The moment I ceased to be satisfied with merely studying the tape I ceased to concern myself exclusively with the daily fluctuations in specific stocks, and when that happened I simply had to study the game from a different angle. I worked back from the quotation to first principles; from price fluctuations to basic conditions.

Of course I had been reading the daily dope regularly for a long time. All traders do. But much of it was gossip, some of it deliberately false, and the rest merely the personal opinion of the writers. The reputable weekly reviews when they touched upon underlying conditions were not entirely satisfactory to me. The point of view of the financial editors was not mine as a rule. It was not a vital matter for them to marshal their facts and draw their conclusions from them, but it was for me. Also there was a vast difference in our appraisal of the element of time. The analysis of the week that had passed was less important to me than the forecast of the weeks that were to come.

For years I had been the victim of an unfortunate combination of inexperience, youth and insufficient capital. But now I felt the elation of a discoverer. My new attitude toward the game explained my repeated failures to make big money in New York. But now with adequate resources, experience and confidence, I was in such a hurry to try the new key that I did not notice that there was another lock on the door a time lock! It was a perfectly natural oversight. I had to pay the usual tuition a good whack per each step forward.

I studied the situation in 1906 and I thought that the money outlook was particularly serious. Much actual wealth the world over had been destroyed. Everybody must sooner or later feel the pinch, and therefore nobody would be in position to help anybody. It would not be the kind of hard times that comes from the swapping of a house worth ten thousand dollars for a carload of race horses worth eight thousand dollars. It was the complete destruction of the house by fire and of most of the horses by a railroad wreck. It was good hard cash that went up in cannon smoke in the Boer War, and the millions spent for feeding nonproducing soldiers in South Africa meant no help from British investors as in the past. Also, the earthquake and the fire in San Francisco and other disasters touched everybody manufacturers, farmers, merchants, labourers and millionaires. The railroads must suffer greatly. I figured that nothing could stave off one peach of a smash. Such being the case there was but one thing to do sell stocks!

I told you I had already observed that my initial transaction, after I made up my mind which way I was going to trade, was apt to show me a profit. And now when I decided to sell I plunged. Since we undoubtedly were entering upon a genuine bear market I was sure I should make the biggest killing of my career.

The market went off. Then it came back. It shaded off and then it began to advance steadily. My paper profits vanished and my paper losses grew. One day it looked as if not a bear would be left to tell the tale of the strictly genuine bear market. I couldn't stand the gaff. I covered. It was just as well. If I hadn't I wouldn't have had enough left to buy a postal card. I lost most of my fur, but it was better to live to fight another day.

I had made a mistake. But where? I was bearish in a bear market. That was wise. I had sold stocks short. That was proper. I had sold them too soon. That was costly. My position was right but my play was wrong. However, every day brought the market nearer to the inevitable smash. So I waited and when the rally began to falter and pause I let them have as much stock as my sadly diminished margins permitted. I was right this time for exactly one whole day, for on the next there was another rally. Another big bite out of yours truly! So I read the tape and covered and waited. In due course I sold again and again they went down promisingly and then they rudely rallied.

It looked as if the market were doing its best to make me go back to my old and simple ways of bucket-shop trading. It was the first time I had worked with a definite forward-looking plan embracing the entire market instead of one or two stocks. I figured that I must win if I held out. Of course at that time I had not developed my system of placing my bets or I would have put out my short line on a declining market, as I explained to you the last time. I would not then have lost so much of my margin. I would have been wrong but not hurt. You see, I had observed certain facts but had not learned to co- ordinate them. My incomplete observation not only did not help but actually hindered.

I have always found it profitable to study my mistakes. Thus I eventually discovered that it was all very well not to lose your bear position in a bear market, but that at all times the tape should be read to determine the propitiousness of the time for operating. If you begin right you will not see your profitable position seriously menaced; and then you will find no trouble in sitting tight.

Of course to-day I have greater confidence in the accuracy of my observations in which neither hopes nor hobbies play any part and also I have greater facilities for verifying my facts as well as for variously testing the correctness of my views. But in 1906 the succession of rallies dangerously impaired my margins.

I was nearly twenty-seven years old. I had been at the game twelve years. But the first time I traded because of a crisis that was still to come I found that I had been using a telescope. Between my first glimpse of the storm cloud and the time for cashing in on the big break the stretch was evidently so much greater than I had thought that I began to wonder whether I really saw what I thought I saw so clearly. We had had many warnings and sensational ascensions in call-money rates. Still some of the great financiers talked hopefully at least to newspaper reporters and the ensuing rallies in the stock market gave the lie to the calamity howlers. Was I fundamentally wrong in being bearish or merely temporarily wrong in having begun to sell short too soon?

I decided that I began too soon, but that I really couldn't help it. Then the market began to sell off. That was my opportunity. I sold all I could, and then stocks rallied again, to quite a high level.

It cleaned me out.

There I was right and busted!

I tell you it was remarkable. What happened was this: I looked ahead and saw a big pile of dollars. Out of it stuck a sign. It had "Help yourself," on it, in huge letters. Beside it stood a cart with "Lawrence Livingston Trucking Corporation" painted on its side. I had a brand-new shovel in my hand. There was not another soul in sight, so I had no competition in the gold-shoveling, which is one beauty of seeing the dollar-heap ahead of others. The people who might have seen it if they had stopped to look were just then looking at baseball games instead, or motoring or buying houses to be paid for with the very dollars that I saw. That was the first time that I had seen big money ahead, and I naturally started toward it on the run. Before I could reach the dollar-pile my wind went back on me and I fell to the ground. The pile of dollars was still there, but I had lost the shovel, and the wagon was gone. So much for sprinting too soon! I was too eager to prove to myself that I had seen real dollars and not a mirage. I saw, and knew that I saw. Thinking about the reward for my excellent sight kept me from considering the distance to the dollar-heap. I should have walked and not sprinted.

That is what happened. I didn't wait to determine whether or not the time was right for plunging on the bear side. On the one occasion when I should have invoked the aid of my tape-reading I didn't do it. That is how I came to learn that even when one is properly bearish at the very beginning of a bear market it is well not to begin selling in bulk until there is no danger of the engine back-firing.

I had traded in a good many thousands of shares at Harding's office in all those years, and, moreover, the firm had confidence in me and our relations were of the pleasantest. I think they felt that I was bound to be right again very shortly and they knew that with my habit of pushing my luck all I needed was a start and I'd more than recover what I had lost. They had made a great deal of money out of my trading and they would make more. So there was no trouble about my being able to trade there again as long as my credit stood high.

The succession of spankings I had received made me less aggressively cocksure; perhaps I should say less careless, for of course I knew I was just so much nearer to the smash. All I could do was wait watchfully, as I should have done before plunging. It wasn't a case of locking the stable after the horse was stolen. I simply had to be sure, the next time I tried. If a man didn't make mistakes he'd own the world in a month. But if he didn't profit by his mistakes he wouldn't own a blessed thing.

Well, sir, one fine morning I came downtown feeling cocksure once more. There wasn't any doubt this time. I had read an advertisement in the financial pages of all the newspapers that was the high sign I hadn't had the sense to wait for before plunging. It was the announcement of a new issue of stock by the Northern Pacific and Great Northern roads. The payments were to be made on the installment plan for the convenience of the stockholders. This consideration was something new in Wall Street. It struck me as more than ominous.

For years the unfailing bull item on Great Northern preferred had been the announcement that another melon was to be cut, said melon consisting of the right of the lucky stockholders to subscribe at par to a new issue of Great Northern stock.

These rights were valuable, since the market price was always way above par. But now the money market was such that the most powerful banking houses in the country were none too sure the stockholders would be able to pay cash for the bargain. And Great Northern preferred was selling at about 330!

As soon as I got to the office I told Ed Harding, "The time to sell is right now. This is when I should have begun. Just look at that ad, will you?"

He had seen it. I pointed out what the bankers' confession amounted to in my opinion, but he couldn't quite see the big break right on top of us. He thought it better to wait before putting out a very big short line by reason of the market's habit of having big rallies. If I waited prices might be lower, but the operation would be safer.

"Ed," I said to him, "the longer the delay in starting the sharper the break will be when it does start. That ad is a signed confession on the part of the bankers. What they fear is what I hope. This is a sign for us to get aboard the bear wagon. It is all we needed. If I had ten million dollars I'd stake every cent of it this minute."

I had to do some more talking and arguing. He wasn't content with the only inferences a sane man could draw from that amazing advertisement. It was enough for me, but not for most of the people in the office. I sold a little; too little.

A few days later St. Paul very kindly came out with an announcement of an issue of its own; either stock or notes, I forget which. But that doesn't matter. What mattered then was that I noticed the moment I read it that the date of payment was set ahead of the Great Northern and Northern Pacific payments, which had been announced earlier. It was as plain as though they had used a megaphone that grand old St. Paul was trying to beat the two other railroads to what little money there was floating around in Wall Street. The St. Paul's bankers quite obviously feared that there wasn't enough for all three and they were not saying, "After you, my dear Alphonse!" If money already was that scarce and you bet the bankers knew what would it be later? The railroads needed it desperately. It wasn't there. What was the answer?

Sell 'em! Of course! The public, with their eyes fixed on the stock market, saw little that week. The wise stock operators saw much that year. That was the difference.

For me, that was the end of doubt and hesitation. I made up my mind for keeps then and there. That same morning I began what really was my first campaign along the lines that I have since followed. I told Harding what I thought and how I stood, and he made no objections to my selling Great Northern preferred at around 330, and other stocks at high prices. I profited by my earlier and costly mistakes and sold more intelligently.

My reputation and my credit were reestablished In a jiffy. That is the beauty of being right in a broker's office, whether by accident or not. But this time I was cold-bloodedly right, not because of a hunch or from skilful reading of the tape, but as the result of my analysis of conditions affecting the stock market in general. I wasn't guessing. I was anticipating the inevitable. It did not call for any courage to sell stocks. I simply could not see anything but lower prices, and I had to act on it, didn't I? What else could I do?

The whole list was soft as mush. Presently there was a rally and people came to me to warn me that the end of the decline had been reached. The big fellows, knowing the short interest to be enormous, had decided to squeeze the stuffing out of the bears, and so forth. It would set us pessimists back a few millions. It was a cinch that the big fellows would have no mercy. I used to thank these kindly counsellors. I wouldn't even argue, because then they would have thought that I wasn't grateful for the warnings.

The friend who had been in Atlantic City with me was in agony. He could understand the hunch that was followed by the earthquake. He couldn't disbelieve in such agencies, since I had made a quarter of a million by intelligently obeying my blind impulse to sell Union Pacific. He even said it was Providence working in its mysterious way to make me sell stocks when he himself was bullish. And he could understand my second UP. trade in Saratoga because he could understand any deal that involved one stock, on which the tip definitely fixed the movement in advance, either up or down. But this thing of predicting that all stocks were bound to go down used to exasperate him. What good did that kind of dope do anybody? How in blazes could a gentleman tell what to do?

I recalled old Partridge's favourite remark "Well, this is a bull market, you know" as though that were tip enough for anybody who was wise enough; as in truth it was. It was very curious how, after suffering tremendous losses from a break of fifteen or twenty points, people who were still hanging on, welcomed a three-point rally and were certain the bottom had been reached and complete recovery begun.

One day my friend came to me and asked me, "Have you covered?" "Why should I?" I said

“For the best reason in the world.” “What reason is that?”

“To make money. They’ve touched bottom and what goes down must come up. Isn’t that so?”

“Yes,” I answered. “First they sink to the bottom. Then they come up; but not right away. They’ve got to be good and dead a couple of days. It isn’t time for these corpses to rise to the surface. They are not quite dead yet.”

An old-timer heard me. He was one of those chaps that are always reminded of something. He said that William R. Travers, who was bearish, once met a friend who was bullish. They exchanged market views and the friend said, “Mr. Travers, how can you be bearish with the market so stiff?” and Travers retorted, “Yes! Th-the s-s-stiffness of d-death!” It was Travers who went to the office of a company and asked to be allowed to see the books. The clerk asked him, “Have you an interest in this company?” and Travers answered, “I sh-should s-say I had! I’m sh-short t-t-twenty thousand sh-shares of the stock!”

Well, the rallies grew feebler and feebler. I was pushing my luck for all I was worth. Every time I sold a few thousand shares of Great Northern preferred the price broke several points. I felt out weak spots elsewhere and let ‘em have a few. All yielded, with one impressive exception; and that was Reading.

When everything else hit the toboggan slide Reading stood like the Rock of Gibraltar. Everybody said the stock was cornered. It certainly acted like it. They used to tell me it was plain suicide to sell Reading short. There were people in the office who were now as bearish on everything as I was. But when anybody hinted at selling Reading they shrieked for help. I myself had sold some short and was standing pat on it. At the same time I naturally preferred to seek and hit the soft spots instead of attacking the more strongly protected specialties. My tape reading found easier money for me in other stocks.

I heard a great deal about the Reading bull pool. It was a mighty strong pool. To begin with they had a lot of low-priced stock, so that their average was actually below the prevailing level, according to friends who told me. Moreover, the principal members of the pool had close connections of the friendliest character with the banks whose money they were using to carry their huge holdings of Reading. As long as the price stayed up the bankers' friendship was staunch and steadfast. One pool member's paper profit was upward of three millions. That allowed for some decline without causing fatalities. No wonder the stock stood up and defied the bears. Every now and then the room traders looked at the price, smacked their lips and proceeded to test it with a thousand shares or two. They could not dislodge a share, so they covered and went looking elsewhere for easier money. Whenever I looked at it I also sold a little more just enough to convince myself that I was true to my new trading principles and wasn't playing favourites.

In the old days the strength of Reading might have fooled me. The tape kept on saying, "Leave it alone!" But my reason told me differently. I was anticipating a general break, and there were not going to be any exceptions, pool or no pool.

I have always played a lone hand. I began that way in the bucket shops and have kept it up. It is the way my mind works. I have to do my own seeing and my own thinking.

But I can tell you after the market began to go my way I felt for the first time in my life that I had allies the strongest and truest in the world: underlying conditions. They were helping me with all their might. Perhaps they were a trifle slow at times in bringing up the reserves, but they were dependable, provided I did not get too impatient. I was not pitting my tape-reading knack or my hunches against chance. The inexorable logic of events was making money for me.

The thing was to be right; to know it and to act accordingly. General conditions, my true allies, said "Down!" and Reading disregarded the command. It was an insult to us. It began to annoy me to see Reading holding firmly, as though everything were serene. It ought to be the best short sale in the entire list because it had not gone down and the pool was carrying a lot of stock that it would not be able to carry when the money stringency grew more pronounced. Some day the bankers' friends would fare no better than the friendless public. The stock must go with the others. If Reading didn't decline, then my theory was wrong; I was wrong; facts were wrong; logic was wrong.

I figured that the price held because the Street was afraid to sell it. So on day I gave to two brokers each an order to sell four thousand shares, at the same time. You ought to have seen that cornered stock, that it was sure suicide to go short of, take a headlong dive when those competitive orders struck it. I let 'em have a few thousand more. The price was in when I started selling it. Within a few minutes I took in my entire short line at 92.

I had a wonderful time after that, and in February of 1907 I cleaned up. Great Northern preferred had gone down sixty or seventy points, and other stocks in proportion. I had made a good bit, but the reason I cleaned up was that I figured that the decline had discounted the immediate future. I looked for a fair recovery, but I wasn't bullish enough to play for a turn. I wasn't going to lose my position entirely. The market would not be right for me to trade in for a while. The first ten thousand dollars I made in the bucket shops I lost because I traded in and out of season, every day, whether or not conditions were right. I wasn't making that mistake twice. Also, don't forget that I had gone broke a little while before because I had seen this break too soon and started selling before it was time. Now when I had a big profit I wanted to cash in so that I could feel I had been right. The rallies had broken me before. I wasn't going to let the next rally wipe me out. Instead of sitting tight I went to Florida. I love fishing and I needed a rest. I could get both down there. And besides, there are direct wires between Wall Street and Palm Beach.

Chapter IX

\I cruised off the coast of Florida. The fishing was good. I was out of stocks. My mind was easy. I was having a fine time. One day off Palm Beach some friends came alongside in a motor boat. One of them brought a newspaper with him. I hadn't looked at one in some days and had not felt any desire to see one. I was not interested in any news it might print. But I glanced over the one my friend brought to the yacht, and I saw that the market had had a big rally; ten points and more.

I told my friends that I would go ashore with them. Moderate rallies from time to time were reasonable. But the bear market was not over; and here was Wall Street or the fool public or desperate bull interests disregarding monetary conditions and marking up prices beyond reason or letting somebody else do it. It was too much for me. I simply had to take a look at the market. I didn't know what I might or might not do. But I knew that my pressing need was the sight of the quotation board.

My brokers, Harding Brothers, had a branch office in Palm Beach. When I walked in I found there a lot of chaps I knew. Most of them were talking bullish. They were of the type that trade on the tape and want quick action. Such traders don't care to look ahead very far because they don't need to with their style of play. I told you how I'd got to be known in the New York office as the Boy Plunger. Of course people always magnify a fellow's winnings and the size of the line he swings. The fellows in the office had heard that I had made a killing in New York on the bear side and they now expected that I again would plunge on the short side. They themselves thought the rally would go to a good deal further, but they rather considered it my duty to fight it.

I had come down to Florida on a fishing trip. I had been under a pretty severe strain and I needed my holiday. But the moment I saw how far the recovery in prices had gone I no longer felt the need of a vacation. I had not thought of just what I was going to do when I came ashore. But now I knew I must sell stocks. I was right, and I must prove it in my old and only way by saying it with money. To sell the general list would be a proper, prudent, profitable and even patriotic action.

The first thing I saw on the quotation board was that Anaconda was on the point of crossing 300. It had been going up by leaps and bounds and there was apparently an aggressive bull party in it. It was an old trading theory of mine that when a stock crosses 100 or 200 or 300 for the first time the price does not stop at the even figure but goes a good deal higher, so that if you buy it as soon as it crosses the line it is almost certain to show you a profit. Timid people don't like to buy a stock at a new high record. But I had the history of such movements to guide me.

Anaconda was only quarter stock that is, the par of the shares was only twenty-five dollars. It took four hundred shares of it to equal the usual one hundred shares of other stocks, the par value of which was one hundred dollars. I figured that when it crossed 300 it ought to keep on going and probably touch 340 in a jiffy.

I was bearish, remember, but I was also a tape-reading trader. I knew Anaconda, if it went the way I figured, would move very quickly. Whatever moves fast always appeals to me. I have learned patience and how to sit tight, but my personal preference is for fleet movements, and Anaconda certainly was no sluggard. My buying it because it crossed 300 was prompted by the desire, always strong in me, of confirming my observations.

Just then the tape was saying that the buying was stronger than the selling, and therefore the general rally might easily go a bit further. It would be prudent to wait before going short. Still I might as well pay myself wages for waiting. This would be accomplished by taking a quick thirty points out of Anaconda. Bearish on the entire market and bullish on that one stock! So I bought thirty-two thousand shares of Anaconda that is, eight thousand full shares. It was a nice little flyer but I was sure of my premises and I figured that the profit would help to swell the margin available for bear operations later on.

On the next day the telegraph wires were down on account of a storm up North or something of the sort. I was in Harding's office waiting for news. The crowd was chewing the rag and wondering all sorts of things, as stock traders will when they can't trade. Then we got a quotation the only one that day: Anaconda, 292.

There was a chap with me, a broker I had met in New York. He knew I was long eight thousand full shares and I suspect that he had some of his own, for when we got that one quotation he certainly had a fit. He couldn't tell whether the stock at that very moment had gone off another ten points or not. The way Anaconda had gone up it wouldn't have been anything unusual for it to break twenty points. But I said to him, "Don't you worry, John. It will be all right to-morrow."

That was really the way I felt. But he looked at me and shook his head. He knew better. He was that kind. So I laughed, and I waited in the office in case some quotation trickled through. But no, sir. That one was all we got: Anaconda, 292. It meant a paper loss to me of nearly one hundred thousand dollars. I had wanted quick action. Well, I was getting it.

The next day the wires were working and we got the quotations as usual. Anaconda opened at 298 and went up to 302^4, but pretty soon it began to fade away. Also, the rest of the market was not acting just right for a further rally. I made up my mind that if Anaconda went back to 301 I must" consider the whole thing a fake movement. On a legitimate advance the price should have gone to 310 without stopping. If instead it reacted it meant that precedents had failed me and I was wrong: and the only thing to do when a man is wrong is to be right by ceasing to be wrong. I had bought eight thousand full shares in expectation of a thirty or forty point rise. It would not be my first mistake; nor my last.

Sure enough, Anaconda fell back to 301. The moment it touched that figure I sneaked over to the telegraph operator they had a direct wire to the New York office and I said to him, "Sell all my Anaconda, eight thousand full shares." I said it in a low voice. I didn't want anybody else to know what I was doing.

He looked up at me almost in horror. But I nodded and said, "All I've got!"

"Surely, Mr. Livingston, you don't meant at the market?" and he looked as if he was going to lose a couple of millions of his own through bum execution by a careless broker. But I just told him, "Sell it! Don't argue about it!"

The two Black boys, Jim and Ollie, were in the office, out of hearing of the operator and myself. They were big traders who had come originally from Chicago, where they had been famous plungers in wheat, and were now heavy traders on the New York Stock Exchange. They were very wealthy and were high rollers for fair.

As I left the telegraph operator to go back to my seat in front of the quotation board Oliver Black nodded to me and smiled.

"You'll be sorry, Larry," he said.

I stopped and asked him, "What do you mean?" "To-morrow you'll be buying it back."

"Buying what back?" I said. I hadn't told a soul except the telegraph operator.

"Anaconda," he said. "You'll be paying 320 for it. That wasn't a good move of yours, Larry." And he smiled again.

"What wasn't?" And I looked innocent.

"Selling your eight thousand Anaconda at the market; in fact, insisting on it," said Ollie Black.

I knew that he was supposed to be very clever and always traded on inside news. But how he knew my business so accurately was beyond me. I was sure the office hadn't given me away.

"Ollie, how did you know that?" I asked him.

He laughed and told me: "I got it from Charlie Kratzer." That was the telegraph operator. "But he never budged from his place," I said.

"I couldn't hear you and him whispering," he chuckled. "But I heard every word of the message he sent to the New York office for you. I learned telegraphy years ago after I had a big row over a mistake in a message. Since then when I do what you did just now give an order by word of mouth to an operator I want to be sure the operator sends the message as I give it to him. I know what he sends in my name. But you will be sorry you sold that Anaconda. It's going to 500."

"Not this trip, Ollie," I said.

He stared at me and said, "You're pretty cocky about it."

"Not I; the tape," I said. There wasn't any ticker there so there wasn't any tape. But he knew what I meant.

"I've heard of those birds," he said, "who look at the tape and instead of seeing prices they see a railroad time-table of the arrival and departure of stocks. But they were in padded cells where they couldn't hurt themselves."

I didn't answer him anything because about that time the boy brought me a memorandum. They had sold five thousand shares at 299-3/4. I knew our quotations were a little behind the market. The price on the board at Palm Beach when I gave the operator the order to sell was 301. I felt so certain that at that very moment the price at which the stock was actually selling on the Stock Exchange in New York was less, that if anybody had offered to take the stock off my hands at 296 I'd have been tickled to death to accept. What happened shows you that I am right in never trading at limits. Suppose I had limited my selling price to 300? I'd never have got it off. No, sir! When you want to get out, get out.

Now, my stock cost me about 300. They got off five hundred shares full shares, of course at 299-3/4. The next thousand they sold at 299-5/8. Then a hundred at 1/2; two hundred at 3/8 and two hundred at 1/4. The last of my stock went at 298-3/4. It took Harding's cleverest floor man fifteen minutes to get rid of that last one hundred shares. They didn't want to crack it wide open.

The moment I got the report of the sale of the last of my long stock I started to do what I had really come ashore to do that is, to sell stocks. I simply had to. There was the market after its outrageous rally, begging to be sold. Why, people were beginning to talk bullish again. The course of the market, however, told me that the rally had run its course. It was safe to sell them. It did not require reflection.

The next day Anaconda opened below 296. Oliver Black, who was waiting for a further rally, had come down early to be Johnny-on-the-spot when the stock crossed 320. I don't know how much of it he was long of or whether he was long of it at all. But he didn't laugh when he saw the opening prices, nor later in the day when the stock broke still more and the report came back to us in Palm Beach that there was no market for it at all.

Of course that was all the confirmation any man needed. My growing paper profit kept reminding me that I was right, hour by hour. Naturally I sold some more stocks.

Everything! It was a bear market. They were all going down. The next day was Friday, Washington's Birthday. I couldn't stay in Florida and fish because I had put out a very fair short line, for me. I was needed in New York. Who needed me? I did! Palm Beach was too far, too remote. Too much valuable time was lost telegraphing back and forth.

I left Palm Beach for New York. On Monday I had to lie in St. Augustine three hours, waiting for a train. There was a broker's office there, and naturally I had to see how the market was acting while I was waiting. Anaconda had broken several points since the last trading day. As a matter of fact, it didn't stop going down until the big break that fall.

I got to New York and traded on the bear side for about four months. The market had frequent rallies as before, and I kept covering and putting them out again. I didn't, strictly speaking, sit tight. Remember, I had lost every cent of the three hundred thousand dollars I made out of the San Francisco earthquake break. I had been right, and nevertheless had gone broke. I was now playing safe because after being down a man enjoys being up, even if he doesn't quite make the top. The way to make money is to make it. The way to make big money is to be right at exactly the right time. In this business a man has to think of both theory and practice. A speculator must not be merely a student, he must be both a student and a speculator.

I did pretty well, even if I can now see where my campaign was tactically inadequate. When summer came the market got dull. It was a cinch that there would be nothing doing in a big way until well along in the fall. Everybody I knew had gone or was going to Europe. I though that would be a good move for me. So I cleaned up. When I sailed for Europe I was a trifle more than three-quarters of a million to the good. To me that looked like some balance.

I was in Aix-les-Bains enjoying myself. I had earned my vacation. It was good to be in a place like that with plenty of money and friends and acquaintances and everybody intent upon having a good time. Not much trouble about having that, in Aix. Wall Street was so far away that I never thought about it, and that is more than I could say of any resort in the United States. I didn't have to listen to talk about the stock market. I didn't need to trade. I had enough to last me quite a long time, and besides, when I got back I knew what to do to make much more than I could spend in Europe that summer.

One day I saw in the Paris Herald a dispatch from New York that Smelters had declared an extra dividend. They had run up the price of the stock and the entire market had come back quite strong. Of course that changed everything for me in Aix. The news simply meant that the bull cliques were still fighting desperately against conditions against common sense and against common honesty, for they knew what was coming and were resorting to such schemes to put up the market in order to unload stocks before the storm struck them. It is possible they really did not believe the danger was as serious or as close at hand as I thought. The big men of the Street are as prone to be wishful thinkers as the politicians or the plain suckers. I myself can't work that way. In a speculator such an attitude is fatal. Perhaps a manufacturer of securities or a promoter of new enterprises can afford to indulge in hope-jags.

At all events, I knew that all bull manipulation was foredoomed to failure in that bear market. The instant I read the dispatch I knew there was only one thing to do to be comfortable, and that was to sell Smelters short. Why, the insiders as much as begged me on their knees to do it, when they increased the dividend rate on the verge of a money panic. It was as infuriating as the old "dares" of your boyhood. They dared me to sell that particular stock short.

I cabled some selling orders in Smelters and advised my friends in New York to go short of it. When I got my report from the brokers I saw the price they got was six points below the quotations I had seen in the Paris Herald. It shows you what the situation was.

My plans had been to return to Paris at the end of the month and about three weeks later sail for New York, but as soon as I received the cabled reports from my brokers I went back to Paris. The same day I arrived I called at the steamship offices and found there was a fast boat leaving for New York the next day. I took it.

There I was, back in New York, almost a month ahead of my original plans, because it was the most comfortable place to be short of the market in. I had well over half a million in cash available for margins. My return was not due to my being bearish but to my being logical.

I sold more stocks. As money got tighter call-money rates went higher and prices of stocks lower. I had foreseen it. At first, my foresight broke me. But now I was right and prospering. However, the real joy was in the consciousness that as a trader I was at last on the right track. I still had much to learn but I knew what to do. No more floundering, no more half-right methods. Tape reading was an important part of the game; so was beginning at the right time; so was sticking to your position. But my greatest discovery was that a man must study general conditions, to size them so as to be able to anticipate probabilities. In short, I had learned that I had to work for my money. I was no longer betting blindly or concerned with mastering the techniques of the game, but with earning my successes by hard study and clear thinking. I also had found out that nobody was immune from the danger of making sucker plays. And for a sucker play a man gets sucker pay; for the paymaster is on the job and never loses the pay envelope that is coming to you.

Our office made a great deal of money. My own operations were so successful that they began to be talked about and, of course, were greatly exaggerated. I was credited with starting the breaks in various stocks. People I didn't know by name used to come and congratulate me. They all thought the most wonderful thing was the money I had made. They did not say a word about the time when I first talked bearish to them and they thought I was a crazy bear with a stock-market loser's vindictive grouch. That I had foreseen the money troubles was nothing. That my brokers' bookkeeper had used a third of a drop of ink on the credit side of the ledger under my name was a marvelous achievement to them.

Friends used to tell me that in various offices the Boy Plunger in Harding Brothers' office was quoted as making all sorts of threats against the bull cliques that had tried to mark up prices of various stocks long after it was plain that the market was bound to seek a much lower level. To this day they talk of my raids.

From the latter part of September on, the money market was megaphoning warnings to the entire world. But a belief in miracles kept people from selling what remained of their speculative holdings. Why, a broker told me a story the first week of October that made me feel almost ashamed of my moderation.

You remember that money loans used to be made on the

floor of the Exchange around the Money Post. Those brokers who had received notice from their banks to pay call loans knew in a general way how much money they would have to borrow afresh. And of course the banks knew their position so far as loanable funds were concerned, and those which had money to loan would send it to the Exchange. This bank money was handled by a few brokers whose principal business was time loans. At about noon the renewal rate for the day was posted. Usually this represented a fair average of the loans made up to that time. Business was as a rule transacted openly by bids and offers, so that everyone knew what was going on. Between noon and about two o'clock there was ordinarily not much business done in money, but after delivery time namely, 2:15 p.m. brokers would know exactly what their cash position for the day would be, and they were able either to go to the Money Post and lend the balances that they had over or to borrow what they required. This business also was done openly.

Well, sometime early in October the broker I was telling you about came to me and told me that brokers were getting so they didn't go to the Money Post when they had money to loan. The reason was that members of a couple of well-known commission houses were on watch there, ready to snap up any offerings of money. Of course no lender who offered money publicly could refuse to lend to these firms. They were solvent and the collateral was good enough. But the trouble was that once these firms borrowed money on call there was no prospect of the lender getting that money back. They simply said they couldn't pay it back and the lender would willy-nilly have to renew the loan. So any Stock Exchange house that had money to loan to its fellows used to send its men about the floor instead of to the Post, and they would whisper to good friends, "Want a hundred?" meaning,

“Do you wish to borrow a hundred thousand dollars?” The money brokers who acted for the banks presently adopted the same plan, and it was a dismal sight to watch the Money Post. Think of it!

Why, he also told me that it was a matter of Stock Exchange etiquette in those October days for the borrower to make his own rate of interest. You see, it fluctuated between 100 and 150 per cent per annum. I suppose by letting the borrower fix the rate the lender in some strange way didn’t feel so much like a usurer. But you bet he got as much as the rest. The lender naturally did not dream of not paying a high rate. He played fair and paid whatever the others did. What he needed was the money and was glad to get it.

Things got worse and worse. Finally there came the awful day of reckoning for the bulls and the optimists and the wishful thinkers and those vast hordes that, dreading the pain of a small loss at the beginning, were now about to suffer total amputation without anaesthetics. A day I shall never forget, October 24, 1907.

Reports from the money crowd early indicated that borrowers would have to pay whatever the lenders saw fit to ask. There wouldn’t be enough to go around. That day the money crowd was much larger than usual. When delivery time came that afternoon there must have been a hundred brokers around the Money Post, each hoping to borrow the money that his firm urgently needed. Without money they must sell what stocks they were carrying on margin sell at any price they could get in a market where buyers were as scarce as money and just then there was not a dollar in sight.

My friend’s partner was as bearish as I was. The firm

therefore did not have to borrow, but my friend, the broker I told you about, fresh from seeing the haggard faces around the Money Post, came to me. He knew I was heavily short of the entire market.

He said, "My God, Larry! I don't know what's going to happen. I never saw anything like it. It can't go on. Something has got to give. It looks to me as if everybody is busted right now. You can't sell stocks, and there is absolutely no money in there."

"How do you mean?" I asked.

But what he answered was, "Did you ever hear of the classroom experiment of the mouse in a glass-bell when they begin to pump the air out of the bell? You can see the poor mouse breathe faster and faster, its sides heaving like overworked bellows, trying to get enough oxygen out of the decreasing supply in the bell. You watch it suffocate till its eyes almost pop out of their sockets, gasping, dying. Well, that is what I think of when I see the crowd at the Money Post! No money anywhere, and you can't liquidate stocks because there is nobody to buy them. The whole Street is broke at this very moment, if you ask me!"

It made me think. I had seen a smash coming, but not, I admit, the worst panic in our history. It might not be profitable to anybody if it went much further.

Finally it became plain that there was no use in waiting at the Post for money. There wasn't going to be any. Then hell broke loose.

The president of the Stock Exchange, Mr. R. H. Thomas,

so I heard later in the day, knowing that every house in the Street was headed for disaster, went out in search of succour. He called on James Stillman, president of the National City Bank, the richest bank in the United States. Its boast was that it never loaned money at a higher rate than 6 per cent.

Stillman heard what the president of the New York Stock Exchange had to say. Then he said, "Mr. Thomas, we'll have to go and see Mr. Morgan about this."

The two men, hoping to stave off the most disastrous panic in our financial history, went together to the office of J. P. Morgan & Co. and saw Mr. Morgan. Mr. Thomas laid the case before him. The moment he got through speaking Mr. Morgan said, "Go back to the Exchange and tell them that there will be money for them."

"Where?"

"At the banks!"

So strong was the faith of all men in Mr. Morgan in those critical times that Thomas didn't wait for further details but rushed back to the floor of the Exchange to announce the reprieve to his death-sentenced fellow members.

Then, before half past two in the afternoon, J. P. Morgan sent John T. Atterbury, of Van Emburgh & Atterbury, who was known to have close relations with J. P. Morgan & Co., into the money crowd. My friend said that the old broker walked quickly to the Money Post. He raised his hand like an exhorter at a revival meeting. The crowd, that at first had been calmed down somewhat by President Thomas' announcement, was beginning to fear that the relief plans had miscarried and the worst was still to come. But when they looked at Mr. Atterbury's face and saw him raise his hand they promptly petrified themselves.

In the dead silence that followed, Mr. Atterbury said, "I am authorized to lend ten million dollars. Take it easy! There will be enough for everybody!"

Then he began. Instead of giving to each borrower the name of the lender he simply jotted down the name of the borrower and the amount of the loan and told the borrower, "You will be told where your money is." He meant the name of the bank from which the borrower would get the money later.

I heard a day or two later that Mr. Morgan simply sent word to the frightened bankers of New York that they mnst provide the money the Stock Exchange needed.

"But we haven't got any. We're loaned up to the hilt," the banks protested. "You've got your reserves," snapped J. P.

"But we're already below the legal limit," they howled

"Use them! That's what reserves are for!" And the banks obeyed and invaded the reserves to the extent of about twenty million dollars. It saved the stock market. The bank panic didn't come until the following week. He was a man, J. P. Morgan was. They don't come much bigger.

That was the day I remember most vividly of all the days of my life as a stock operator. It was the day when my winnings exceeded one million dollars. It marked the successful ending of my first deliberately planned trading campaign. What I had foreseen had come to pass. But more than all these things was this: a wild dream of mine had been realised. I had been king for a day!

I'll explain, of course. After I had been in New York a couple of years I used to cudgel my brains trying to determine the exact reason why I couldn't beat in a Stock Exchange house in New York the game that I had beaten as a kid of fifteen in a bucket shop in Boston. I knew that some day I would find out what was wrong and I would stop being wrong. I would then have not alone the will to be right but the knowledge to insure my being right. And that would mean power.

Please do not misunderstand me. It was not a deliberate dream of grandeur or a futile desire born of overweening vanity. It was rather a sort of feeling that the same old stock market that so baffled me in Fullerton's office and in Hoarding's would one day eat out of my hand. I just felt that such a day would come. And it did October 24, 1907.

The reason why I say it is this: That morning a broker who had done a lot of business for my brokers and knew that I had been plunging on the bear side rode down in the company of one of the partners of the foremost banking house in the Street. My friend told the banker how heavily I had been trading, for I certainly pushed my luck to the limit. What is the use of being right unless you get all the good possible out of it?

Perhaps the broker exaggerated to make his story sound important. Perhaps I had more of a following than I knew. Perhaps the banker knew far better than I how critical the situation was. At all events, my friend said to me: "He listened with great interest to what I told him you said the market was going to do when the real selling began, after another push or two. When I got through he said he might have something for me to do later in the day."

When the commission houses found out there was not a cent to be had at any price I knew the time had come. I sent brokers into the various crowds. Why, at one time there wasn't a single bid for Union Pacific. Not at any price! Think of it! And in other stocks the same thing. No money to hold stocks and nobody to buy them.

I had enormous paper profits and the certainty that all that I had to do to smash prices still more was to send in orders to sell ten thousand shares each of Union Pacific and of a half dozen other good dividend-paying stocks and what would follow would be simply hell. It seemed to me that the panic that would be precipitated would be of such an intensity and character that the board of governors would deem it advisable to close the Exchange, as was done in August, 1914, when the World War broke out.

It would mean greatly increased profits on paper. It might also mean an inability to convert those profits into actual cash. But there were other things to consider, and one was that a further break would retard the recovery that I was beginning to figure on, the compensating improvement after all that bloodletting. Such a panic would do much harm to the country generally.

I made up my mind that since it was unwise and unpleasant to continue actively bearish it was illogical for me to stay short. So I turned and began to buy.

It wasn't long after my brokers began to buy in for me and, by the way, I got bottom prices that the banker sent for my friend.

"I have sent for you," he said, "because I want you to go instantly to your friend Livingston and say to him mat we hope he will not sell any more stocks to-day. The market can't stand much more pressure. As it is, it will be an immensely difficult task to avert a devastating panic. Appeal to your friend's patriotism. This is a case where a man has to work for the benefit of all. Let me know at once what he says."

My friend came right over and told me. He was very tactful. I suppose he thought that having planned to smash the market I would consider his request as equivalent to throwing away the chance to make about ten million dollars. He knew I was sore on some of the big guns for the way they had acted trying to land the public with a lot of stock when they knew as well as I did what was coming.

As a matter of fact, the big men were big sufferers and lots of the stocks I bought at the very bottom were in famous financial names. I didn't know it at the time, but it did not matter. I had practically covered all my shorts and it seemed to me there was a chance to buy stocks cheap and help the needed recovery in prices at the same time if nobody hammered the market.

So I told my friend, "Go back and tell Mr. Blank that I agree with them and that I fully realised the gravity of the situation even before he sent for you. I not only will not sell any more stocks to-day, but I am going in and buy as much as I can carry." And I kept my word. I bought one hundred thousand shares that day, for the long account. I did not sell another stock short for nine months.

That is why I said to friends that my dream had come true

and that I had been king for a moment. The stock market at one time that day certainly was at the mercy of anybody who wanted to hammer it. I do not surfer from delusions of grandeur; in fact you know how I feel about being accused of raiding the market and about the way my operations are exaggerated by the gossip of the Street.

I came out of it in fine shape. The newspapers said that Larry Livingston, the Boy Plunger, had made several millions. Well, I was worth over one million after the close of business that day. But my biggest winnings were not in dollars but in the intangibles: I had been right, I had looked ahead and followed a clear-cut plan. I had learned what a man must do in order to make big money; I was permanently out of the gambler class; I had at last learned to trade intelligently in a big way. It was a day of days for me.

Chapter X

The recognition of our own mistakes should not benefit us any more than the study of our successes. But there is a natural tendency in all men to avoid punishment. When you associate certain mistakes with a licking, you do not hanker for a second dose, and, of course, all stock-market mistakes wound you in two tender spots your pocketbook and your vanity. But I will tell you something curious : A stock speculator sometimes makes mistakes and knows that he is making them. And after he makes them he will ask himself why he made them; and after thinking over it cold-bloodedly a long time after the pain of punishment is over he may learn how he came to make them, and when, and at what particular point of his trade ; but not why. And then he simply calls himself names and lets it go at that.

Of course, if a man is both wise and lucky, he will not make the same mistake twice. But he will make any one of the ten thousand brothers or cousins of the original. The Mistake family is so large that there is always one of them around when you want to see what you can do in the fool-play line.

To tell you about the first of my million-dollar mistakes I shall have to go back to this time when I first became a millionaire, right after the big break of October, 1907. As far as my trading went, having a million merely meant more reserves. Money does not give a trader more comfort, because, rich or poor, he can make mistakes and it is never comfortable to be wrong. And when a millionaire is right his money is merely one of his several servants. Losing money is the least of my troubles. A loss never bothers me after I take it. I forget it Overnight. But being wrong not taking the loss that is what does the damage to the pocketbook and to the soul. You remember Dickson G. Watts' story about the man who was so nervous that a friend asked him what was the matter.

"I can't sleep," answered the nervous one.

"Why not?" asked the friend.

"I am carrying so much cotton that I can't sleep thinking about it. It is wearing me out. What can I do?"

"Sell down to the sleeping point," answered the friend.

As a rule a man adapts himself to conditions so quickly that he loses the perspective. He does not feel the difference much that is, he does not vividly remember how it felt not to be a millionaire. He only remembers that there were things he could not do that he can do now. It does not take a reasonably young and normal man very long to lose the habit of being poor. It requires a little longer to forget that he used to be rich. I suppose that is because money creates needs or encourages their multiplication. I mean that after a man makes money in the stock market he very quickly loses the habit of not spending. But after he loses his money it takes him a long time to lose the habit of spending.

After I took in my shorts and went long in October, 1907, I decided to take it easy for a while. I bought a yacht and planned to go off on a cruise in Southern waters. I am crazy about fishing and I was due to have the time of my life. I looked forward to it and expected to go any day. But I did not. The market wouldn't let me.

I always have traded in commodities as well as in stocks. I began as a youngster in the bucket shops. I studied those markets for years, though perhaps not so assiduously as the stock market. As a matter of fact, I would rather play commodities than stocks. There is no question about their greater legitimacy, as it were. It partakes more of the nature of a commercial venture than trading in stocks does. A man can approach it as he might any mercantile problem. It may be possible to use fictitious arguments for or against a certain trend in a commodity market; but success will be only temporary, for in the end the facts are bound to prevail, so that a trader gets dividends on study and observation, as he does in a regular business. He can watch and weigh conditions and he knows as much about it as anyone else. He need not guard against inside cliques. Dividends are not unexpectedly passed or increased overnight in the cotton market or in wheat or corn. In the long run commodity prices are governed but by one law the economic law of demand and supply. The business of the trader in commodities is simply to get facts about the demand and the supply, present and prospective. He does not indulge in guesses about a dozen things as he does in stocks. It always appealed to me trading in commodities.

Of course the same things happen in all speculative markets. The message of the tape is the same. That will be perfectly plain to anyone who will take the trouble to think. He will find if he asks himself questions and considers conditions, that the answers will supply themselves directly. But people never take the trouble to ask questions, leave alone seeking answers. The average American is from Missouri everywhere and at all times except when he goes to the brokers' offices and looks at the tape, whether it is stocks or commodities. The one game of all games that really requires study before making a play is the one he goes into without his usual highly intelligent preliminary and precautionary doubts. He will risk half his fortune in the stock market with less reflection than he devotes to the selection of a medium-priced automobile.

This matter of tape reading is not so complicated as it appears. Of course you need experience. But it is even more important to keep certain fundamentals in mind. To read the tape is not to have your fortune told. The tape does not tell you how much you will surely be worth next Thursday at 1:35 p.m. The object of reading the tape is to ascertain, first, how and, next, when to trade that is, whether it is wiser to buy than to sell. It works exactly the same for stocks as for cotton or wheat or corn or oats.

You watch the market that is, the course of prices as recorded by the tape with one object: to determine the direction that is, the price tendency. Prices, we know, will move either up or down according to the resistance they encounter. For purposes of easy explanation we will say that prices, like everything else, move along the line of least resistance. They will do whatever comes easiest, therefore they will go up if there is less resistance to an advance than to a decline; and vice versa.

Nobody should be puzzled as to whether a market is a bull or a bear market after it fairly starts. The trend is evident to a man who has an open mind and reasonably clear sight, for it is never wise for a speculator to fit his facts to his theories. Such a man will, or ought to, know whether it is a bull or a bear market, and if he knows that he knows whether to buy or to sell. It is therefore at the very inception of the movement that a man needs to know whether to buy or to sell.

Let us say, for example, that the market, as it usually does in those between-swings times, fluctuates within a range of ten points; up to 130 and down to 120. It may look very weak at the bottom; or, on the way up, after a rise of eight or ten points, it may look as strong as anything. A man ought not to be led into trading by tokens. He should wait until the tape tells him that the time is ripe. As a matter of fact, millions upon millions of dollars have been lost by men who bought stocks because they looked cheap or sold them because they looked dear. The speculator is not an investor. His object is not to secure a steady return on his money at a good rate of interest, but to profit by either a rise or a fall in the price of whatever he may be speculating in. Therefore the thing to determine is the speculative line of least resistance at the moment of trading; and what he should wait for is the moment when that line defines itself, because that is his signal to get busy.

Reading the tape merely enables him to see that at 130 the selling had been stronger than the buying and a reaction in the price logically followed. Up to the point where the selling prevailed over the buying, superficial students of the tape may conclude that the price is not going to stop short of 150, and they buy. But after the reaction begins they hold on, or sell out at a small loss, or they go short and talk bearish. But at 120 there is stronger resistance to the decline. The buying prevails over the selling, there is a rally and the shorts cover. The public is so often whipsawed that one marvels at their persistence in not learning their lesson.

Eventually something happens that increases the power of

either the upward or the downward force and the point of greatest resistance moves up or down that is, the buying at 130 will for the first time be stronger than the selling, or the selling at 120 be stronger than the buying. The price will break through the old barrier or movement-limit and go on. As a rule, there is always a crowd of traders who are short at 120 because it looked so weak, or long at 130 because it looked so strong, and, when the market goes against them they are forced, after a while, either to change their minds and turn or to close out, In either event they help to define even more clearly the price line of least resistance. Thus the intelligent trader who has patiently waited to determine this line will enlist the aid of fundamental trade conditions and also of the force of the trading of that part of the community that happened to guess wrong and must now rectify mistakes. Such corrections tend to push prices along the line of least resistance.

And right here I will say that, though I do not give it as a mathematical certainty or as an axiom of speculation, my experience has been that accidents that is, the unexpected or unforeseen have always helped me in my market position whenever the latter has been based upon my determination of the line of least resistance. Do you remember that Union Pacific episode at Saratoga that I told you about? Well, I was long because I found out that the line of least resistance was upward. I should have stayed long instead of letting my broker tell me that insiders were selling stocks. It didn't make any difference what was going on in the directors' minds. That was something I couldn't possibly know. But I could and did know that the tape said: "Going up!" And then came the unexpected raising of the dividend rate and the thirty-point rise in the stock. At 164 prices looked mighty high, but as I told you before, stocks are never too high to buy or too low to sell. The price, per se, has nothing to do with establishing my line of least resistance.

You will find in actual practice that if you trade as I have indicated any important piece of news given out between the closing of one market and the opening of another is usually in harmony with the line of least resistance. The trend has been established before the news is published, and in bull markets bear items are ignored and bull news exaggerated, and vice versa. Before the war broke out the market was in a very weak condition. There came the proclamation of Germany's submarine policy. I was short one hundred and fifty thousand shares of stock, not because I knew the news was coming, but because I was going along the line of least resistance. What happened came out of a clear sky, as far as my play was concerned. Of course I took advantage of the situation and I covered my shorts that day.

It sounds very easy to say that all you have to do is to watch the tape, establish your resistance points and be ready to trade along the line of least resistance as soon as you have determined it. But in actual practice a man has to guard against many things, and most of all against himself that is, against human nature. That is the reason why I say that the man who is right always has two forces working in his favor basic conditions and the men who are wrong. In a bull market bear factors are ignored. That is human nature, and yet human beings profess astonishment at it. People will tell you that the wheat crop has gone to pot because there has been bad weather in one or two sections and some farmers have been ruined. When the entire crop is gathered and all the farmers in all the wheat-growing sections begin to take their wheat to the elevators the bulls are surprised at the smallness of the damage. They discover that they merely have helped the bears.

When a man makes his play in a commodity market he must not permit himself set opinions. He must have an open mind and flexibility. It is not wise to disregard the message of the tape, no matter what your opinion of crop conditions or of the probable demand may be. I recall how I missed a big play just by trying to anticipate the starting signal. I felt so sure of conditions that I thought it was not necessary to wait for the line of least resistance to define itself. I even thought I might help it arrive, because it looked as if it merely needed a little assistance.

I was very bullish on cotton. It was hanging around twelve cents, running up and down within a moderate range. It was in one of those in-between places and I could see it. I knew I really ought to wait. But I got to thinking that if I gave it a little push it would go beyond the upper resistance point.

I bought fifty thousand bales. Sure enough, it moved up. And sure enough, as soon as I stopped buying it stopped going up. Then it began to settle back to where it was when I began buying it. I got out and it stopped going down. I thought I was now much nearer the starting signal, and presently I thought I'd start it myself again. I did. The same thing happened. I bid it up, only to see it go down when I stopped. I did this four or five times until I finally quit in disgust. It cost me about two hundred thousand dollars. I was done with it. It wasn't very long after that when it began to go up and never stopped till it got to a price that would have meant a killing for me if I hadn't been in such a great hurry to start.

This experience has been the experience of so many traders so many times that I can give this rule: In a narrow market, when prices are not getting anywhere to speak of but move within a narrow range, there is no sense in trying to anticipate what the next big movement is going to be up or down. The thing to do is to watch the market, read the tape to determine the limits of the get-nowhere prices, and make up your mind that you will not take an interest until the price breaks through the limit in either direction. A speculator must concern himself with making money out of the market and not with insisting that the tape must agree with him. Never argue with it or ask it for reasons or explanations. Stock-market postmortems don't pay dividends.

Not so long ago I was with a party of friends. They got to talking wheat. Some of them were bullish and others bearish. Finally they asked me what I thought. Well, I had been studying the market for some time. I knew they did not want any statistics or analyses of conditions. So I said: "If you want to make some money out of wheat I can tell you how to do it."

They all said they did and I told them, "If you are sure you wish to make money in wheat just you watch it. Wait. The moment it crosses $1.20 buy it and you will get a nice quick play in it!"

"Why not buy it now, at $1.14?" one of the party asked.

"Because I don't know yet that it is going up at all." "Then why buy it at $1.20? It seems a mighty high price."

"Do you wish to gamble blindly in the hope of getting a great big profit or do you wish to speculate intelligently and get a smaller but much more probable profit?"

They all said they wanted the smaller but surer profit, so I said, “Then do as I tell you. If it crosses $1.20 buy.”

As I told you, I had watched it a long time. For months it sold between $1.10 and $1.20, getting nowhere in particular. Well, sir, one day it closed at above $1.19. I got ready for it, Sure enough the next day it opened at $1.20-1/2, and I bought. It went to $1.21, to $1.22, to $1.23, to $1.25, and I went with it.

Now I couldn’t have told you at the time just what was going on. I didn’t get any explanations about its behaviour during the course of the limited fluctuations. I couldn’t tell whether the breaking through the limit would be up through $1.20 or down through $1.10, though I suspected it would be up because there was not enough wheat in the world for a big break in prices.

As a matter of fact, it seems Europe had been buying quietly and a lot of traders had gone short of it at around $1.19. Owing to the European purchases and other causes, a lot of wheat had been taken out of the market, so that finally the big movement got started. The price went beyond the $1.20 mark. That was all the point I had and it was all I needed. I knew that when it crossed $1.20 it would be because the upward movement at last had gathered force to push it over the limit and something had to happen. In other words, by crossing $1.20 the line of least resistance of wheat prices was established. It was a different story then.

I remember that one day was a holiday with us and all our markets were closed. Well, in Winnipeg wheat opened up six cents a bushel. When our market opened on the following day, it also was up six cents a bushel. The price just went along the line of least resistance.

What I have told you gives you the essence of my trading system as based on studying the tape. I merely learn the way prices are most probably going to move. I check up my own trading by additional tests, to determine the psychological moment. I do that by watching the way the price acts after I begin.

It is surprising how many experienced traders there are who look incredulous when I tell them that when I buy stocks for a rise I like to pay top prices and when I sell I must sell low or not at all. It would not be so difficult to make money if a trader always stuck to his speculative guns that is, waited for the line of least resistance to define itself and began buying only when the tape said up or selling only when it said down. He should accumulate his line on the way up. Let him buy one-fifth of his full line. If that does not show him a profit he must not increase his holdings because he has obviously begun wrong; he is wrong temporarily and there is no profit in being wrong at any time. The same tape that said UP did not necessarily lie merely because it is now saying NOT YET.

In cotton I was very successful in my trading for a long time. I had my theory about it and I absolutely lived up to it. Suppose I had decided that my line would be forty to fifty thousand bales. Well, I would study the tape as I told you, watching for an opportunity either to buy or to sell. Suppose the line of least resistance indicated a bull movement. Well, I would buy ten thousand bales. After I got through buying that, if the market went up ten points over my initial purchase price, I would take on another ten thousand bales. Same thing. Then, if I could get twenty points' profit, or one dollar a bale, I would buy twenty thousand more. That would give me my line my basis for my trading. But if after buying the first ten or twenty thousand bales, it showed me a loss, out I'd go. I was wrong. It might be I was only temporarily wrong. But as I have said before it doesn't pay to start wrong in anything.

What I accomplished by sticking to my system was that I always had a line of cotton in every real movement. In the course of accumulating my full line I might chip out fifty or sixty thousand dollars in these feeling-out plays of mine. This looks like a very expensive testing, but it wasn't. After the real movement started, how long would it take me to make up the fifty thousand dollars I had dropped in order to make sure that I began to load up at exactly the right time? No time at all! It always pays a man to be right at the right time.

As I think I also said before, this describes what I may call my system for placing my bets. It is simple arithmetic to prove that it is a wise thing to have the big bet down only when you win, and when you lose to lose only a small exploratory bet, as it were. If a man trades in the way I have described, he will always be in the profitable position of being able to cash in on the big bet.

Professional traders have always had some system or other based upon their experience and governed either by their attitude toward speculation or by their desires. I remember I met an old gentleman in Palm Beach whose name I did not catch or did not at once identify. I knew he had been in the Street for years, way back in Civil War times, and somebody told me that he was a very wise old codger who had gone through so many booms and panics that he was always saying there was nothing new under the sun and least of all in the stock market.

The old fellow asked me a lot of questions. When I got through telling him about my usual practice in trading he nodded and said, "Yes! Yes! You're right. The way you're built, the way your mind runs, makes your system a good system for you. It comes easy for you to practice what you preach, because the money you bet is the least of your cares. I recollect Pat Hearne. Ever hear of him? Well, he was a very well-known sporting man and he had an account with us. Clever chap and nervy. He made money in stocks, and that made people ask him for advice. He would never give any. If they asked him point-blank for his opinion about the wisdom of their commitments he used a favourite race-track maxim of his: "You can't tell till you bet." He traded in our office. He would buy one hundred shares of some active stock and when, or if, it went up I per cent he would buy another hundred. On another point's advance, another hundred shares; and so on. He used to say he wasn't playing the game to make money for others and therefore he would put in a stop-loss order one point below the price of his last purchase. When the price kept going tip he simply moved up his stop with it. On a I per cent reaction he was stopped out. He declared he did not see any sense in losing more than one point, whether it came out of his original margin or out of his paper profits.

"You know, a professional gambler is not looking for long shots, but for sure money. Of course long shots are fine when they come in. In the stock market Pat wasn't after tips or playing to catch twenty-points-a-week advances, but sure money in sufficient quantity to provide him with a good living. Of all the thousands of outsiders that I have run across in Wall Street, Pat Hearne was the only one who saw in stock speculation merely a game of chance like faro or roulette, but, nevertheless, had the sense to stick to a relatively sound betting method.

"After Hearne's death one of our customers who had always traded with Pat and used his system made over one hundred thousand dollars in Lackawanna. Then he switched over to some other stock and because he had made a big stake he thought he need not stick to Pat's way. When a reaction came, instead of cutting short his losses he let them run as though they were profits. Of course every cent went. When he finally quit he owed us several thousand dollars.

"He hung around for two or three years. He kept the fever long after the cash had gone; but we did not object as long as he behaved himself. I remember that he used to admit freely that he had been ten thousand kinds of an ass not to stick to Pat Hearne's style of play. Well, one day he came to me greatly excited and asked me to let him sell some stock short in our office. He was a nice enough chap who had been a good customer in his day and I told him I personally would guarantee his account for one hundred shares.

"He sold short one hundred shares of Lake Shore. That was the time Bill Travers hammered the market, in 1875. My friend Roberts put out that Lake Shore at exactly the right time and kept selling it on the way down as he had been wont to do in the old successful days before he forsook Pat Hearne's system and instead listened to hope's whispers.

"Well, sir, in four days of successful pyramiding, Roberts' account showed him a profit of fifteen thousand dollars. Observing that he had not put in a stop-loss order I spoke to him about it and he told me that the break hadn't fairly begun and he wasn't going to be shaken out by any one-point reaction. This was in August. Before the middle of

September he borrowed ten dollars from me for a baby carriage his fourth, He did not stick to his own proved system. That's the trouble with most of them," and the old fellow shook his head at me.

And he was right. I sometimes think that speculation must be an unnatural sort of business, because I find that the average speculator has arrayed against him his own nature. The weaknesses that all men are prone to are fatal to success in speculation usually those very weaknesses that make him likable to his fellows or that he himself particularly guards against in those other ventures of his where they are not nearly so dangerous as when he is trading in stocks or commodities.

The speculator's chief enemies are always boring from within. It is inseparable from human nature to hope and to fear. In speculation when the market goes against you you hope that every day will be the last day and you lose more than you should had you not listened to hope to the same ally that is so potent a success-bringer to empire builders and pioneers, big and little. And when the market goes your way you become fearful that the next day will take away your profit, and you get out too soon. Fear keeps you from making as much money as you ought to. The successful trader has to fight these two deep-seated instincts. He has to reverse what you might call his natural impulses. Instead of hoping he must fear; instead of fearing he must hope. He must fear that his loss may develop into a much bigger loss, and hope that his profit may become a big profit. It is absolutely wrong to gamble in stocks the way the average man does.

I have been in the speculative game ever since I was fourteen. It is all I have ever done. I think I know what I am talking about. And the conclusion that I have reached after nearly thirty years of constant trading, both on a shoestring and with millions of dollars back of me, is this: A man may beat a stock or a group at a certain time, but no man living can beat the stock market! A man may make money out of individual deals in cotton or grain, but no man can beat the cotton market or the grain market. It's like the track. A man may beat a horse race, but he cannot beat horse racing.

If I knew how to make these statements stronger or more emphatic I certainly would. It does not make any difference what anybody says to the contrary. I know I am right in saying these are incontrovertible statements.

Chapter XI

And now I'll get back to October, 1907. I bought a yacht and made all preparations to leave New York for a cruise in Southern waters. I am really daffy about fishing and this was the time when I was going to fish to my heart's content from my own yacht, going wherever I wished whenever I felt like it. Everything was ready. I had made a killing in stocks, but at the last moment corn held me back.

I must explain that before the money panic which gave me ray first million I had been trading in grain at Chicago. I was short ten million bushels of wheat and ten million bushels of corn. I had studied the grain markets for a long time and was as bearish on corn and wheat as I had been on stocks.

Well, they both started down, but while wheat kept on dedining the biggest of all the Chicago operators I'll call him Stratton took it into his head to run a corner in corn. After I cleaned up in stocks and was ready to go South on my yacht I found that wheat showed me a handsome profit, but in corn Stratton had run up the price and I had quite a loss.

I knew there was much more corn in the country than the price indicated. The law of demand and supply worked as always. But the demand came chiefly from Stratton and the supply was not coming at all, because there was an acute congestion in the movement of corn. I remember that I used to pray for a cold spell that would freeze the impassable roads and enable the farmers to bring their corn into the market. But no such luck.

There I was, waiting to go on my joyously planned fishing trip and that loss in corn holding me back. I couldn't go away with the market as it was. Of course Stratton kept pretty close tabs on the short interest. He knew he had me, and I knew it quite as well as he did. But, as I said, I was hoping I might convince the weather that it ought to get busy and help me. Perceiving that neither the weather nor any other kindly wonder-worker was paying any attention to my needs I studied how I might work out of my difficulty by my own efforts.

I closed out my line of wheat at a good profit. But the problem in corn was infinitely more difficult. If I could have covered my ten million bushels at the prevailing prices I instantly and gladly would have done so, large though the loss would have been. But, of course, the moment I started to buy in my corn Stratton would be on the job as squeezer in chief, and I no more relished running up the price on myself by reason of my own purchases than cutting my own throat with my own knife.

Strong though corn was, my desire to go fishing was even stronger, so it was up to me to find a way out at once. I must conduct a strategic retreat. I must buy back the ten million bushels I was short of and in so doing keep down my loss as much as I possibly could.

It so happened that Stratton at that time was also running a deal in oats and had the market pretty well sewed up. I had kept track of all the grain markets in the way of crop news and pit gossip, and I heard that the powerful Armour interests were not friendly, marketwise, to Stratton. Of course I knew that Stratton would not let me have the corn I needed except at his own price, but the moment I heard the rumors about

Armour being against Stratton it occurred to me that I might look to the Chicago traders for aid. The only way in which they could possibly help me was for them to sell me the corn that Stratton wouldn't. The rest was easy.

First, I put in orders to buy five hundred thousand bushels of corn every eighth of a cent down. After these orders were in I gave to each of four houses an order to sell simultaneously fifty thousand bushels of oats at the market. That, I figured, ought to make a quick break in oats. Knowing how the traders' minds worked, it was a cinch that they would instantly think that Armour was gunning for Stratton. Seeing the attack opened in oats they would logically conclude that the next break would be in corn and they would start to sell it. If that corner in corn was busted, the pickings would be fabulous.

My dope on the psychology of the Chicago traders was absolutely correct. When they saw oats breaking on the scattered selling they promptly jumped on corn and sold it with great enthusiasm. I was able to buy six million bushels of corn in the next ten minutes.

The moment I found that their selling of corn ceased I simply bought in the other four million bushels at the market. Of course that made the price go up again, but the net result of my maneuver was that I covered the entire line of ten million bushels within one-half cent of the price prevailing at the time I started to cover on the traders' selling. The two hundred thousand bushels of oats that I sold short to start the traders' selling of corn I covered at a loss of only three thousand dollars. That was pretty cheap bear bait. The profits I had made in wheat offset so much of my deficit in corn that my total loss on all my grain trades that time was only twenty-five thousand dollars. Afterwards corn went up twenty-five cents a bushed. Stratton undoubtedly had me at his mercy. If I had set about buying my ten million bushels of corn without bothering to think of the price there is no telling what I would have had to pay.

A man can't spend years at one thing and not acquire a habitual attitude towards it quite unlike that of the average beginner. The difference distinguishes the professional from the amateur. It is the way a man looks at things that makes or loses money for him in the speculative markets. The public has the dilettante's point of view toward his own effort. The ego obtrudes itself unduly and the thinking therefore is not deep or exhaustive. The professional concerns himself with doing the right thing rather than with making money, knowing that the profit takes care of itself if the other things are attended to. A trader gets to play the game as the professional billiard player does that is, he looks far ahead instead of considering the particular shot before him. It gets to be an instinct to play for position.

I remember hearing a story about Addison Cammack that illustrates very nicely what I wish to point out. From all I have heard, I am inclined to think that Cammack was one of the ablest stock traders the Street ever saw. He was not a chronic bear as many believe, but he felt the greater appeal of trading on the bear side, of utilising in his behalf the two great human factors of hope and fear. He is credited with coining the warning: "Don't sell stocks when the sap is running up the trees!" and the old-timers tell me that his biggest winnings were made on the bull side, so that it is plain he did not play prejudices but conditions. At all events, he was a consummate trader. It seems that once this was way back at the tag end of a bull market Cammack was bearish, and J. Arthur Joseph, the financial writer and raconteur, knew it. The market, however, was not only strong but still rising, in response to prodding by the bull leaders and optimistic reports by the newspapers. Knowing what use a trader like Cammack could make of bearish information, Joseph rushed to Cammack's office one day with glad tidings.

"Mr. Cammack, I have a very good friend who is a transfer clerk in the St. Paul office and he has just told me something which I think you ought to know."

"What is it?" asked Cammack listlessly.

"You've turned, haven't you? You are bearish now?" asked Joseph, to make sure. If Cammack wasn't interested he wasn't going to waste precious ammunition.

"Yes. What's the wonderful information?"

"I went around to the St. Paul office to-day, as I do in my news-gathering rounds two or three times a week, and my friend there said to me: 'The Old Man is selling stock.' He meant William Rockefeller. 'Is he really, Jimmy?' I said to him, and he answered, 'Yes; he is selling fifteen hundred shares every three-eighths of a point up. I've been transferring the stock for two or three days now.' I didn't lose any time, but came right over to tell you."

Cammack was not easily excited, and, moreover, was so accustomed to having all manner of people rush madly into his office with all manner of news, gossip, rumors, tips and lies that he had grown distrustful of them all. He merely said now, "Are you sure you heard right, Joseph?"

"Am I sure? Certainly I am sure! Do you think" I am

deaf?" said Joseph. "Are you sure of your man?"

"Absolutely!" declared Joseph. "I've known him for years. He has never lied to me. He wouldn't! No object! I know he is absolutely reliable and I'd stake my life on what he tells me. I know him as well as I know anybody in this world a great deal better than you seem to know me, after all these years."

"Sure of him, eh?" And Cammack again looked at Joseph. Then he said, "Well, you ought to know." He called his broker, W. B. Wheeler. Joseph expected to hear him give an order to sell at least fifty thousand shares of St. Paul. William Rockefeller was disposing of his holdings in St. Paul, taking advantage of the strength of the market. Whether it was investment stock or speculative holdings was irrelevant. The one important fact was that the best stock trader of the Standard Oil crowd was getting out of St. Paul. What would the average man have done if he had received the news from a trustworthy source? No need to ask.

But Cammack, the ablest bear operator of his day, who was bearish on the market just then, said to his broker, "Billy, go over to the board and buy fifteen hundred St. Paul every three-eighths up." The stock was then in the nineties.

"Don't you mean sell?" interjected Joseph hastily. He was no novice in Wall Street, but he was thinking of the market from the point of view of the newspaper man and, incidentally, of the general public. The price certainly ought to go down on the news of inside selling. And there was no better inside selling than Mr. William Rockefeller's. The Standard Oil getting out and Cammack buying! It couldn't be!

"No," said Cammack; "I mean buy!" "Don't you believe

me?"

"Yes!"

"Don't you believe my information?" "Yes." '

"Aren't you bearish?" "Yes."

"Well, then?"

"That's why I'm buying. Listen to me now: You keep in touch with that reliable friend of yours and the moment the scaled selling stops, let me know. Instantly! Do you understand?"

"Yes," said Joseph, and went away, not quite sure he could fathom Cammack's motives in buying William Rockefeller's stock. It was the knowledge that Cammack was bearish on the entire market that made his manoeuvre so difficult to explain. However, Joseph saw his friend the transfer clerk and told him he wanted to be tipped off when the Old Man got through selling. Regularly twice a day Joseph called on his friend to inquire.

One day the transfer clerk told him, "There isn't any more stock coming from the Old Man." Joseph thanked him and ran to Cammack's office with the information.

Cammack listened attentively, turned to Wheeler and asked, "Billy, how much St. Paul have we got in the office?" Wheeler looked it up and reported that they had accumulated about sixty thousand shares.

Cammack, being bearish, had been putting out short lines in the other Grangers as well as in various other stocks, even before he began to buy St. Paul. He was now heavily short of the market. He promptly ordered Wheeler to sell the sixty thousand shares of St. Paul that they were long of, and more besides. He used his long holdings of St. Paul as a lever to depress the general list and greatly benefit his operations for a decline.

St. Paul didn't stop on that move until it reached forty-four and Cammack made a killing in it. He played his cards with consummate skill and profited accordingly. The point I would make is his habitual attitude toward trading. He didn't have to reflect. He saw instantly what was far more important to him than his profit on that one stock. He saw that he had providentially been offered an opportunity to begin his big bear operations not only at the proper time but with a proper initial push. The St. Paul tip made him buy instead of sell because he saw at once that it gave him a vast supply of the best ammunition for his bear campaign.

To get back to myself. After I closed my trade in wheat and corn I went South in my yacht. I cruised about in Florida waters, having a grand old time. The fishing was great. Everything was lovely. I didn't have a care in the world and I wasn't looking for any.

One day I went ashore at Palm Beach. I met a lot of Wall Street friends and others. They were all talking about the most picturesque cotton speculator of the day. A report from New York had it that Percy Thomas had lost every cent. It wasn't a commercial bankruptcy; merely the rumor of the world-famous operator's second Waterloo in the cotton market.

I had always felt a great admiration for him. The first I ever heard of him was through the newspapers at the time of the failure of the Stock Exchange house of Sheldon & Thomas, when Thomas tried to corner cotton. Sheldon, who did not have the vision or the courage of his partner, got cold feet on the very verge of success. At least, so the Street said at the time. At all events, instead of making a killing they made one of the most sensational failures in years. I forget how many millions. The firm was wound up and Thomas went to work alone. He devoted himself exclusively to cotton and it was not long before he was on his feet again. He paid off his creditors in full with interest debts he was not legally obliged to discharge and withal had a million dollars left for himself. His comeback in the cotton market was in its way as remarkable as Deacon S. V. White's famous stock-market exploit of paying off one million dollars in one year. Thomas' pluck and brains made me admire him immensely.

Everybody in Palm Beach was talking about the collapse of Thomas' deal in March cotton. You know how the talk goes and grows; the amount of misinformation and exaggeration and improvements that you hear. Why, I've seen a rumor about myself grow so that the fellow who started it did not recognise it when it came back to him in less than twenty-four hours, swollen with new and picturesque details.

The news of Percy Thomas' latest misadventure turned my mind from the fishing to the cotton market. I got files of the trade papers and read them to get a line on conditions. When I got back to New York I gave myself up to studying the market. Everybody was bearish and everybody was selling July cotton. You know how people are. I suppose it is the contagion of example that makes a man do something because everybody around him is doing the same thing. Perhaps it is some phase or variety of the herd instinct. In any case it was, in the opinion of hundreds of traders, the wise and proper thing to sell July cotton and so safe too! You couldn't call that general selling reckless; the word is too conservative. The traders simply saw one side to the market and a great big profit. They certainly expected a collapse in prices.

I saw all this, of course, and it struck me that the chaps who were short didn't have a terrible lot of time to cover in. The more I studied the situation the clearer I saw this, until I finally decided to buy July cotton. I went to work and quickly bought one hundred thousand bales. I experienced no trouble in getting it because it came from so many sellers. It seemed to me that I could have offered a reward of one million dollars for the capture, dead or alive, of a single trader who was not selling July cotton and nobody would have claimed it.

I should say this was in the latter part of May. I kept buying more and they kept on selling it to me until I had picked up all the floating contracts and I had one hundred and twenty thousand bales. A couple of days after I had bought the last of it it began to go up. Once it started the market was kind enough to keep on doing very well indeed -that is, it went up from forty to fifty points a day.

One Saturday this was about ten days after I began operations the price began to creep up. I did not know whether there was any more July cotton for sale. It was up to me to find out, so I waited until the last ten minutes. At that time, I knew, it was usual for those fellows to be short and if the market closed up for the day they would be safely hooked. So I sent in four different orders to buy five thousand bales each, at the market, at the same time. That ran the price up thirty points and the shorts were doing their best to wriggle away. The market closed at the top. All I did, remember, was to buy that last twenty thousand bales.

The next day was Sunday. But on Monday, Liverpool was due to open up twenty points to be on a parity with the advance in New York. Instead, it came fifty points higher. That meant that Liverpool had exceeded our advance by 100 per cent. I had nothing to do with the rise in that market. This showed me that my deductions had been sound and that I was trading along the line of least resistance. At the same time I was not losing sight of the fact that I had a whopping big line to dispose of. A market may advance sharply or rise gradually and yet not possess the power to absorb more than a certain amount of selling.

Of course the Liverpool cables made our own market wild. But I noticed the higher it went the scarcer July cotton seemed to be. I wasn't letting go any of mine. Altogether that Monday was an exciting and not very cheerful day for the bears; but for all that, I could detect no signs of an impending bear panic; no beginnings of a blind stampede to cover. And I had one hundred and forty thousand bales for which I must find a market.

On Tuesday morning as I was walking to my office I met a friend at the entrance of the building.

"That was quite a story in the World this morning," he said with a smile. "What story?" I asked.

"What? Do you mean to tell me you haven't seen it?" "I never see the World," I said. "What is the story?"

"Why, it's all about you. It says you've got July cotton

cornered."

"I haven't seen it," I told him and left him. I don't know whether he believed me or not. He probably thought it was highly inconsiderate of me not to tell him whether it was true or not.

When I got to the office I sent out for a copy of the paper. Sure enough, there it was, on the front page, in big headlines:

JULY COTTON CORNERED BY LARRY LIVINGSTON

Of course I knew at once that the article would play the dickens with the market. If I had deliberately studied ways and means of disposing of my one hundred and forty thousand bales to the best advantage I couldn't have hit upon a better plan. It would not have been possible to find one. That article at that very moment was being read all over the country either in the World or in other papers quoting it. It had been cabled to Europe. That was plain from the Liverpool prices. That market was simply wild. No wonder, with such news.

Of course I knew what New York would do, and what I ought to do. The market here opened at ten o'clock. At ten minutes after ten I did not own any cotton. I let them have every one of my one hundred and forty thousand bales. For most of my line I received what proved to be the top prices of the day. The traders made the market for me. All I really did was to see a heaven-sent opportunity to get rid of my cotton. I grasped it because I couldn't help it. What else could I do?

The problem that I knew would take a great deal of hard

thinking to solve was thus solved for me by an accident. If the World had not published that article I never would have been able to dispose of my line without sacrificing the greater portion of my paper profits. Selling one hundred and forty thousand bales of July cotton without sending the price down was a trick beyond my powers. But the World story turned it for me very nicely.

Why the World published it I cannot tell you. I never knew. I suppose the writer was tipped off by some friend in the cotton market and he thought he was printing a scoop. I didn't see him or anybody from the World. I didn't know it was printed that morning until after nine o'clock; and if it had not been for my friend calling my attention to it I would not have known it then.

Without it I wouldn't have had a market big enough to unload in. That is one trouble about trading on a large scale. You cannot sneak out as you can when you pike along. You cannot always sell out when you wish or when you think it wise. You have to get out when you can; when you have a market that will absorb your entire line. Failure to grasp the opportunity to get out may cost you millions. You cannot hesitate. If you do you are lost. Neither can you try stunts like running up the price on the bears by means of competitive buying, for you may thereby reduce the absorbing capacity. And I want to tell you that perceiving your opportunity is not as easy as it sounds. A man must be on the lookout so alertly that when his chance sticks in its head at his door he must grab it.

Of course not everybody knew about my fortunate accident. In Wall Street, and, for that matter, everywhere else, any accident that makes big money for a man is regarded with suspicion. When the accident is unprofitable it is never considered an accident but the logical outcome of your hoggish-ness or of the swelled head. But when there is a profit they call it loot and talk about how well unscrupulousness fares, and how ill conservatism and decency.

It was not only the evil-minded shorts smarting under punishment brought about by their own recklessness who accused me of having deliberately planned the coup. Other people thought the same thing.

One of the biggest men in cotton in the entire world met me a day or two later and said, "That was certainly the slickest deal you ever put over, Livingston. I was wondering how much you were going to lose when you came to market that line of yours. You knew this market was not big enough to take more than fifty or sixty thousand bales without selling off, and how you were going to work off the rest and not lose all your paper profits was beginning to interest me. I didn't think of your scheme. It certainly was slick."

"I had nothing to do with it," I assured him as earnestly as I could.

But all he did was to repeat: "Mighty slick, my boy. Mighty slick! Don't be so modest!"

It was after that deal that some of the papers referred to me as the Cotton King. But, as I said, I really was not entitled to that crown. It is not necessary to tell you that there is not enough money in the United States to buy the columns of the New York World or enough personal pull to secure the publication of a story like that. It gave me an utterly unearned reputation that time.

But I have not told this story to moralize on the crowns that are sometimes pressed down upon the brows of undeserving traders or to emphasize the need of seizing the opportunity, no matter when or how it comes. My object merely was to account for the vast amount of newspaper notoriety that came to me as the result of my deal in July cotton. If it hadn't been for the newspapers I never would have met that remarkable man, Percy Thomas.

Chapter XII

Not long after I closed my July cotton deal more successfully than I had expected I received by mail a request for an interview. The letter was signed by Percy Thomas. Of course I immediately answered that I'd be glad to see him at my office at any time he cared to call. The next day he came.

I had long admired him. His name was a household word wherever men took an interest in growing or buying or selling cotton. In Europe as well as all over this country people quoted Percy Thomas' opinions to me. I remember once at a Swiss resort talking to a Cairo banker who was interested in cotton growing in Egypt in association with the late Sir Ernest Cassel. When he heard I was from New York he immediately asked me about Percy Thomas, whose market reports he received and read with unfailing regularity.

Thomas, I always thought, went about his business scientifically. He was a true speculator, a thinker with the vision of a dreamer and the courage of a fighting man an unusually well-informed man, who knew both the theory and the practice of trading in cotton. He loved to hear and to express ideas and theories and abstractions, and at the same time there was mighty little about the practical side of the cotton market or the psychology of cotton traders that he did not know, for he had been trading for years and had made and lost vast sums.

After the failure of his old Stock Exchange firm of Sheldon & Thomas he went it alone. Inside of two years he came back, almost spectacularly. I remember reading in the Sun that the first thing he did when he got on his feet financially was to pay off his old creditors in full, and the next was to hire an expert to study and determine for him how he had best invest a million dollars. This expert examined the properties and analysed the reports of several companies and then recommended the purchase of Delaware & Hudson stock.

Well, after having failed for millions and having come back with more millions, Thomas was cleaned out as the result of his deal in March cotton. There wasn't much time wasted after he came to see me. He proposed that we form a working alliance. Whatever information he got he would immediately turn over to me before passing it on to the public. My part would be to do the actual trading, for which he said I had a special genius and he hadn't.

That did not appeal to me for a number of reasons. I told him frankly that I did not think I could run in double harness and wasn't keen about trying to learn. But he insisted that it would be an ideal combination until I said flatly that I did not want to have anything to do with influencing other people to trade.

"If I fool myself," I told him, "I alone suffer and I pay the bill at once. There are no drawn-out payments or unexpected annoyances. I play a lone hand by choice and also because it is the wisest and cheapest way to trade. I get my pleasure out of matching my brains against the brains of other traders men whom I have never seen and never talked to and never advised to buy or sell and never expect to meet or know. When I make money I make it backing my own opinions. I don't sell them or capitalise them. If I made money in any other way I would imagine I had not earned it. Your proposition does not interest me because I am interested in the game only as I play it for myself and in my own way."

He said he was sorry I felt the way I did, and tried to convince me that I was wrong in rejecting his plan. But I stuck to my views. The rest was a pleasant talk. I told him I knew he would "come back" and that I would consider it a privilege if he would allow me to be of financial assistance to him. But he said he could not accept any loans from me. Then he asked me about my July deal and I told him all about it; how I had gone into it and how much cotton I bought and the price and other details. We chatted a little more and then he went away.

When I said to you some time ago that a speculator has a host of enemies, many of whom successfully bore from within, I had in mind my many mistakes. I have learned that a man may possess an original mind and a lifelong habit of independent thinking and withal be vulnerable to attacks by a persuasive personality. I am fairly immune from the commoner speculative ailments, such as greed and fear and hope. But being an ordinary man I find I can err with great ease.

I ought to have been on my guard at this particular time because not long before that I had had an experience that proved how easily a man may be talked into doing something against his judgment and even against his wishes. It happened in Harding's office. I had a sort of private office a room that they let me occupy by myself and nobody was supposed to get to me during market hours without my consent. I didn't wish to be bothered and, as I was trading on a very large scale and my account was fairly profitable, I was pretty well guarded.

One day just after the market closed I heard somebody say,

"Good afternoon, Mr. Livingston."

I turned and saw an utter stranger a chap of about thirty or thirty-five. I could not understand how he'd got in, but there he was. I concluded his business with me had passed him. But I didn't say anything. I just looked at him and pretty soon he said, "I came to see you about that Walter Scott," and he was off.

He was a book agent. Now, he was not particularly pleasing of manner or skillful of speech. Neither was he especially attractive to look at. But he certainly had personality. He talked and I thought I listened. But I do not know what he said. I don't think I ever knew, not even at the time. When he finished his monologue he handed me first his fountain pen and then a blank form, which I signed. It was a contract to take a set of Scott's works for five hundred dollars.

The moment I signed I came to. But he had the contract safe in his pocket. I did not want the books. I had no place for them. They weren't of any use whatever to me. I had nobody to give them to. Yet I had agreed to buy them for five hundred dollars.

I am so accustomed to losing money that I never think first of that phase of my mistakes. It is always the play itself, the reason why. In the first place I wish to know my own limitations and habits of thought. Another reason is that I do not wish to make the same mistake a second time. A man can excuse his mistakes only by capitalising them to his subsequent profit.

Well, having made a five-hundred dollar mistake but not yet having localised the trouble, I just looked at the fellow to size him up as a first step. I'll be hanged if he didn't actually smile at me an understanding little smile! He seemed to read my thoughts. I somehow knew that I did not have to explain anything to him; he knew it without my telling him. So I skipped the explanations and the preliminaries and asked him, "How much commission will you get on that five hundred dollar order?"

He promptly shook his head and said, "I can't do it! Sorry!" "How much do you get?" I persisted.

"A third. But I can't do it!" he said.

"A third of five hundred dollars is one hundred and sixty-six dollars and sixty-six cents. I'll give you two hundred dollars cash if you give me back that signed contract" And to prove it I took the money out of my pocket.

"I told you I couldn't do it," he said.

"Do all your customers make the same offer to you?" I asked. "No," he answered.

"Then why were you so sure that I was going to make it?"

"It is what your type of sport would do. You are a first-class loser and that makes you a first-class business man. I am much obliged to you, but I can't do it."

"Now tell me why you do not wish to make more than your commission?" "It isn't that, exactly," he said. "I am not working just for the commission." "What are you working for then?"

“For the commission and the record,” he answered. “What record?”

“Mine.”

“What are you driving at?”

“Do you work for money alone?” he asked me.

“Yes,” I said.

“No.” And he shook his head. “No, you don’t. You wouldn’t get enough fun out of it. You certainly do not work merely to add a few more dollars to your bank account and you are not in Wall Street because you like easy money. You get your fun some other way. Well, same here.”

I did not argue but asked him, “And how do you get your fun?” “Well,” he confessed, “we’ve all got a weak spot.”

“And what’s yours?” “Vanity,” he said.

“Well,” I told him, “you succeeded in getting me to sign on. Now I want to sign off, and I am paying you two hundred dollars for ten minutes’ work. Isn’t that enough for your pride?”

“No,” he answered. “You see, all the rest of the bunch have been working Wall Street for months and failed to make expenses. They said it was the fault of the goods and the territory. So the office sent for me to prove that the fault was with their salesmanship and not with the books or the place. They were working on a 25 per cent commission. I was in Cleveland, where I sold eighty-two sets in two weeks. I am here to sell a certain number of sets not only to people who did not buy from the other agents but to people they couldn't even get to see. That's why they give me 33-1/3 percent."

"I can't quite figure out how you sold me that set." "Why," he said consolingly, "I sold J. P. Morgan a set."

"No, you didn't," I said. He wasn't angry. He simply said, "Honest, I did!"

"A set of Walter Scott to J. P. Morgan, who not only has some fine editions but probably the original manuscripts of some of the novels as well?"

"Well, here's his John Hancock." And he promptly flashed on me a contract signed by J.

P. Morgan himself. It might not have been Mr. Morgan's signature, but it did not occur to me to doubt it at the time.

Didn't he have mine in his pocket? All I felt was curiosity. So I asked him, "How did you get past the librarian?"

"I didn't see any librarian. I saw the Old Man himself. In his office."

"That's too much!" I said. Everybody knew that it was much harder to get into Mr. Morgan's private office empty handed than into the White House with a parcel that ticked like an alarm clock.

But he declared, "I did."

"But how did you get into his office?" "How did I get into

yours?" he retorted. "I don't know. You tell me," I said.

"Well, the way I got into Morgan's office and the way I got into yours are the same. I just talked to the fellow at the door whose business it was not to let me in. And the way I got Morgan to sign was the same way I got you to sign. You weren't signing a contract for a set of books. You just took the fountain pen I gave you and did what I asked you to do with it. No difference. Same as you."

"And is that really Morgan's signature?" I asked him, about three minutes late with my skepticism.

"Sure! He learned how to write his name when he was a boy." "And that's all there's to it?"

"That's all," he answered. "I know exactly what I am doing. That's all the secret there is. I am much obliged to you. Good day, Mr. Livingston." And he started to go out.

"Hold on," I said. "I'm bound to have you make an even two hundred dollars out of me." And I handed him thirty-five dollars.

He shook his head. Then: "No," he said. "I can't do that. But I can do this!" And he took the contract from his pocket, tore it in two and gave me the pieces.

I counted two hundred dollars and held the money before him, but he again shook his head.

"Isn't that what you meant?" I said. "No."

"Then, why did you tear up the contract?"

"Because you did not whine, but took it as I would have taken it myself had I been in your place."

"But I offered you the two hundred dollars of my own accord," I said. "I know; but money isn't everything."

Something in his voice made me say, "You're right; it isn't And now what do you really want me to do for you?"

"You're quick, aren't you?" he said. "Do you really want to do something for me?"

"Yes," I told him, "I do. But whether I will or not depends what it is you have in mind."

"Take me with you into Mr. Ed Harding's office and tell him to let me talk to him three minutes by the clock. Then leave me alone with him."

I shook my head and said, "He is a good friend of mine."

"He's fifty years old and a stock broker," said the book agent That was perfectly true, so I took him into Ed's office. I did not hear anything more from or about that book agent. But one evening some weeks later when I was going uptown I ran across him in a Sixth Avenue L train. He raised his hat very politely and I nodded back. He came over and asked me, "How do you do, Mr. Livingston? And how is Mr. Harding?"

"He's well. Why do you ask?" I felt he was holding back a story.

"I sold him two thousand dollars' worth of books that day you took me in to see him." "He never said a word to me about it," I said, "No; that kind doesn't talk about it." "What kind doesn't talk?"

"The kind that never makes mistakes on account of its being bad business to make them. That kind always knows what he wants and nobody can tell him different. That is the kind that's educating my children and keeps my wife in good humor. You did me a good turn, Mr. Livingston. I expected it when I gave up the two hundred dollars you were so anxious to present to me."

"And if Mr. Harding hadn't given you an order?"

"Oh, but I knew he would. I had found out what kind of man he was. He was a cinch." "Yes. But if he hadn't bought any books?" I persisted.

"I'd have come back to you and sold you something. Good day, Mr. Livingston. I am going to see the mayor." And he got up as we pulled up at Park Place.

"I hope you sell him ten sets," I said. His Honor was a Tammany man.

"I'm a Republican, too," he said, and went out, not hastily, but leisurely, confident that the train would wait. And it did.

I have told you this story in such detail because it concerned a remarkable man who made me buy what I did not wish to buy. He was the first man who did that to me. There never should have been a second, but there was. You can never bank on there being but one remarkable salesman in the world or on complete immunization from the influence of personality.

When Percy Thomas left my office, after I had pleasantly but definitely declined to enter into a working alliance with him, I would have sworn that our business paths would never cross. I was not sure I'd ever even see him again. But on the very next day he wrote me a letter thanking me for my offers of help and inviting me to come and see him. I answered that I would. He wrote again. I called.

I got to see a great deal of him. It was always a pleasure for me to listen to him, he knew so much and he expressed his knowledge so interestingly. I think he is the most magnetic man I ever met.

We talked of many things, for he is a widely read man with an amazing grasp of many subjects and a remarkable gift for interesting generalization. The wisdom of his speech is impressive; and as for plausibility, he hasn't an equal. I have heard many people accuse Percy Thomas of many things, including insincerity, but I sometimes wonder if his remarkable plausibility does not come from the fact that he first convinces himself so thoroughly as to acquire thereby a greatly increased power to convince others.

Of course we talked about market matters at great length. I was not bullish on cotton, but he was. I could not see the bull side at all, but he did. He brought up so many facts and figures that I ought to have been overwhelmed, but I wasn't. I couldn't disprove them because I could not deny their authenticity, but they did not shake my belief in what I read for myself. But he kept at it until I no longer felt sure of my own information as gathered from the trade papers and the dailies. That meant I couldn't see the market with my own eyes. A man cannot be convinced against his own convictions, but he can be talked into a state of uncertainty and indecision, which is even worse, for that means that he cannot trade with confidence and comfort.

I cannot say that I got all mixed up, exactly, but I lost my poise; or rather, I ceased to do my own thinking. I cannot give you in detail the various steps by which I reached the state of mind that was to prove so costly to me. I think it was his assurances of the accuracy of his figures, which were exclusively his, and the undependability of mine, which were not exclusively mine, but public property. He harped on the utter reliability, as proved time and again, of all his ten thousand correspondents throughout the South. In the end I came to read conditions as he himself read them because we were both reading from the same page of the same book, held by him before my eyes. He has a logical mind. Once I accepted his facts it was a cinch that my own conclusions, derived from his facts, would agree with his own.

When he began his talks with me about the cotton situation I not only was bearish but I was short of the market. Gradually, as I began to accept his facts and figures, I began to fear I had been basing my previous position on misinformation. Of course I could not feel that way and not cover. And once I had covered because Thomas made me think I was wrong, I simply had to go long. It is the way my mind works. You know, I have done nothing in my life but trade in stocks and commodities. I naturally think that if it is wrong to be bearish it must be right to be a bull. And if it is right to be a bull it is imperative to buy. As my old Palm Beach friend said Pat Hearne used to say, "You can't tell till you bet!" I must prove whether I am right on the market or not; and the proofs are to be read only in my brokers' statements at the end of the month.

I started in to buy cotton and in a jiffy I had my usual line,' about sixty thousand bales. It was the most asinine play of my career. Instead of standing or falling by my own observation and deductions I was merely playing another man's game. It was eminently fitting that my silly plays should not end with that. I not only bought when I had no business to be bullish but I didn't accumulate my line in accordance with the promptings of experience. I wasn't trading right. Having listened, I was lost.

The market was not going my way. I am never afraid or impatient when I am sure of my position. But the market didn't act the way it should have acted had Thomas been right. Having taken the first wrong step I took the second and the third, and of course it muddled me all up. I allowed myself to be persuaded not only into not taking my loss but into holding up the market. That is a style of play foreign to my nature and contrary to my trading principles and theories. Even as a boy in the bucket shops I had known better. But I was not myself. I was another man a Thomas-ized person.

I not only was long of cotton but I was carrying a heavy line of wheat. That was doing famously and showed me a handsome profit. My fool efforts to bolster up cotton had increased my line to about one hundred and fifty thousand bales. I may tell you that about this time I was not feeling very well. " I don't say this to furnish an excuse for my blunders, but merely to state a pertinent fact. I remember I went to Bayshore for a rest.

While there I did some thinking. It seemed to me that my speculative commitments were overlarge. I am not timid as a rule, but I got to feeling nervous and that made me decide to lighten my load. To do this I must clean up either tht cotton or the wheat.

It seems incredible that knowing the game as well as I did and with an experience of twelve or fourteen years of speculating in stocks and commodities I did precisely the wrong thing. The cotton showed me a loss and I kept it. The wheat showed me a profit and I sold it out. It was an utterly foolish play, but all I can say in extenuation is that it wasn't really my deal, but Thomas'. Of all speculative blunders there are few greater than trying to average a losing game. My cotton deal proved it to the hilt a little later. Always sell what shows you a loss and keep what shows you a profit. That was so obviously the wise thing to do and was so well known to me that even now I marvel at myself for doing the reverse.

And so I sold my wheat, deliberately cut short my profit in it. After I got out of it the price went up twenty cents a bushel without stopping. If I had kept it I might have taken a profit of about eight million dollars. And having decided to keep on with the losing proposition I bought more cotton!

I remember very clearly how every day I would buy cotton, more cotton. And why do you think I bought it? To keep the price from going down! If that isn't a supersucker play, what is? I simply kept on putting up more and more money more money to lose eventually. My brokers and my intimate friends could not understand it; and they don't to this day. Of course if the deal had turned out differently I would have been a wonder. More than once I was warned against placing too much reliance on Percy Thomas' brilliant analyses. To this I paid no heed, but kept on buying cotton to keep it from going down. I was even buying it in Liverpool. I accumulated four hundred and forty thousand bales before I realised what I was doing. And then it was too late. So I sold out my line.

I lost nearly all that I had made out of all my other deals in stocks and commodities. I was not completely cleaned out, but I had left fewer hundreds of thousands than I had millions before I met my brilliant friend Percy Thomas. For me of all men to violate all the laws that experience had taught me to observe in order to prosper was more than asinine.

To learn that a man can make foolish plays for no reason whatever was a valuable lesson. It cost me millions to learn that another dangerous enemy to a trader is his susceptibility to the urgings of a magnetic personality when plausibly expressed by a brilliant mind. It has always seemed to me, however, that I might have learned my lesson quite as well if the cost had been only one million. But Fate does not always let you fix the tuition fee. She delivers the educational wallop and presents her own bill, knowing you have to pay it, no matter what the amount may be. Having learned what folly I was capable of I closed that particular incident. Percy Thomas went out of my life.

There I was, with more than nine-tenths of my stake, as Jim Fisk used to say, gone where the woodbine twineth up the spout. I had been a millionaire rather less than a year. My millions I had made by using brains, helped by luck. I had lost them by reversing the process. I sold my two yachts and was decidedly less extravagant in my manner of living.

But that one blow wasn't enough. Luck was against me. I ran up first against illness and then against the urgent need of two hundred thousand dollars in cash. A few months before that sum would have been nothing at all; but now it meant almost the entire remnant of my fleet-winged fortune. I had to supply the money and the question was: Where could I get it? I didn't want to take it out of the balance I kept at my brokers' because if I did I wouldn't have much of a margin left for my own trading; and I needed trading facilities more than ever if I was to win back my millions quickly. There was only one alternative that I could see, and that was to take it out of the stock market!

Just think of it! If you know much about the average customer of the average commission house you will agree with me that the hope of making the stock market pay your bill is one of the most prolific sources of loss in Wall Street. You will chip out all you have if you adhere to your determination.

Why, in Harding's office one winter a little bunch of high flyers spent thirty or forty thousand dollars for an overcoat and not one of them lived to wear it. It so happened that a prominent floor trader who since has become world-famous as one of the dollar-a-year men came down to the Exchange wearing a fur overcoat lined with sea otter. In those days, before furs went up sky high, that coat was valued at only ten thousand dollars. Well, one of the chaps in Harding's office, Bob Keown, decided to get a coat lined with Russian sable. He priced one uptown. The cost was about the same, ten thousand dollars.

"That's the devil of a lot of money," objected one of the fellows.

"Oh, fair! Fair!" admitted Bob Keown amiably. "About a week's wages unless you guys promise to present it to me as a slight but sincere token of the esteem in which you hold the nicest man in the office. Do I hear the presentation speech? No? Very well. I shall let the stock market buy it for me!"

"Why do you want a sable coat?" asked Ed Harding.

"It would look particularly well on a man of my inches," replied Bob, drawing himself up.

"And how did you say you were going to pay for it?" asked Jim Murphy, who was the star tip-chaser of the office.

"By a judicious investment of a temporary character, James. That's how," answered Bob, who knew that Murphy merely wanted a tip.

Sure enough, Jimmy asked, "What stock are you going to buy?"

"Wrong as usual, friend. This is no time to buy anything. I propose to sell five thousand Steel. It ought to go down ten points at the least. I'll just take two and a half points net.

That is conservative, isn't it?"

"What do you hear about it?" asked Murphy eagerly. He was a tall thin man with black hair and a hungry look, due to his never going out to lunch for fear of missing something on the tape.

"I hear that coat's the most becoming I ever planned to get." He turned to Harding and said, "Ed, sell five thousand U. S. Steel common at the market. Today darling!"

He was a plunger, Bob was, and liked to indulge in humorous talk. It was his way of letting the world know that he had an iron nerve. He sold five thousand Steel, and the stock promptly went up. Not being half as big an ass as he seemed when he talked, Bob stopped his loss at one and a half points and confided to the office that the New York climate was too benign for fur coats. They were unhealthy and ostentatious. The rest of the fellows jeered. But it was not long before one of them bought some Union Pacific to pay for the coat. He lost eighteen hundred dollars and said sables were all right for the outside of a woman's wrap, but not for the inside of a garment intended to be worn by a modest and intelligent man.

After that, one after another of the fellows tried to coax the market to pay for that coat. One day I said I would buy it to keep the office from going broke. But they all said that it wasn't a sporting thing to do; that if I wanted the coat for myself I ought to let the market give it to me. But Ed Harding strongly approved of my intention and that same afternoon I went to the furrier's to buy it. I found out that a man from Chicago had bought it the week before.

That was only one case. There isn't a man in Wall Street who has not lost money trying to make the market pay for an automobile or a bracelet or a motor boat or a painting. I could build a huge hospital with the birthday presents that the tight-fisted stock market has refused to pay for. In fact, of all hoodoos in Wall Street I think the resolve to induce the stock market to act as a fairy godmother is the busiest and most persistent.

Like all well-authenticated hoodoos this has its reason for being. What does a man do when he sets out to make the stock market pay for a sudden need? Why, he merely hopes. He gambles. He therefore runs much greater risks than he would if he were speculating intelligently, in accordance with opinions or beliefs logically arrived at after a dispassionate study of underlying conditions. To begin with, he is after an immediate profit. He cannot afford to wait. The market must be nice to him at once if at all. He flatters himself that he is not asking more than to place an even-money bet. Because he is prepared to run quick say, stop his loss at two points when all he hopes to make is two points he hugs the fallacy that he is merely taking a fifty-fifty chance. Why, I've known men to lose thousands of dollars on such trades, particularly on purchases made at the height of a bull market just before a moderate reaction. It certainly is no way to trade. Well, that crowning folly of my career as a stock operator was the last straw. It beat me. I lost what little my cotton deal had left me. It did even more harm, for I kept on trading and losing. I persisted in thinking that the stock market must perforce make money for me in the end. But the only end in sight was the end of my resources. I went into debt, not only to my principal brokers but to other houses that accepted business from me without my putting up an adequate margin. I not only got in debt but I stayed in debt from then on.

Chapter XIII

There I was, once more broke, which was bad, and dead wrong in my trading, which was a sight worse. I was sick, nervous, upset and unable to reason calmly. That is, I was in the frame of mind in which no speculator should be when he is trading. Everything went wrong with me. Indeed, I began to think that I could not recover my departed sense of proportion. Having grown accustomed to swinging a big line say, more than a hundred thousand shares of stock I feared I would not show good judgment trading in a small way. It scarcely seemed worth while being right when all you carried was a hundred shares of stock. After the habit of taking a big profit on a big line I wasn't sure I would know when to take my profit on a small line. I can't describe to you how weaponless I felt.

Broke again and incapable of assuming the offensive vigorously. In debt and wrong! After all those long years of successes, tempered by mistakes that really served to pave the way for greater successes, I was now worse off than when I began in the bucket shops. I had learned a great deal about the game of stock speculation, but I had not learned quite so much about the play of human weaknesses. There is no mind so machinelike that you can depend upon it to function with equal efficiency at all times. I now learned that I could not trust myself to remain equally unaffected by men and misfortunes at all times.

Money losses have never worried me in the slightest. But other troubles could and did. I studied my disaster in detail and of course found no difficulty in seeing just where I had been silly. I spotted the exact time and place. A man must know himself thoroughly if he is going to make a good job out of trading in the speculative markets. To know what I was capable of in the line of folly was a long educational step. I sometimes think that no price is too high for a speculator to pay to learn that which will keep him from getting the swelled head. A great many smashes by brilliant men can be traced directly to the swelled head an expensive disease everywhere to everybody, but particularly in Wall Street to a speculator.

I was not happy in New York, feeling the way I did. I didn't want to trade, because I wasn't in good trading trim. I decided to go away and seek a stake elsewhere. The change of scene could help me to find myself again, I thought. So once more I left New York, beaten by the game of speculation. I was worse than broke, since I owed over one hundred thousand dollars spread among various brokers.

I went to Chicago and there found a stake. It was not a very substantial stake, but that merely meant that I would need a little more time to win back my fortune. A house that I once had done business with had faith in my ability as a trader and they were willing to prove it by allowing me to trade in their office in a small way.

I began very conservatively. I don't know how I might have fared had I stayed there. But one of the most remarkable experiences in my career cut short my stay in Chicago It is an almost incredible story.

One day I got a telegram from Lucius Tucker. I had known him when he was the office manager of a Stock Exchange firm that I had at times given some business to, but I had lost track of him. The telegram read:

Come to New York at once. L. TUCKER.

I knew that he knew from mutual friends how I was fixed and therefore it was certain he had something up his sleeve. At the same time I had no money to throw away on an unnecessary trip to New York; so instead of doing what he asked me to do I got him on the long distance.

"I got your telegram," I said. "What does it mean?"

"It means that a big banker in New York wants to see you/' he answered. "Who is it?" I asked. I couldn't imagine who it could be.

"I'll tell you when you get to New York. No use otherwise." "You say he wants to see me?"

"He does." "What about?"

"He'll tell you that in person if you give him a chance," said Lucius. "Can't you write me?"

"No."

"Then tell me more plainly," I said. "I don't want to."

"Look here, Lucius," I said, "just tell me this much: Is this a fool trip?" "Certainly not. It will be to your advantage to come."

"Can't you give me an inkling?"

"No," he said. "It wouldn't be fair to him. And besides, I

don't know just how much he wants to do for you. But take my advice: Come, and come quick." "Are you sure it is I that he wishes to see?"

"Nobody else but you will do. Better come, I tell you. Telegraph me what train you take and I'll meet you at the station."

"Very well," I said, and hung up.

I didn't like quite so much mystery, but I knew that Lucius was friendly and that he must have a good reason for talking the way he did. I wasn't faring so sumptuously in Chicago that it would break my heart to leave it. At the rate I was trading it would be a long time before I could get together enough money to operate on the old scale.

I came back to New York, not knowing what would happen. Indeed, more than once during the trip I feared nothing at all would happen and that I'd be out my railroad fare and my time. I could not guess that I was about to have the most curious experience of my entire life.

Lucius met me at the station and did not waste any time in telling me that he had sent for me at the urgent request of Mr. Daniel Williamson, of the well-known Stock Exchange house of Williamson & Brown. Mr. Williamson told Lucius to tell me that he had a business proposition to make to me that he was sure I would accept since it would be very profitable for me. Lucius swore he didn't know what the proposition was. The character of the firm was a guaranty that nothing improper would be demanded of me.

Dan Williamson was the senior member of the firm, which

was founded by Egbert Williamson way back in the '70s. There was no Brown and hadn't been one in the firm for years. The house had been very prominent in Dan's father's time and Dan had inherited a considerable fortune and didn't go after much outside business. They had one customer who was worth a hundred average customers and that was Alvin Marquand, Williamson's brother-in-law, who in addition to being a director in a dozen banks and trust companies was the president of the great Chesapeake and Atlantic Railroad system. He was the most picturesque personality in the railroad world after James J. Hill, and was the spokesman and dominant member of the powerful banking coterie known as the Fort Dawson gang. He was worth from fifty million to five hundred million dollars, the estimate depending upon the state of the speaker's liver. When he died they found out that he was worth two hundred and fifty million dollars, all made in Wall Street. So you see he was some customer.

Lucius told me he had just accepted a position with Williamson & Brown one that was made for him. He was supposed to be a sort of circulating general business getter. The firm was after a general commission business and Lucius had induced Mr. Williamson to open a couple of branch offices, one in one of the big hotels uptown and the other in Chicago. I rather gathered that I was going to be offered a position in the latter place, possibly as office manager, which was something I would not accept. I didn't jump on Lucius because I thought I'd better wait until the offer was made before I refused it.

Lucius took me into Mr. Williamson's private office, introduced me to his chief and left the room in a hurry, as though he wished to avoid being called as witness in a case in which he knew both parties. I prepared to listen and then to say no.

Mr. Williamson was very pleasant. He was a thorough gentleman, with polished manners and a kindly smile. I could see that he made friends easily and kept them. Why not? He was healthy and therefore good-humored. He had slathers of money and therefore could not be suspected of sordid motives. These things, together with his education and social training, made it easy for him to be not only polite but friendly, and not only friendly but helpful.

I said nothing. I had nothing to say and, besides, I always let the other man have his say in full before I do any talking. Somebody told me that the late James Stillman, president of the National City Bank who, by the way, was an intimate friend of Williamson's made it his practice to listen in silence, with an impassive face, to anybody who brought a proposition to him. After the man got through Mr. Stillman continued to look at him, as though the man had not finished. So the man, feeling urged to say something more, did so. Simply by looking and listening Stillman often made the man offer terms much more advantageous to the bank than he had meant to offer when he began to speak.

I don't keep silent just to induce people to offer a better bargain, but because I like to know all the facts of the case. By letting a man have his say in full you are able to decide at once. It is a great time-saver. It averts debates and prolonged discussions that get nowhere. Nearly every business proposition that is brought to me can be settled, as far as my participation in it is concerned, by my saying yes or no. But I cannot say yes or no right off unless I have the complete proposition before me.

Dan Williamson did the talking and I did the listening. He

told me he had heard a great deal about my operations in the stock market and how he regretted that I had gone outside of my bailiwick and come a cropper in cotton. Still it was to my bad luck that he owed the pleasure of that interview with me. He thought my forte was the stock market, that I was born for it and that I should not stray from it.

"And that is the reason, Mr. Livingston," he concluded pleasantly, "why we wish to do business with you."

"Do business how?" I asked him.

"Be your brokers," he said. "My firm would like to do your stock business." "I'd like to give it to you," I said, "but I can't."

"Why not?" he asked.

"I haven't any money," I answered.

"That part is all right," he said with a friendly smile. "I'll furnish it." He took out a pocket check book, wrote out a check for twenty-five thousand dollars to my order, and gave it to me.

"What's this for?" I asked.

"For you to deposit in your own bank. You will draw your own checks. I want you to do your trading in our office. I don't care whether you win or lose. If that money goes 1 will give you another personal check. So you don't have to be so very careful with this one. See?"

I knew that the firm was too rich and prosperous to need

anybody's business, much less to give a fellow the money to put up as margin. And then he was so nice about it! Instead of giving me a credit with the house he gave me the actual cash, so that he alone knew where it came from, the only string being that if I traded I should do so through his firm. And then the promise that there would be more if that went! Still, there must be a reason.

"What's the idea?" I asked him.

"The idea is simply that we want to have a customer in this office who is known as a big active trader. Everybody knows that you swing a big line on the short side, which is what I particularly like about you. You are known as a plunger."

"I still don't get it," I said.

"I'll be frank with you, Mr. Livingston. We have two or three very wealthy customers who buy and sell stocks in a big way. I don't want the Street to suspect them of selling long stock every time we sell ten or twenty thousand shares of any stock. If the Street knows that you are trading in our office it will not know whether it is your short selling or the other customers' long stock that is coming on the market."

I understood at once. He wanted to cover up his brother-in-law's operations with my reputation as a plunger! It so happened that I had made my biggest killing on the bear side a year and a half before, and, of course, the Street gossips and the stupid rumor mongers had acquired the habit of blaming me for every decline in prices. To this day when the market is very weak they say I am raiding it.

I didn't have to reflect. I saw at a glance that Dan Williamson was offering me a chance to come back and come back quickly. I took the check, banked it, opened an account with his firm and began trading. It was a good active market, broad enough for a man not to have to stick to one or two specialties. I had begun to fear, as I told you, that I had lost the knack of hitting it right. But it seems I hadn't. In three weeks' time I had made a profit of one hundred and twelve thousand dollars out of the twenty-five thousand that Dan Williamson lent me.

I went to him and said, "I've come to pay you back that twenty-five thousand dollars."

"No, no!" he said and waved me away exactly as if I had offered him a castor-oil cocktail. "No, no, my boy. Wait until your account amounts to something. Don't think about it yet. You've only got chicken feed there."

There is where I made the mistake that I have regretted more than any other I ever made in my Wall Street career. It was responsible for long and dreary years of suffering. I should have insisted on his taking the money. I was on my way to a bigger fortune than I had lost and walking pretty fast. For three weeks my average profit was 150 per cent per week. From then on my trading would be on a steadily increasing scale. But instead of freeing myself from all obligation I let him have his way and did not compel him to accept the twenty-five thousand dollars. Of course, since he didn't draw out the twenty- five thousand dollars he had advanced me I felt I could not very well draw out my profit. I was very grateful to him, but I am so constituted that I don't like to owe money or favours. I can pay the money back with money, but the favours and kindnesses I must pay back in kind and you are apt to find these moral obligations mighty high priced at times. Moreover there is no statute of limitations.

I left the money undisturbed and resumed my trading. I was getting on very nicely. I was recovering my poise and I was sure it would not be very long before I should get back into my 1907 stride. Once I did that, all I'd ask for would be for the market to hold out a little while and I'd more than make up my losses. But making or not making the money was not bothering me much. What made me happy was that I was losing the habit of being wrong, of not being myself. It had played havoc with me for months but I had learned my lesson.

Just about that time I turned bear and I began to sell short several railroad stocks. Among them was Chesapeake & Atlantic. I think I put out a short line in it; about eight thousand shares.

One morning when I got downtown Dan Williamson called me into his private office before the market opened and said to me: "Larry, don't do anything in Chesapeake & Atlantic just now. That was a bad play of yours, selling eight thousand short. I covered it for you this morning in London and went long."

I was sure Chesapeake & Atlantic was going down. The tape told it to me quite plainly; and besides I was bearish on the whole market, not violently or insanely bearish, but enough to feel comfortable with a moderate short line out. I said to Williamson, "What did you do that for? I am bearish on the whole market and they are all going lower."

But he just shook his head and said, "I did it because I happen to know something about Chesapeake & Atlantic that you couldn't know. My advice to you is not to sell that stock short until I tell you it is safe to do so."

What could I do? That wasn't an asinine tip. It was advice that came from the brother-in- law of the chairman of the board of directors. Dan was not only Alvin Marquand's closest friend but he had been kind and generous to me. He had shown his faith in me and confidence in my word. I couldn't do less than to thank him. And so my feelings again won over my judgment and I gave in. To subordinate my judgment to his desires was the undoing of me. Gratitude is something a decent man can't help feeling, but it is for a fellow to keep it from completely tying him up. The first thing I knew I not only had lost all my profit but I owed the firm one hundred and fifty thousand dollars besides. I felt pretty badly about it, but Dan told me not to worry.

"I'll get you out of this hole," he promised. "I know I will. But I can only do it if you let me. You will have to stop doing business on your own hook. I can't be working for you and then have you completely undo all my work in your behalf. Just you lay off the market and give me a chance to make some money for you. Won't you, Larry?"

Again I ask you: What could I do? I thought of his kindliness and I could not do anything that might be construed as lacking in appreciation. I had grown to like him. He was very pleasant and friendly. I remember that all I got from him was encouragement. He kept on assuring me that everything would come out O.K. One day, perhaps six months later, he came to me with a pleased smile and gave me some credit slips.

"I told you I would puil you out of that hole," he said, "and I have." And then I discovered that not only had he wiped out the debt entirely but I had a small credit balance besides.

I think I could have run that up without much trouble, for the market was right, but he said to me, “I have bought you ten thousand shares of Southern Atlantic.” That was another road controlled by his brother-in-law, Alvin Marquand, who also ruled the market destinies of the stock.

When a man does for you what Dan Williamson did for me you can’t say anything but “Thank you” no matter what your market views may be. You may be sure you’re right, but as Pat Hearne used to say: “You can’t tell till you bet!” and Dan Williamson had bet for me with his money.

Well, Southern Atlantic went down and stayed down and I lost, I forget how much, on my ten thousand shares before Dan sold me out. I owed him more than ever. But you never saw a nicer or less importunate creditor in your life. Never a whimper from him. Instead, encouraging words and admonitions not to worry about it. In the end the loss was made up for me in the same generous but mysterious way.

He gave no details whatever. They were all numbered accounts. Dan Williamson would just say to me, “We made up your Southern Atlantic loss with profits on this other deal,” and he’d tell me how he had sold seventy-five hundred shares of some other stock and made a nice thing out of it. I can truthfully say that I never knew a blessed thing about those trades of mine until I was told that the indebtedness was wiped out.

After that happened several times I began to think, and I got to look at my case from a different angle. Finally I tumbled. It was plain that I had been used by Dan Williamson. It made me angry to think it, but still angrier that I had not tumbled to it quicker. As soon as I had gone over the whole thing in my mind I went to Dan Williamson, told him I was through with the firm, and I quit the office of Williamson & Brown. I had no words with him or any of his partners. What good would that have done me? But I will admit that I was sore at myself quite as much as at Williamson & Brown.

The loss of the money didn't bother me. Whenever I have lost money in the stock market I have always considered that I have learned something; that if I have lost money I have gained experience, so that the money really went for a tuition fee. A man has to have experience and he has to pay for it. But there was something that hurt a whole lot in that experience of mine in Dan Williamson's office, and that was the loss of a great opportunity. The money a man loses is nothing; he can make it up. But opportunities such as I had then do not come every day.

The market, you see, had been a fine trading market. I was right; I mean, I was reading it accurately. The opportunity to make millions was there. But I allowed my gratitude to interfere with my play. I tied my own hands. I had to do what Dan Williamson in his kindness wished done. Altogether it was more unsatisfactory than doing business with a relative. Bad business!

And that wasn't the worst thing about it. It was that after that there was practically no opportunity for me to make big money. The market flattened out. Things drifted from bad to worse. I not only lost all I had but got into debt again more heavily than ever. Those were long lean years, 1911, 1912, 1913 and 1914. There was no money to be made. The opportunity simply wasn't there and so I was worse off than ever.

It isn't uncomfortable to lose when the loss is not

accompanied by a poignant vision of what might have been. That was precisely what I could not keep my mind from dwelling on, and of course it unsettled me further. I learned that the weaknesses to which a speculator is prone are almost numberless. It was proper for me as a man to act the way I did in Dan Williamson's office, but it was improper and unwise for me as a speculator to allow myself to be influenced by any consideration to act against my own judgment. Noblesse oblige but not in the stock market, because the tape is not chivalrous and moreover does not reward loyalty. I realise that I couldn't have acted differently. I couldn't make myself over just because I wished to trade in the stock market. But business is business always, and my business as a speculator is to back my own judgment always.

It was a very curious experience. I'll tell you what I think happened. Dan Williamson was perfectly sincere in what he told me when he first saw me. Every time his firm did a few thousand shares in any one stock the Street jumped at the conclusion that Alvin Marquand was buying or selling. He was the big trader of the office, to be sure, and he gave this firm all his business; and he was one of the best and biggest traders they have ever had in Wall Street. Well, I was to be used as a smoke screen, particularly for Marquand's selling.

Alvin Marquand fell sick shortly after I went in. His ailment was early diagnosed as incurable, and Dan Williamson of course knew it long before Marquand himself did. That is why Dan covered my Chesapeake & Atlantic stock. He had begun to liquidate some of his brother-in-law's speculative holdings of that and other stocks.

Of course when Marquand died the estate had to liquidate his speculative and semispeculative lines, and by that time we had run into a bear market. By tying me up the way he did, Dan was helping the estate a whole lot. I do not speak boastfully when I say that I was a very heavy trader and that I was dead right in my views on the stock market. I know that Williamson remembered my successful operations in the bear market of 1907 and he couldn't afford to run the risk of having me at large. Why, if I had kept on the way I was going I'd have made so much money that by the time he was trying to liquidate part of Alvin Marquand's estate I would have been trading in hundreds of thousands of shares. As an active bear I would have done damage running into the millions of dollars to the Marquand heirs, for Alvin left only a little over a couple of hundred millions.

It was much cheaper for them to let me get into debt and then to pay off the debt than to have me in some other office operating actively on the bear side. That is precisely what 1 would have been doing but for my feeling that I must not be outdone in decency by Dan Williamson.

I have always considered this the most interesting and most unfortunate of all my experiences as a stock operator. As a lesson it cost me a disproportionately high price. It put off the time of my recovery several years. I was young enough to wait with patience for the strayed millions to come back. But five years is a long time for a man to be poor. Young or old, it is not to be relished. I could do without the yachts a great deal easier than I could without a market to come back on. The greatest opportunity of a lifetime was holding before my very nose the purse I had lost. I could not put out my hand and reach for it. A very shrewd boy, that Dan Williamson; as slick as they make them; farsighted, ingenious, daring. He is a thinker, has imagination, detects the vulnerable spot in any man and can plan cold-bloodedly to hit it. He did his own sizing up and soon doped out just what to do to me in order to reduce me to complete inoffensiveness in the market. He did not actually do me out of any money. On the contrary, he was to all appearances extremely nice about it. He loved his sister, Mrs. Marquand, and he did his duty toward her as he saw it.

Chapter XIV

It has always rankled in my mind that after I left Williamson & Brown's office the cream was off the market. We ran smack into a long moneyless period; four mighty lean years. There was not a penny to be made. As Billy Hen-riquez once said, "It was the kind of market in which not even a skunk could make a scent."

It looked to me as though I was in Dutch with destiny. It might have been the plan of Providence to chasten me, but really I had not been filled with such pride as called for a fall. I had not committed any of those speculative sins which a trader must expiate on the debtor side of the account. I was not guilty of a typical sucker play. What I had done, or, rather, what I had left undone, was something for which I would have received praise and not blame north of Forty-second Street. In Wall Street it was absurd and costly. But by far the worst thing about it was the tendency it had to make a man a little less inclined to permit himself human feelings in the ticker district.

I left Williamson's and tried other brokers' offices. In every one of them I lost money. It served me right, because I was trying to force the market into giving me what it didn't have to give to wit, opportunities for making money. I did not find any trouble in getting credit, because those who knew me had faith in me. You can get an idea of how strong their confidence was when I tell you that when I finally stopped trading on credit I owed well over one million dollars.

The trouble was not that I had lost my grip but that during those four wretched years the opportunities for making money simply didn't exist. Still I plugged along, trying to make a stake and succeeding only in increasing my indebtedness. After I ceased trading on my own hook because I wouldn't owe my friends any more money I made a living handling accounts for people who believed I knew the game well enough to beat it even in a dull market. For my services I received a percentage of the profits when there were any. That is how I lived. Well, say that is how I sustained life.

Of course, I didn't always lose, but I never made enough to allow me materially to reduce what I owed. Finally, as things got worse, I felt the beginnings of discouragement for the first time in my life.

Everything seemed to have gone wrong with me. I did not go about bewailing the descent from millions and yachts to debts and the simple life. I didn't enjoy the situation, but I did not fill up with self-pity. I did not propose to wait patiently for time and Providence to bring about the cessation of my discomforts. I therefore studied my problem. It was plain that the only way out of my troubles was by making money. To make money I needed merely to trade successfully. I had so traded before and I must do so once more. More than once in the past I had run up a shoe string into hundreds of thousands. Sooner or later the market would offer me an opportunity.

I convinced myself that whatever was wrong was wrong with me and not with the market. Now what could be the trouble with me? I asked myself that question in the same spirit in which I always study the various phases of my trading problems. I thought about it calmly and came to the conclusion that my main trouble came from worrying over the money I owed. I was never free from the mental discomfort of it. I must explain to you that it was not the mere consciousness of my indebtedness. Any business man contracts debts in the course of his regular business. Most of my debts were really nothing but business debts, due to what were unfavourable business conditions for me, and no worse than a merchant suffers from, for instance, when there is an unusually prolonged spell of unseasonable weather.

Of course as time went on and I could not pay I began to feel less philosophical about my debts. I'll explain: I owed over a million dollars all of it stock-market losses, remember. Most of my creditors were very nice and didn't bother me; but there were two who did bedevil me. They used to follow me around. Every time I made a winning each of them was Johnny-on-the-spot, wanting to know all about it and insisting on getting theirs right off. One of them, to whom I owed eight hundred dollars, threatened to sue me, seize my furniture, and so forth. I can't conceive why he thought I was concealing assets, unless it was that I didn't quite look like a stage hobo about to die of destitution.

As I studied the problem I saw that it wasn't a case that called for reading the tape but for reading my own self. I quite cold-bloodedly reached the conclusion that I would never be able to accomplish anything useful so long as I was worried, and it was equally plain that I should be worried so long as I owed money. I mean, as long as any creditor had the power to vex me or to interfere with my coming back by insisting upon being paid before I could get a decent stake together. This was all so obviously true that I said to myself, "I must go through bankruptcy." What else could relieve my mind?

It sounds both easy and sensible, doesn't it? But it was more than unpleasant, I can tell you. I hated to do it. I hated to put myself in a position to be misunderstood or misjudged. I myself never cared much for money. I never thought enough of it to consider it worth while lying for. But I knew that everybody didn't feel that way. Of course I also knew that if I got on my feet again I'd pay everybody off, for the obligation remained. But unless I was able to trade in the old way I'd never be able to pay back that million.

I nerved myself and went to see my creditors. It was a mighty difficult thing for me to do, for all that most of them were personal friends or old acquaintances.

I explained the situation quite frankly to them. I said: "I am not going to take this step because I don't wish to pay you but because, in justice to both myself and you, I must put myself in a position to make money. I have been thinking of this solution off and on for over two years, but I simply didn't have the nerve to come out and say so frankly to you. It would have been infinitely better for all of us if I had. It all simmers down to this: I positively cannot be my old self while I am harassed or upset by these debts. I have decided to do now what I should have done a year ago. I have no other reason than the one I have just given you."

What the first man said was to all intents and purposes what all of them said. He spoke for his firm.

"Livingston," he said, "we understand. We realise your position perfectly. I'll tell you what we'll do: we'll just give you a release. Have your lawyer prepare any kind of paper you wish, and we'll sign it."

That was in substance what all my big creditors said. That

is one side of Wall Street for you. It wasn't merely careless good nature or sportsmanship. It was also a mighty intelligent decision, for it was clearly good business. I appreciated both the good will and the business gumption.

These creditors gave me a release on debts amounting to over a million dollars. But there were the two minor .creditors who wouldn't sign off. One of them was the eight- hundred-dollar man I told you about. I also owed sixty thousand dollars to a brokerage firm which had gone into bankruptcy, and the receivers, who didn't know me from Adam, were on my neck early and late. Even if they had been disposed to follow the example set by my largest creditors I don't suppose the court would have let them sign off. At all events my schedule of bankruptcy amounted to only about one hundred thousand dollars; though, as I said, I owed well over a million.

It was extremely disagreeable to see the story in the newspapers. I had always paid my debts in full and this new experience was most mortifying to me. I knew I'd pay off everybody some day if I lived, but everybody who read the article wouldn't know it. I was ashamed to go out after I saw the report in the newspapers. But it all wore off presently and I cannot tell you how intense was my feeling of relief to know that I wasn't going to be harried any more by people who didn't understand how a man must give his entire mind to his business if he wishes to succeed in stock speculation.

My mind now being free to take up trading with some prospect of success, unvexed by debts, the next step was to get another stake. The Stock Exchange had been closed from July thirty-first to the middle of December, 1914, and Wall Street was in the dumps. There hadn't been any business whatever in a long time. I owed all my friends. I couldn't very well ask them to help me again just because they had been so pleasant and friendly to me, when I knew that nobody was in a position to do much for anybody.

It was a mighty difficult task, getting a decent stake, for with the closing of the Stock Exchange there was nothing that I could ask any broker to do for me. I tried in a couple of places. No use.

Finally I went to see Dan Williamson. This was in February, 1915. I told him that I had rid myself of the mental incubus of debt and I was ready to trade as of old. You will recall that when he needed me he offered me the use of twenty-five thousand dollars without my asking him.

Now that I needed him he said, "When you see something' that looks good to you and you want to buy five hundred shares go ahead and it will be all right."

I thanked him and went away. He had kept me from making a great deal of money and the office had made a lot in commissions from me. I admit I was a little sore to think that Williamson & Brown didn't give me a decent stake. I intended to trade conservatively at first. It would make my financial recovery easier and quicker if I could begin with a line a little better than five hundred shares. But, anyhow, I realised that, such as it was, there was my chance to come back.

I left Dan Williamson's office and studied the situation in general and my own problem in particular. It was a bull market. That was as plain to me as it was to thousands of traders. But my stake consisted merely of an offer to carry five hundred shares for me. That is, I had no leeway, limited as I was. I couldn't afford even a slight setback at the beginning. I must build up my stake with my very first play. That initial purchase of mine of five hundred shares must be profitable. I had to make real money. I knew that unless I had sufficient trading capital I would not be able to use good judgment. Without adequate margins it would be impossible to take the cold-blooded, dispassionate attitude toward the game that comes from the ability to afford a few minor losses such as I often incurred in testing the market before putting down the big bet.

I think now that I found myself then at the most critical period of my career as a speculator. If I failed this time there was no telling where or when, if ever, I might get another stake for another try. It was very clear that I simply must wait for the exact psychological moment.

I didn't go near Williamson & Brown's. I mean, I purposely kept away from them for six long weeks of steady tape reading. I was afraid that if I went to the office, knowing that I could buy five hundred shares, I might be tempted into trading at the wrong time or in the wrong stock. A trader, in addition to studying basic conditions, remembering market precedents and keeping in mind the psychology of the outside public as well as the limitations of his brokers, must also know himself and provide against his own weaknesses. There is no need to feel anger over being human. I have come to feel that it is as necessary to know how to read myself as to know how to read the tape. I have studied and reckoned on my own reactions to given impulses or to the inevitable temptations of an active market, quite in the same mood and spirit as I have considered crop conditions or analysed reports of earnings.

So day after day, broke and anxious to resume trading, I

sat in front of a quotation-board in another broker's office where I couldn't buy or sell as much as one share of stock, studying the market, not missing a single transaction on the tape, watching for the psychological moment to ring the full-speed-ahead bell.

By reason of conditions known to the whole world the stock 1 was most bullish on in those critical days of early 1915 was Bethlehem Steel. I was morally certain it was going way up, but in order to make sure that I would win on my very first play, as I must, I decided to wait until it crossed par.

I think I have told you it has been my experience that whenever a stock crosses 100 or 200 or 300 for the first time, it nearly always keeps going up for 30 to 50 points and after 300 faster than after 100 or 200. One of my first big coups was in Anaconda, which I bought when it crossed 200 and sold a day later at 260. My practice of buying a stock just after it crossed par dated back to my early bucket-shop days. It is an old trading principle.

You can imagine how keen I was to get back to trading on my old scale. I was so eager to begin that I could not think of anything else; but I held myself in leash. I saw Bethlehem Steel climb, every day, higher and higher, as I was sure it would, and yet there I was checking my impulse to run over to Williamson & Brown's office and buy five hundred shares. I knew I simply had to make my initial operation as nearly a cinch as was humanly possible.

Every point that stock went up meant five hundred dollars I had not made. The first ten points' advance meant that I would have been able to pyramid, and instead of five hundred snares I might now be carrying one thousand shares that would be earning for me one thousand dollars a point. But I sat tight and instead of listening to my loud- mouthed hopes or to my clamorous beliefs I heeded only the level voice of my experience and the counsel of common sense. Once I got a decent stake together I could afford to take chances. But without a stake, taking chances, even slight chances, was a luxury utterly beyond my reach. Six weeks of patience but, in the end, a victory for common sense over greed and hope!

I really began to waver and sweat blood when the stock got up to 90. Think of what I had not made by not buying, when I was so bullish. Well, when it got to 98 I said to myself, "Bethlehem is going through 100, and when it does the roof is going to blow clean off!" The tape said the same thing more than plainly. In fact, it used a megaphone. I tell you, I saw 100 on the tape when the ticker was only printing 98. And I knew that wasn't the voice of my hope or the sight of my desire, but the assertion of my tape-reading instinct. So I said to myself, "I can't wait until it gets through 100. I have to get it now. It is as good as gone through par."

I rushed to Williamson & Brown's office and put in an order to buy five hundred shares of Bethlehem Steel. The market was then 98. I got five hundred shares at 98 to 99. After that she shot right up, and closed that night, I think, at 114 or 115. I bought five hundred shares more.

The next day Bethlehem Steel was 145 and I had my stake. But I earned it. Those six weeks of waiting for the right moment were the most strenuous and wearing six weeks I ever put in. But it paid me, for I now had enough capital to trade in fair-sized lots. I never would have got anywhere just on five hundred shares of stock.

There is a great deal in starting right, whatever the enterprise may be, and I did very well after my Bethlehem deal so well, indeed, that you would not have believed it was the selfsame man trading. As a matter of fact I wasn't the same man, for where I had been harassed and wrong I was now at ease and right. There were no creditors to annoy and no lack of funds to interfere with my thinking or with my listening to the truthful voice of experience, and so I was winning right along.

All of a sudden, as I was on my way to a sure fortune, we had the Lusitania break. Every once in a while a man gets a crack like that in the solar plexus, probably that he may be reminded of the sad fact that no human being can be so uniformly right on the market as to be beyond the reach of unprofitable accidents. I have heard people say that no professional speculator need have been hit very hard by the news of the torpedoing of the Lusitania, and they go on to tell how they had it long before the Street did. I was not clever enough to escape by means of advance information, and all I can tell you is that on account of what I lost through the Lusitania break and one or two other reverses that I wasn't wise enough to foresee, I found myself at the end of 1915 with a balance at my brokers' of about one hundred and forty thousand dollars. That was all I actually made, though I was consistently right on the market throughout the greater part of the year.

I did much better during the following year. I was very lucky. I was rampantly bullish in a wild bull market. Things were certainly coming my way so that there wasn't anything to do but to make money. It made me remember a saying of the late H. H. Rogers, of the Standard Oil Company, to the effect that there were times when a man could no more help making money than he could help getting wet if he went out in a rainstorm without an umbrella. It was the most clearly defined bull market we ever had. It was plain to everybody that the Allied purchases of all kinds of supplies here made the United States the most prosperous nation in the world. We had all the things that no one else had for sale, and we were fast getting all the cash in the world. I mean that the wide world's gold was pouring into this country in torrents. Inflation was inevitable, and, of course, that meant rising prices for everything.

All this was so evident from the first that little or no manipulation for the rise was needed. That was the reason why the preliminary work was so much less than in other bull markets. And not only was the war-bride boom more naturally developed than all others but it proved unprecedentedly profitable for the general public. That is, the stock- market winnings during 1915 were more widely distributed than in any other boom in the history of Wall Street. That the public did not turn all their paper profits into good hard cash or that they did not long keep what profits they actually took was merely history repeating itself. Nowhere does history indulge in repetitions so often or so uniformly as in Wall Street. When you read contemporary accounts of booms or panics the one thing that strikes you most forcibly is how little either stock speculation or stock speculators to-day differ from yesterday. The game does not change and neither does human nature.

I went along with the rise in 1916. I was as bullish as the next man, but of course I kept my eyes open. I knew, as everybody did, that there must be an end, and I was on the watch for warning signals. I wasn't particularly interested in guessing from which quarter the tip would come and so I didn't stare at just one spot. I was not, and I never have felt that I was, wedded indissolubly to one or the other side of the market. That a bull market has added to my bank account or a bear market has been particularly generous I do not consider sufficient reason for sticking to the bull or the bear side after I receive the get-out warning. A man does not swear eternal allegiance to either the bull or the bear side. His concern lies with being right.

And there is another thing to remember, and that is that a market does not culminate in one grand blaze of glory. Neither does it end with a sudden reversal of form. A market can and does often cease to be a bull market long before prices generally begin to break. My long expected warning came to me when I noticed that, one after another, those stocks which had been the leaders of the market reacted several points from the top and for the first time in many months did not come back. Their race evidently was run, and that clearly necessitated a change in my trading tactics.

It was simple enough. In a bull market the trend of prices, of course, is decidedly and definitely upward. Therefore whenever a stock goes against the general trend you are justified in assuming that there is something wrong with that particular stock. It is enough for the experienced trader to perceive that something is wrong. He must not expect the tape to become a lecturer. His job is to listen for it to say "Get out!" and not wait for it to submit a legal brief for approval.

As I said before, I noticed that stocks which had been the leaders of the wonderful advance had ceased to advance. They dropped six or seven points and stayed there. At the same time the rest of the market kept on advancing under new standard bearers. Since nothing wrong had developed with the companies themselves, the reason had to be sought elsewhere. Those stocks had gone with the current for months. When they ceased to do so, though the bull tide was still running strong, it meant that for those particular stocks the bull market was over. For the rest of the list the tendency was still decidedly upward.

There was no need to be perplexed into inactivity, for there were really no cross currents. I did not turn bearish on the market then, because the tape didn't tell me to do so. The end of the bull market had not come, though it was within hailing distance. Pending its arrival there was still bull money to be made. Such being the case, I merely turned bearish on the stocks which had stopped advancing and as the rest of the market had rising power behind it I both bought and sold.

The leaders that had ceased to lead I sold. I put out a short line of five thousand shares in each of them; and then I went long of the new leaders. The stocks I was short of didn't do much, but my long stocks kept on rising. When finally these in turn ceased to advance I sold them out and went short five thousand shares of each. By this time I was more bearish than bullish, because obviously the next big money was going to be made on the down side. While I felt certain that the bear market had really begun before the bull market had really ended, I knew the time for being a rampant bear was not yet. There was no sense in being more royalist than the king; especially in being so too soon. The tape merely said that patrolling parties from the main bear army had dashed by. Time to get ready.

I kept on both buying and selling until after about a month's trading I had out a short line of sixty thousand shares five thousand shares each in a dozen different stocks which earlier in the year had been the public's favourites because they had been the leaders of the great bull market. It was not a very heavy line; but don't forget that neither was the market definitely bearish.

Then one day the entire market became quite weak and prices of all stocks began to fall. When I had a profit of at least four points in each and every one of the twelve stocks that I was short of, I knew that I was right. The tape told me it was now safe to be bearish, so I promptly doubled up.

I had my position. I was short of stocks in a market that now was plainly a bear market. There wasn't any need for me to push things along. The market was bound to go my way, and, knowing that, I could afford to wait. After I doubled up I didn't make another trade for a long tune. About seven weeks after I put out my full line, we had the famous "leak," and stocks broke badly. It was said that somebody had advance news from Washington that President Wilson was going to issue a message that would bring back the dove of peace to Europe in a hurry. Of course the war-bride boom was started and kept up by the World War, and peace was a bear item. When one of the cleverest traders on the floor was accused of profiting by advance information he simply said he had sold stocks not on any news but because he considered that the bull market was overripe. I myself had doubled my line of shorts seven weeks before.

On the news the market broke badly and I naturally covered. It was the only play possible. When something happens on which you did not count when you made your plans it behooves you to utilise the opportunity that a kindly fate offers you. For one thing, on a bad break like that you have a big market, one that you can turn around in, and that is the time to turn your paper profits into real money. Even in a bear market a man cannot always cover one hundred and twenty thousand shares of stock without putting up the price on himself. He must wait for the market that will allow him to buy that much at no damage to his profit as it stands him on paper.

I should like to point out that I was not counting on that particular break at that particular time for that particular reason. But, as I have told you before, my experience of thirty years as a trader is that such accidents are usually along the line of least resistance on which I base my position in the market. Another thing to bear in mind is this: Never try to sell at the top. It isn't wise. Sell after a reaction if there is no rally.

I cleared about three million dollars in 1916 by being bullish as long as the bull market lasted and then by being bearish when the bear market started. As I said before, a man does not have to marry one side of the market till death do them part.

That winter I went South, to Palm Beach, as I usually do for a vacation, because I am very fond of saltwater fishing.

I was short of stocks and wheat, and both lines showed me a handsome profit. There wasn't anything to annoy me and I was having a good time. Of course unless I go to Europe I cannot really be out of touch with the stock or commodities markets. For instance, in the Adirondacks I have a direct wire from my broker's office to my house.

In Palm Beach I used to go to my broker's branch office regularly. I noticed that cotton, in which I had no interest, was strong and rising. About that time this was in 1917 -I heard a great deal about the efforts that President Wilson was making to bring about peace. The reports came from Washington, both in the shape of press dispatches and private advices to friends in Palm Beach. That is the reason why one day I got the notion that the course of the various markets reflected confidence in Mr. Wilson's success. With peace supposedly close at hand, stocks and wheat ought to go down and cotton up. I was all set as far as stocks and wheat went, but I had not done anything in cotton in some time.

At 2:20 that afternoon I did not own a single bale, but at 2:25 my belief that peace was impending made me buy fifteen thousand bales as a starter. I proposed to follow my old system of trading that is, of buying my full line which I have already described to you.

That very afternoon, after the market closed, we got the Unrestricted Warfare note. There wasn't anything to do except to wait for the market to open the next day. I recall that at Gridley's that night one of the greatest captains of industry in the country was offering to sell any amount of United States Steel at five points below the closing price that afternoon. There were several Pittsburgh millionaires within hearing. Nobody took the big man's offer. They knew there was bound to be a whopping big break at the opening.

Sure enough, the next morning the stock and commodity markets were in an uproar, as you can imagine. Some stocks opened eight points below the previous night's close. To me that meant a heaven-sent opportunity to cover all my shorts profitably. As I said before, in a bear market it is always wise to cover if complete demoralisation suddenly develops.

That is the only way, if you swing a good-sized line, of

turning a big paper profit into real money both quickly and without regrettable reductions. For instance, I was short fifty thousand shares of United States Steel alone. Of course I was short of other stocks, and when I saw I had the market to cover in, I did. My profits amounted to about one and a half million dollars. It was not a chance to disregard.

Cotton, of which I was long fifteen thousand bales, bought in the last half hour of the trading the previous afternoon, opened down five hundred points. Some break! It meant an overnight loss of three hundred and seventy-five thousand dollars. While it was perfectly clear that the only wise play in stocks and wheat was to cover on the break I was not so clear as to what I ought to do in cotton. There were various things to consider, and while I always take my loss the moment I am convinced I am wrong, I did not like to take that loss that morning. Then I reflected that I had gone South to have a good time fishing instead of perplexing myself over the course of the cotton market. And, moreover, I had taken such big profits in my wheat and in stocks that I decided to take my Joss in cotton. I would figure that my profit had been a little more than one million instead of over a million and a half. It was all a matter of bookkeeping, as promoters are apt to tell you when you ask too many questions.

If I hadn't bought that cotton just before the market closed the day before, I would have saved that four hundred thousand dollars. It shows you how quickly a man may lose big money on a moderate line. My main position was absolutely correct and I benefited by an accident of a nature diametrically opposite to the considerations that led me to take the position I did in stocks and wheat. Observe, please, that the speculative line of least resistance again demonstrated its value to a trader. Prices went as I expected, notwithstanding the unexpected market factor introduced by the German note. If things had turned out as I had figured I would have been 100 per cent right in all three of my lines, for with peace stocks and wheat would have gone down and cotton would have gone kiting up. I would have cleaned up in all three. Irrespective of peace or war, I was right in my position on the stock market and in wheat and that is why the unlooked-for event helped. In cotton I based my play on something that might happen outside of the market that is, I bet on Mr. Wilson's success in his peace negotiations. It was the German military leaders who made me lose the cotton bet.

When I returned to New York early in 1917 I paid back all the money I owed, which was over a million dollars. 16 was a great pleasure to me to pay my debts. I might have paid it back a few months earlier, but I didn't for a very simple reason. I was trading actively and successfully and I needed all the capital I had. I owed it to myself as well as to the men I considered my creditors to take every advantage of the wonderful markets we had in 1915 and 1916. I knew that I would make a great deal of money and I wasn't worrying because I was letting them wait a few months longer for money many of them never expected to get back. I did not wish to pay off my obligations in driblets or to one man at a time, but in full to all at once. So as long as the market was doing all it could for me I just kept on trading on as big a scale as my resources permitted.

I wished to pay interest, but all those creditors who had signed releases positively refused to accept it. The man I paid off the last of all was the chap I owed the eight hundred dollars to, who had made my life a burden and had upset me until I couldn't trade. I let him wait until he heard that I had paid off all the others. Then he got his money. I wanted to teach him to be considerate the next time somebody owed him a few hundreds.

And that is how I came back.

After I paid off my debts in full I put a pretty fair amount into annuities. I made up my mind I wasn't going to be strapped and uncomfortable and minus a stake ever again. Of course, after I married I put some money in trust for my wife. And after the boy came I put some in trust for him.

The reason I did this was not alone the fear that the stock market might, take it away from me, but because I knew that a man will spend anything he can lay his hands on. By doing what I did my wife and child are safe from me.

More than one man I know has done the same thing, but has coaxed his wife to sign off when he needed the money, and he has lost it. But I have fixed it up so that no matter what I want or what my wife wants, that trust holds. It is absolutely safe from all attacks by either of us; safe from my market needs; safe even from a devoted wife's love. I'm taking no chances!

Chapter XV

Among the hazards of speculation the happening of the unexpected I might even say of the unexpectable ranks high. There are certain chances that the most prudent man is justified in taking chances that he must take if he wishes to be more than a mercantile mollusk. Normal business hazards are no worse than the risks a man runs when he goes out of his house into the street or sets out on a railroad journey. When I lose money by reason of some development which nobody could foresee I think no more vindictively of it than I do of an inconveniently timed storm. Life itself from the cradle to the grave is a gamble and what happens to me because I do not possess the gift of second sight I can bear undisturbed. But there have been times in my career as a speculator when I have both been right and played square and nevertheless I have been cheated out of my earnings by the sordid unfairness of unsportsmanlike opponents.

Against misdeeds by crooks, cowards and crowds a quick-thinking or far-sighted business man can protect himself. I have never gone up against downright dishonesty except in a bucket shop or two because even there honesty was the best policy; the big money was in being square and not in welshing. I have never thought it good business to play any game in any place where it was necessary to keep an eye on the dealer because he was likely to cheat if unwatched. But against the whining welsher the decent man is powerless. Fair play is fair play. I could tell you a dozen instances where I have been the victim of my own belief in the sacredness of the pledged word or of the inviolability of a gentlemen's agreement. I shall not do so because no useful purpose can be served thereby.

Fiction writers, clergymen and women are fond of alluding to the floor of the. Stock Exchange as a boodlers' battlefield and to Wall Street's daily business as a fight. It is quite dramatic but utterly misleading. I do not think that my business is strife and contest. I never fight either individuals or speculative cliques. I merely differ in opinion that is, in my reading of basic conditions. What playwrights call battles of business are not fights between human beings. They are merely tests of business vision. I try to stick to facts and facts only, and govern my actions accordingly. That is Bernard M. Baruch's recipe for success in wealth-winning. Sometimes I do not see the facts all the facts clearly enough or early enough; or else I do not reason logically. Whenever any of these things happen I lose. I am wrong. And it always costs me money to be wrong.

No reasonable man objects to paying for his mistakes. There are no preferred creditors in mistake-making and no exceptions or exemptions. But I object to losing money when I am right. I do not mean, either, those deals that have cost me money because of sudden changes in the rules of some particular exchange. I have in mind certain hazards of speculation that from time to time remind a man that no profit should be counted safe until it is deposited in your bank to your credit.

After the Great War broke out in Europe there began the rise in the prices of commodities that was to be expected. It was as easy to foresee that as to foresee war inflation. Of course the general advance continued as the war prolonged itself. As you may remember, I was busy "coming back" in 1915. The boom in stocks was there and it was my duty to utilise it. My safest, easiest and quickest big play was in the stock market, and I was lucky, as you know.

By July, 1917, I not only had been able to pay off all my debts but was quite a little to the good besides. This meant that I now had the time, the money and the inclination to consider trading in commodities as well as in stocks. For many years I have made it my practice to study all the markets. The advance in commodity prices over the pre-war level ranged from 100 to 400 per cent. There was only one exception, and that was coffee. Of course there was a reason for this. The breaking out of the war meant the closing up of European markets and huge cargoes were sent to this country, which was the one big market. That led in time to an enormous surplus of raw coffee here, and that, in turn, kept the price low. Why, when I first began to consider its speculative possibilities coffee was actually selling below pre-war prices. If the reasons for this anomaly were plain, no less plain was it that the active and increasingly efficient operation by the German and Austrian submarines must mean an appalling reduction in the number of ships available for commercial purposes. This eventually in turn must lead to dwindling imports of coffee. With reduced receipts and an unchanged consumption the surplus stocks must be absorbed, and when that happened the price of coffee must do what the prices of all other commodities had done, which was, go way up.

It didn't require a Sherlock Holmes to size up the situation. Why everybody did not buy coffee I cannot tell you. When I decided to buy it I did not consider it a speculation. It was much more of an investment. I knew it would take time to cash in, but I knew also that it was bound to yield a good profit. That made it a conservative investment operation a banker's act rather than a gambler's play.

I started my buying operations in the winter of 1917. I took quite a lot of coffee. The market, however, did nothing to speak of. It continued inactive and as for the price, it did not go up as I had expected. The outcome of it all was that I simply carried my line to no purpose for nine long months. My contracts expired then and I sold out all my options. I took a whopping big loss on that deal and yet I was sure my views were sound. I had been clearly wrong in the matter of time, but I was confident that coffee must advance as all commodities had done, so that no sooner had I sold out my line than I started in to buy again. I bought three times as much coffee as I had so unprofitably carried during those nine disappointing months. Of course I bought deferred options for as long a time as I could get.

I was not so wrong now. As soon as I had taken on my trebled line the market began to go up. People everywhere seemed to realise all of a sudden what was bound to happen in the coffee market. It began to look as if my investment was going to return me a mighty good rate of interest.

The sellers of the contracts I held were roasters, mostly of German names and affiliations, who had bought the coffee in Brazil confidently expecting to bring it to this country. But there were no ships to bring it, and presently they found themselves in the uncomfortable position of having no end of coffee down there and being heavily short of it to me up here. Please bear in mind that I first became bullish on coffee while the price was practically at a pre-war level, and don't forget that after I bought it I carried it the greater part of a year and then took a big loss on it. The punishment for being wrong is to lose money. The reward for being right is to make money. Being clearly right and carrying a big line, I was justified in expecting to make a killing. It would not take much of an advance to make my profit satisfactory to me, for I was carrying several hundred thousand bags. I don't like to talk about my operations in figures because sometimes they sound rather formidable and people might think I was boasting. As a matter of fact I trade in accordance to my means and always leave myself an ample margin of safety. In this instance I was conservative enough. The reason I bought options so freely was because I couldn't see how I could lose. Conditions were in my favour. I had been made to wait a year, but now I was going to be paid both for my waiting and for being right. I could see the profit coming fast. There wasn't any cleverness about it. It was simply that I wasn't blind.

Coming sure and fast, that profit of millions! But it never reached me. No; it wasn't side- tracked by a sudden change in conditions. The market did not experience an abrupt reversal of form. Coffee did not pour into the country. What happened? The unexpectable! What had never happened in anybody's experience; what I therefore had no reason to guard against. I added a new one to the long list of hazards of speculation that I must always keep before me. It was simply that the fellows who had sold me the coffee, the shorts, knew what was in store for them, and in their efforts to squirm out of the position into which they had sold themselves, devised a new way of welshing. They rushed to Washington for help, and got it.

Perhaps you remember that the Government had evolved various plans for preventing further profiteering in necessities. You know how most of them worked. Well, the philanthropic coffee shorts appeared before the Price Fixing Committee of the War Industries Board I think that was the official designation and made a patriotic appeal to that body to protect the American breakfaster. They asserted that a professional speculator, one Lawrence Livingston, had cornered, or was about to corner, coffee. If his speculative plans were not brought to naught he would take advantage of the conditions created by the war and the American people would be forced to pay exorbitant prices for their daily coffee. It was unthinkable to the patriots who had sold me cargoes of coffee they couldn't find ships for, that one hundred millions of Americans, more or less, should pay tribute to conscienceless speculators. They represented the coffee trade, not the coffee gamblers, and they were willing to help the Government curb profiteering actual or prospective.

Now I have a horror of whiners and I do not mean to intimate that the Price Fixing Committee was not doing its honest best to curb profiteering and wastefulness. But that need not stop me from expressing the opinion that the committee could not have gone very deeply into the particular problem of the coffee market. They fixed on a maximum price for raw coffee and also fixed a time limit for closing out all existing contracts. This decision meant, of course, that the Coffee Exchange would have to go out of business. There was only one thing for me to do and I did it, and that was to sell out all my contracts. Those profits of millions that I had deemed as certain to come my way as any I ever made failed completely to materialise. I was and am as keen as anybody against the profiteer in the necessaries of life, but at the time the Price Fixing Committee made their ruling on coffee, all other commodities were selling at from 250 to 400 per cent above pre-war prices while raw coffee was actually below the average prevailing for some years before the war. I can't see that it made any real difference who held the coffee. The price was bound to advance; and the reason for that was not the operations of conscienceless speculators, but the dwindling surplus for which the diminishing importations were responsible, and they in turn were affected exclusively by the appalling destruction of the world's ships by the German submarines. The committee did not wait for coffee to start; they clamped on the brakes.

As a matter of policy and of expediency it was a mistake to force the Coffee Exchange to close just then. If the committee had let coffee alone the price undoubtedly would have risen for the reasons I have already stated, which had nothing to do with any alleged corner. But the high price which need not have been exorbitant would have been an incentive to attract supplies to this market. I have heard Mr. Bernard M. Baruch say that the War Industries Board took into consideration this factor the insuring of a supply in fixing prices, and for that reason some of the complaints about the high limit on certain commodities were unjust. When the Coffee Exchange resumed business, later on, coffee sold at twenty-three cents. The American people paid that price because of the small supply, and the supply was small because the price had been fixed too low, at the suggestion of philanthropic shorts, to make it possible to pay the high ocean freights and thus insure continued importations.

I have always thought that my coffee deal was the most legitimate of all my trades in commodities. I considered it more of an investment than a speculation. I was in it over a year. If there was any gambling it was done by the patriotic roasters with German names and ancestry. They had coffee in Brazil and they sold it to me in New York. The Price Fixing Committee fixed the price of the only commodity that had not advanced. They protected the public against profiteering before it started, but not against the inevitable higher Prices that followed. Not only that, but even when green coffee hung around nine cents a pound, roasted coffee went up with everything else. It was only the roasters who benefited. If the price of green coffee had gone up two or three cents a pound it would have meant several millions for me. And it wouldn't have cost the public as much as the later advance did.

Post-mortems in speculation are a waste of time. They get you nowhere. But this particular deal has a certain educational value. It was as pretty as any I ever went into. The rise was so sure, so logical, that I figured that I simply couldn't help making several millions of dollars. But I didn't.

On two other occasions I have suffered from the action of exchange committees making rulings that changed trading rules without warning. But in those cases my own position, while technically right, was not quite so sound commercially as in my coffee trade. You cannot be dead sure of anything in a speculative operation. It was the experience I have just told you that made me add the unexpectable to the unexpected in my list of hazards.

After the coffee episode I was so successful in other commodities and on the short side of the stock market, that I began to suffer from silly gossip. The professionals in Wall Street and the newspaper writers got the habit of blaming me and my alleged raids for the inevitable breaks in prices. At times my selling was called unpatriotic whether I was really selling or not. The reason for exaggerating the magnitude and the effect of my operations, I suppose, was the need to satisfy the public's insatiable demand for reasons for each and every price movement.

As I have said a thousand times, no manipulation can put stocks down and keep them down. There is nothing mysterious about this. The reason is plain to everybody who will take the trouble to think about it half a minute. Suppose an operator raided a stock that is, put the price down to a level below its real value what would inevitably happen? Why, the raider would at once be up against the best kind of inside buying. The people who know what a stock is worth will always buy it when it is selling at bargain prices. If the insiders are not able to buy, it will be because general conditions are against their free command of their own resources, and such conditions are not bull conditions. When people speak about raids the inference is that the raids are unjustified; almost criminal. But selling a stock down to a price much below what it is worth is mighty dangerous business. It is well to bear in mind that a raided stock that fails to rally is not getting much inside buying and where there is a raid that is, unjustified short selling there is usually apt to be inside buying; and when there is that, the price does not stay down. I should say that in ninety-nine cases out of a hundred, so-called raids are really legitimate declines, accelerated at times but not primarily caused by the operations of a professional trader, however big a line he may be able to swing.

The theory that most of the sudden declines or particular sharp breaks are the results of some plunger's operations probably was invented as an easy way of supplying reasons to those speculators who, being nothing but blind gamblers, will believe anything that is told them rather than do a little thinking. The raid excuse for losses that unfortunate speculators so often receive from brokers and financial gossipers is really an inverted tip. The difference lies in this: A bear tip is distinct, positive advice to sell short. But the inverted tip that is, the explanation that does not explain serves merely to keep you from wisely selling short. The natural tendency when a stock breaks badly is to sell it. There is a reason an unknown reason but a good reason; therefore get out. But it is not wise to get out when the break is the result of a raid by an operator, because the moment he stops the price must rebound. Inverted tips!

Chapter XVI

Tips! How people want tips! They crave not only to get them but to give them. There is greed involved, and vanity. It is very amusing, at times, to watch really intelligent people fish for them. And the tip-giver need not hesitate about the quality, for the tip- seeker is not really after good tips, but after any tip. If it makes good, fine! If it doesn't, better luck with the next. I am thinking of the average customer of the average commission house. There is a type of promoter or manipulator that believes in tips first, last and all the time. A good flow of tips is considered by him as a sort of sublimated publicity work, the best merchandising dope in the world, for, since tip-seekers and tip- takers are invariably tip-passers, tip-broadcasting becomes a sort of endless-chain advertising. The tipster-promoter labours under the delusion that no human being breathes who can resist a tip if properly delivered. He studies the art of handing them out artistically.

I get tips by the hundreds every clay from all sorts of people. I'll tell you a story about Borneo Tin. You remember when the stock was brought out? It was at the height of the boom. The promoter's pool had taken the advice of a very clever banker and decided to float the new company in the open market at once instead of letting an underwriting syndicate take its time about it. It was good advice. The only mistake the members of the pool made came from inexperience. They did not know what the stock market was capable of doing during a crazy boom and at the same time they were not intelligently liberal. They were agreed on the need of marking up the price in order to market the stock, but they started the trading at a figure at which the traders and the speculative pioneers could not buy it without misgivings.

By rights the promoters ought to have got stuck with it, but in the wild bull market their hoggishness turned out to be rank conservatism. The public was buying anything that was adequately tipped. Investments were not wanted. The demand was for easy money; for the sure gambling profit. Gold was pouring into this country through the huge purchases of war material. They tell me that the promoters, while making their plans for bringing out Borneo stock, marked up the opening price three different times before their first transaction was officially recorded for the benefit of the public.

I had been approached to join the pool and I had looked into it but I didn't accept the offer because if there is any market manoeuvring to do, I like to do it myself. I trade on my own information and follow my own methods. When Borneo Tin was brought out, knowing what the pool's resources were and what they had planned to do, and also knowing what the public was capable of, I bought ten thousand shares during the first hour of the first day. Its market debut was successful at least to that extent. As a matter of fact the promoters found the demand so active that they decided it would be a mistake to lose so much stock so soon. They found out that I had acquired my ten thousand shares about at the same time that they found out that they would probably be able to sell every share they owned if they merely marked up the price twenty-five or thirty points. They therefore concluded that the profit on my ten thousand shares would take too big a chunk out of the millions they felt were already as good as banked. So they actually ceased their bull operations and tried to shake me out. But I simply sat tight. They gave me up as a bad job because they didn't want the market to get away from them, and then they began to put up the price, without losing any more stock than they could help.

They saw the crazy height that other stocks rose to and they began to think in billions. Well, when Borneo Tin got up to 120 I let them have my ten thousand shares. It checked the rise and the pool managers let up on their jacking-up process. On the next general rally they again tried to make an active market for it and disposed of quite a little, but the merchandising proved to be rather expensive. Finally they marked it up to 150. But the bloom was off the bull market for keeps, so the pool was compelled to market what stock it could on the way down to those people who love to buy after a good reaction, on the fallacy that a stock that has once sold at 150 must be cheap at 130 and a great bargain at 120. Also, they passed the tip first to the floor traders, who often are able to make a temporary market, and later to the commission houses. Every little helped and the pool was using every device known. The trouble was that the time for bulling stocks had passed. The suckers had swallowed other hooks. The Borneo bunch didn't or wouldn't see it.

I was down in Palm Beach with my wife. One day I made a little money at Gridley's and when I got home I gave Mrs. Livingston a five-hundred-dollar bill out of it. It was a curious coincidence, but that same night she met at a dinner the president of the Borneo Tin Company, a Mr. Wisenstein, who had become the manager of the stock pool. We didn't learn until some time afterward that this Wisenstein deliberately manoeuvred so that he sat next to Mrs. Livingston at dinner.

He laid himself out to be particularly nice to her and talked most entertainingly. In the end he told her, very confidentially, "Mrs. Livingston, I'm going to do something I've never done before. I am very glad to do it because you know exactly what it means." He stopped and looked at Mrs. Livingston anxiously, to make sure she was not only wise but discreet. She could read it on his face, plain as print. But all she said was, "Yes."

"Yes, Mrs. Livingston. It has been a very great pleasure to meet you and your husband, and I want to prove that I am sincere in saying this because I hope to see a great deal of both of you. I am sure I don't have to tell you that what I am going to say is strictly confidential!" Then he whispered, "If you will buy some Borneo Tin you will make a great deal of money."

"Do you think so?" she asked.

"Just before I left the hotel," he said, "I received some cables with news that won't be known to the public for several days at least. I am going to gather in as much of the stock as I can. If you get some at the opening to-morrow you will be buying it at the same time and at the same price as I. I give you my word that Borneo Tin will surely advance. You are the only person that I have told this to. Absolutely the only one!"

She thanked him and then she told him that she didn't know anything about speculating in stocks. But he assured her it wasn't necessary for her to know any more than he had told her. To make sure she heard it correctly he repeated his advice to her:

"All you have to do is to buy as much Borneo Tin as you wish. I can give you my word that if you do you will not lose a cent. I've never before told a woman or a man, for that matter to buy anything in my life. But I am so sure the stock won't stop this side of 200 that I'd like you to make some money. I can't buy all the stock myself, you know, and if somebody besides myself is going to benefit by the rise I'd rather it was you than some stranger. Much rather! I've told you in confidence because I know you won't talk about it. Take my word for it, Mrs. Livingston, and buy Borneo Tin!"

He was very earnest about it and succeeded in so impressing her that she began to think she had found an excellent use for the five hundred dollars I had given her that afternoon. That money hadn't cost me anything and was outside of her allowance. In other words, it was easy money to lose if the luck went against her. But he had said she would surely win. It would be nice to make money on her own hook and tell me all about it afterwards.

Well, sir, the very next morning before the market opened she went into Harding's office and said to the manager:

"Mr. Haley, I want to buy some stock, but I don't want it to go in my regular account because I don't wish my husband to know anything about it until I've made some money. Can you fix it for me?"

Haley, the manager, said, "Oh, yes. We can make it a special account. What's the stock and how much of it do you want to buy?"

She gave him the five hundred dollars and told him, "Listen, please. I do not wish to lose more than this money. If that goes I don't want to owe you anything; and remember, I don't want Mr. Livingston to know anything about this. Buy me as much Borneo Tin as you can for the money, at the opening."

Haley took the money and told her he'd never say a word to a soul, and bought her a hundred shares at the opening. I think she got it at 108. The stock was very active that day and closed at an advance of three points. Mrs. Livingston was so delighted with her exploit that it was all she could do to keep from telling me all about it.

It so happened that I had been getting more and more bearish on the general market. The unusual activity in Borneo Tin drew my attention to it. I didn't think the time was right for any stock to advance, much less one like that. I had decided to begin my bear operations that very day, and I started by selling about ten thousand shares of Borneo. If I had not I rather think the stock would have gone up five or six points instead of three.

On the very next day I sold two thousand shares at the opening and two thousand shares just before the close, and the stock broke to 102.

Haley, the manager of Harding Brothers' Palm Beach Branch, was waiting for Mrs. Livingston to call there on the third morning. She usually strolled in about eleven to see how things were, if I was doing anything.

Haley took her aside and said, "Mrs. Livingston, if you want me to carry that hundred shares of Borneo Tin for you, you will have to give me more margin."

"But I haven't any more," she told him.

"I can transfer it to your regular account," he said.

"No," she objected, "because that way L. L. would learn

about it." "But the account already shows a loss of " he began.

"But I told you distinctly I didn't want to lose more than the five hundred dollars. I didn't even want to lose that," she said.

"I know, Mrs. Livingston, but I didn't want to sell it without consulting you, and now unless you authorise me to hold it I'll have to let it go."

"But it did so nicely the day I bought it," she said, "that I didn't believe it would act this way so soon. Did you?"

"No," answered Haley, "I didn't." They have to be diplomatic in brokers' offices. "What's gone wrong with it, Mr. Haley?"

Haley knew, but he could not tell her without giving me away, and a customer's business is sacred. So he said, "I don't hear anything special about it, one way or another. There she goes! That's low for the move!" and he pointed to the quotation board.

Mrs. Livingston gazed at the sinking stock and cried: "Oh, Mr. Haley! I didn't want to lose my five hundred dollars! What shall I do?"

"I don't know, Mrs. Livingston, but if I were you I'd ask Mr. Livingston."

"Oh, no! He doesn't want me to speculate on my own hook. He's told me so. He'll buy or sell stock for me, if I ask him, but I've never before done trading that he did not know all about. I wouldn't dare tell him."

"That's all right," said Haley soothingly. "He is a wonderful trader and he'll know just what to do." Seeing her shake her head violently he added devilishly: "Or else you put up a thousand or two to take care of your Borneo."

The alternative decided her then and there. She hung about the office, but as the market got weaker and weaker she came over to where I sat watching the board and told me she wanted to speak to me. We went into the private office and she told me the whole story. So I just said to her: "You foolish little girl, you keep your hands off this deal."

She promised that she would, and so I gave her back her five hundred dollars and she went away happy. The stock was par by that time.

I saw what had happened. Wisenstein was an astute person. He figured that Mrs. Livingston would tell me what he had told her and I'd study the stock. He knew that activity always attracted me and I was known to swing a pretty fair line. I suppose he thought I'd buy ten or twenty thousand shares.

It was one of the most cleverly planned and artistically propelled tips I've ever heard of. But it went wrong. It had to. In the first place, the lady had that very day received an unearned five hundred dollars and was therefore in a much more venturesome mood than usual. She wished to make some money all by herself, and womanlike dramatised the temptation so attractively that it was irresistible. She knew how I felt about stock speculation as practised by outsiders, and she didn't dare mention the matter to me. Wisenstein didn't size up her psychology right.

He also was utterly wrong in his guess about the kind of

trader I was. I never take tips and I was bearish on the entire market. The tactics that he thought would prove effective in inducing me to buy Borneo that is, the activity and the three-point rise were precisely what made me pick Borneo as a starter when I decided to sell the entire market.

After I heard Mrs. Livingston's story I was keener than ever to sell Borneo. Every morning at the opening and every afternoon just before closing I let him have some stock regularly, until I saw a chance to take in my shorts at a handsome profit.

It has always seemed to me the height of damfoolishness to trade on tips. I suppose I am not built the way a tip-taker is. I sometimes think that tip-takers are like drunkards. There are some who can't resist the craving and always look forward to those jags which they consider indispensable to their happiness. It is so easy to open your ears and let the tip in. To be told precisely what to do to be happy in such a manner that you can easily obey is the next nicest thing to being happy which is a mighty long first step toward the fulfilment of your heart's desire. It is not so much greed made blind by eagerness as it is hope bandaged by the unwillingness to do any thinking.

And it is not only among the outside public that you find inveterate tip-takers. The professional trader on the floor of the New York Stock Exchange is quite as bad. I am definitely aware that no end of them cherish mistaken notions of me because I never give anybody tips. If I told the average man, "Sell yourself five thousand Steel!" he would do it on the spot. But if I tell him I am quite bearish on the entire market and give him my reasons in detail, he finds trouble in listening and after I'm done talking he will glare at me for wasting his time expressing my views on general conditions instead of giving him a direct and specific tip, like a real philanthropist of the type that is so abundant in Wall Street the sort who loves to put millions into the pockets of friends, acquaintances and utter strangers alike.

The belief in miracles that all men cherish is born of immoderate indulgence in hope. There are people who go on hope sprees periodically and we all know the chronic hope drunkard that is held up before us as an exemplary optimist. Tip-takers are all they really are.

I have an acquaintance, a member of the New York Stock Exchange, who was one of those who thought I was a selfish, cold-blooded pig because I never gave tips or put friends into things. One day this was some years ago he was talking to a newspaper man who casually mentioned that he had had it from a good source that G. O. H. was going up. My broker friend promptly bought a thousand shares and saw the price decline so quickly that he was out thirty-five hundred dollars before he could stop his loss. He met the newspaper man a day or two later, while he still was sore.

"That was a hell of a tip you gave me," he complained.

"What tip was that?" asked the reporter, who did not remember. "About G. O. H. You said you had it from a good source."

"So I did. A director of the company who is a member of the finance committee told me."

"Which of them was it?" asked the broker vindictively.

"If you must know," answered the newspaper man, "it

was your own father-in-law, Mr. Westlake."

"Why in Hades didn't you tell me you meant him!" yelled the broker. "You cost me thirty-five hundred dollars!" He didn't believe in family tips. The farther away the source the purer the tip.

Old Westlake was a rich and successful banker and promoter. He ran across John W. Gates one day. Gates asked him what he knew. "If you will act on it I'll give you a tip. If you won't I'll save my breath," answered old Westlake grumpily.

"Of course I'll act on it," promised Gates cheerfully.

"Sell Reading! There is a sure twenty-five points in it, and possibly more. But twenty- five absolutely certain," said Westlake impressively.

"I'm much obliged to you," and Bet-you-a-million Gates shook hands warmly and went away in the direction of his broker's office.

Westlake had specialized on Reading. He knew all about the company and stood in with the insiders so that the market for the stock was an open book to him and everybody knew it. Now he was advising the western plunger to go short of it.

Well, Reading never stopped going up. It rose something like one hundred points in a few weeks. One day old Westlake ran smack up against John W. in the Street, but he made out he hadn't seen him and was walking on. John W. Gates caught up with him, his face all smiles and held out his hand. Old Westlake shook it dazedly.

"I want to thank you for that tip you gave me on Reading,"

said Gates. "I didn't give you any tip," said Westlake, frowning.

"Sure you did. And it was a Jim Hickey of a tip too. I made sixty thousand dollars."

"Made sixty thousand dollars?"

"Sure! Don't you remember? You told me to sell Reading; so I bought it! I've always made money coppering your tips, Westlake," said John W. Gates pleasantly. "Always!"

Old Westlake looked at the bluff Westerner and presently remarked admiringly, "Gates, what a rich man I'd be if I had your brains!"

The other day I met Mr. W. A. Rogers, the famous cartoonist, whose Wall Street drawings brokers so greatly admire. His daily cartoons in the New York Herald for years gave pleasure to thousands. Well, he told me a story. It was just before we went to war with Spain. He was spending an evening with a broker friend. When he left he picked up his derby hat from the rack, at least he thought it was his hat, for it was the same shape and fitted him perfectly.

The Street at that time was thinking and talking of nothing but war with Spain. Was there to be one or not? If it was to be war the market would go down; not so much on our own selling as on pressure from European holders of our securities. If peace, it would be a cinch to buy stocks, as there had been considerable declines prompted by the sensational clamorings of the yellow papers. Mr. Rogers told me the rest of the story as follows:

"My friend, the broker, at whose house I had been the

night before, stood in the Exchange the next day anxiously debating in his mind which side of the market to play. He went over the pros and cons, but it was impossible to distinguish which were rumours and which were facts. There was no authentic news to guide him. At one moment he thought war was inevitable, and on the next he almost convinced himself that it was utterly unlikely. His perplexity must have caused a rise in his temperature, for he took off his derby to wipe his fevered brow. He couldn't tell whether he should buy or sell.

"He happened to look inside of his hat. There in gold letters was the word WAR. That was all the hunch he needed. Was it not a tip from Providence via my hat? So he sold a raft of stock, war was duly declared, he covered on the break and made a killing." And then W. A. Rogers finished, "I never got back that hat!"

But the prize tip story of my collection concerns one of the most popular members of the New York Stock Exchange, J. T. Hood. One day another floor trader, Bert Walker, told him that he had done a good turn to a prominent director of the Atlantic & Southern. In return the grateful insider told him to buy all the A. & S. he could carry. The directors were going to do something that would put the stock up at least twenty-five points. All the directors were not in the deal, but the majority would be sure to vote as wanted.

Bert Walker concluded that the dividend rate was going to be raised. He told his friend Hood and they each bought a couple of thousand shares of A. & S. The stock was very weak, before and after they bought, but Hood said that was obviously intended to facilitate accumulation by the inside clique, headed by Bert's grateful friend.

On the following Thursday, after the market closed, the

directors of the Atlantic & Southern met and passed the dividend. The stock broke six points in the first six minutes of trading Friday morning.

Bert Walker was sore as a pup. He called on the grateful director, who was broken- hearted about it and very penitent. He said that he had forgotten that he had told Walker to buy. That was the reason he had neglected to call him up to tell him of a change in the plans of the dominant faction in the board. The remorseful director was so anxious to make up that he gave Bert another tip. He kindly explained that a couple of his colleagues wanted to get cheap stock and against his judgment resorted to coarse work. He had to yield to win their votes. But now that they all had accumulated their full lines there was nothing to stop the advance. It was a double, riveted, lead-pipe cinch to buy A. & S. now.

Bert not only forgave him but shook hands warmly with the high financier. Naturally he hastened to find his friend and fellow-victim, Hood, to impart the glad tidings to him. They were going to make a killing. The stock had been tipped for a rise before and they bought. But now it was fifteen points lower. That made it a cinch. So they bought five thousand shares, joint account.

As if they had rung a bell to start it, the stock broke badly on what quite obviously was inside selling. Two specialists cheerfully confirmed the suspicion. Hood sold out their five thousand shares. When he got through Bert Walker said to him, "If that blankety- blank blanker hadn't gone to Florida day before yesterday I'd lick the stuffing out of him. Yes, I would. But you come with me."

"Where to?" asked Hood.

"To the telegraph office. I want to send that skunk a telegram that he'll never forget. Come on."

Hood went on. Bert led the way to the telegraph office. There, carried away by his feelings they had taken quite a loss on the five thousand shares he composed a masterpiece of vituperation. He read it to Hood and finished, "That will come pretty near to showing him what I think of him."

He was about to slide it toward the waiting clerk when Hood said, "Hold on, Bert!" "What's the matter?"

"I wouldn't send it," advised Hood earnestly. "Why not?" snapped Bert.

"It will make him sore as the dickens."

"That's what we want, isn't it?" said Bert, looking at Hood in surprise.

But Hood shook his head disapprovingly and said in all seriousness, "We'll never get another tip from him if you send that telegram!"

A professional trader actually said that. Now what's the use of talking about sucker tip- takers? Men do not take tips because they are bally asses but because they like those hope cocktails I spoke of. Old Baron Rothschild's recipe for wealth winning applies with greater force than ever to speculation. Somebody asked him if making money in the Bourse was not a very difficult matter, and he replied that, on the contrary, he thought it was very easy.

"That is because you are so rich," objected the interviewer.

"Not at all. I have found an easy way and I stick to it. I simply cannot help making money. I will tell you my secret if you wish. It is this : I never buy at the bottom and I always sell too soon."

Investors are a different breed of cats. Most of them go in strong for inventories and statistics of earnings and all sorts of mathematical data, as though that meant facts and certainties. The human factor is minimised as a rule. Very few people like to buy into a one-man business. But the wisest investor I ever knew was a man who began by being a Pennsylvania Dutchman and followed it up by coming to Wall Street and seeing a great deal of Russell Sage.

He was a great investigator, an indefatigable Missourian. He believed in asking his own questions and in doing his seeing with his own eyes. He had no use for another man's spectacles. This was years ago. It seems he held quite a little Atchison. Presently he began to hear disquieting reports about the company and its management. He was told that Mr. Reinhart, the president, instead of being the marvel he was credited with being, in reality was a most extravagant manager whose recklessness was fast pushing the company into a mess. There would be the deuce to pay on the inevitable day of reckoning.

This was precisely the kind of news that was as the breath of life to the Pennsylvania Dutchman. He hurried over to Boston to interview Mr. Reinhart and ask him a few questions. The questions consisted of repeating the accusations he had heard and then asking the president of the Atchison, Topeka & Santa Fe Railroad if they were true.

Mr. Reinhart not only denied the allegations emphatically

but said even more: He proceeded to prove by figures that the allegators were malicious liars. The Pennsylvania Dutchman had asked for exact information and the president gave it to him, showing him what the company was doing and how it stood financially, to a cent.

The Pennsylvania Dutchman thanked President Reinhart, returned to New York and promptly sold all his Atchison holdings. A week or so later he used his idle funds to buy a big lot of Delaware, Lackawanna & Western.

Years afterward we were talking of lucky swaps and he cited his own case. He explained what prompted him to make it.

"You see," he said, "I noticed that President Reinhart, when he wrote down figures, took sheets of letter paper from a pigeonhole in his mahogany roll-top desk. It was fine heavy linen paper with beautifully engraved letterheads in two colors. It was not only very expensive but worse it was unnecessarily expensive. He would write a few figures on a sheet to show me exactly what the company was earning on certain divisions or to prove how they were cutting down expenses or reducing operating costs, and then he would crumple up the sheet of the expensive paper and throw it in the waste-basket. Pretty soon he would want to impress me with the economies they were introducing and he would reach for a fresh sheet of the beautiful notepaper with the engraved letterheads in two colors. A few figures and bingo, into the waste-basket! More money wasted without a thought. It struck me that if the president was that kind of a man he would scarcely be likely to insist upon having or rewarding economical assistants. I therefore decided to believe the people who had told me the management was extravagant instead of accepting the president's version and

I sold what Atchison stock I held.

"It so happened that I had occasion to go to the offices of the Delaware, Lackawanna & Western a few days later. Old Sam Sloan was the president. His office was the nearest to the entrance and his door was wide open. It was always open. Nobody could walk into the general offices of the D. L. & W. in those days and not see the president of the company seated at his desk. Any man could walk in and do business with him right off, if he had any business to do. The financial reporters used to tell me that they never had to beat about the bush with old Sam Sloan, but would ask their questions and get a straight yes or no from him, no matter what the stock-market exigencies of the other directors might be.

"When I walked in I saw the old man was busy. I thought at first that he was opening his mail, but after I got inside close to the desk I saw what he was doing. I learned afterwards that it was his daily custom to do it. After the mail was sorted and opened, instead of throwing away the empty envelopes he had them gathered up and taken to his office. In his leisure moments he would rip the envelope all around. That gave him two bits of paper, each with one clean blank side. He would pile these up and then he would have them distributed about, to be used in lieu of scratch pads for such figuring as Reinhart had done for me on engraved notepaper. No waste of empty envelopes and no waste of the president's idle moments. Everything utilised.

"It struck me that if that was the kind of man the D. L. & W. had for president, the company was managed economically in all departments. The president would see to that! Of course I knew the company was paying regular dividends and had a good property. I bought all the D. L. & W. stock I could. Since that time the capital stock has been doubled and quadrupled. My annual dividends amount to as much as my original investment. I still have my D. L. & W. And Atchison went into the hands of a receiver a few months after I saw the president throwing sheet after sheet of linen paper with engraved letterheads in two colors into the waste-basket to prove to me with figures that he was not extravagant."

And the beauty of that story is that it is true and that no other stock that the Pennsylvania Dutchman could have bought would have proved to be so good an investment as D. L. & W.

Chapter XVII

One of my most intimate friends is very fond of telling stories about what he calls my hunches. He is forever ascribing to me powers that defy analysis. He declares I merely follow blindly certain mysterious impulses and thereby get out of the stock market at precisely the right time. His pet yarn is about a black cat that told me, at his breakfast- table, to sell a lot of stock I was carrying, and that after I got the pussy's message I was grouchy and nervous until I sold every share I was long of. I got practically the top prices of the movement, which of course strengthened the hunch theory of my hard-headed friend.

I had gone to Washington to endeavor to convince a few Congressmen that there was no wisdom in taxing us to death and I wasn't paying much attention to the stock market. My decision to sell out my line came suddenly, hence my friend's yarn.

I admit that I do get irresistible impulses at times to do certain things in the market. It doesn't matter whether I am long or short of stocks. I must get out. I am uncomfortable until I do. I myself think that what happens is that I see a lot of warning-signals. Perhaps not a single one may be sufficiently clear or powerful to afford me a positive, definite reason for doing what I suddenly feel like doing. Probably that is all there is to what they call "ticker-sense" that old traders say James R. Keene had so strongly developed and other operators before him. Usually, I confess, the warning turns out to be not only sound but timed to the minute. But in this particular instance there was no hunch. The black cat had nothing to do with it. What he tells everybody about my getting up so grumpy that morning I suppose can be explained if I in truth was grouchy by my disappointment. I knew I was not convincing the Congressman I talked to and the Committee did not view the problem of taxing Wall Street as I did. I wasn't trying to arrest or evade taxation on stock transactions but to suggest a tax that I as an experienced stock operator felt was neither unfair nor unintelligent. I didn't want Uncle Sam to kill the goose that could lay so many golden eggs with fair treatment. Possibly my lack of success not only irritated me but made me pessimistic over the future of an unfairly taxed business. But I'll tell you exactly what happened.

At the beginning of the bull market I thought well of the outlook in both the Steel trade and the copper market and I therefore felt bullish on stocks of both groups. So I started to accumulate some of them. I began by buying 5000 shares of Utah Copper and stopped because it didn't act right. That is, it did not behave as it should have behaved to make me feel I was wise in buying it. I think the price was around 114. I also started to buy United States Steel at almost the same price. I bought in all 20,000 shares the first day because it did act right. I followed the method I have described before.

Steel continued to act right and I therefore continued to accumulate it until I was carrying 72,000 shares of it in all. But my holdings of Utah Copper consisted of my initial purchase. I never got above the 5000 shares. Its behaviour did not encourage me to do more with it.

Everybody knows what happened. We had a big bull movement. I knew the market was going up. General conditions were favourable. Even after stocks had gone up extensively and my paper-profit was not to be sneezed at, the tape kept trumpeting: Not yet! Not yet! When I arrived in Washington the tape was still saying that to me. Of course, I had no intention of increasing my line at that late day, even though I was still bullish. At the same time, the market was plainly going my way and there was no occasion for me to sit in front of a quotation board all day, in hourly expectation of getting a tip to get out. Before the clarion call to retreat came barring an utterly unexpected catastrophe, of course the market would hesitate or otherwise prepare me for a reversal of the speculative situation. That was the reason why I went blithely about my business with my Congressmen.

At the same time, prices kept going up and that meant that the end of the bull market was drawing nearer.

I did not look for the end on any fixed date. That was something quite beyond my power to determine. But I needn't tell you that I was on the watch for the tip-off. I always am, anyhow. It has become a matter of business habit with me.

I cannot swear to it but I rather suspect that the day before I sold out, seeing the high prices made me think of the magnitude of my paper-profit as well as of the line I was carrying and, later on, of my vain efforts to induce our legislators to deal fairly and intelligently by Wall Street. That was probably the way and the time the seed was sown within me. The subconscious mind worked on it all night. In the morning I thought of the market and began to wonder how it would act that day. When I went down to the office I saw not sa much that prices were still higher and that I had a satisfying profit but that there was a great big market with a tremendous power of absorption. I could sell any amount of stock in that market; and, of course, when a man is carrying his full line of stocks, he must be on the watch for an opportunity to change his paper profit into actual cash. He should try to lose as little of the profit as possible in the swapping. Experience has taught me that a man can always find an opportunity to make his profits real and that this opportunity usually comes at the end of the move. That isn't tape- reading or a hunch.

Of course, when I found that morning a market in which I could sell out all my stocks without any trouble I did so. When you are selling out it is no wiser or braver to sell fifty shares than fifty thousand; but fifty shares you can sell in the dullest market without breaking the price and fifty thousand shares of a single stock is a different proposition. I had seventy-two thousand shares of U. S. Steel. This may not seem a colossal line, but you can't always sell that much without losing some of that profit that looks so nice on paper when you figure it out and that hurts as much to lose as if you actually had it safe in bank.

I had a total profit of about $1,500,000 and I grabbed it while the grabbing was good. But that wasn't the principal reason for thinking that I did the right thing in selling out when I did. The market proved it for me and that was indeed a source of satisfaction to me. It was this way: I succeeded in selling my entire line of seventy-two thousand shares of U. S. Steel at a price which averaged me just one point from the top of the day and of the movement. It proved that I was right, to the minute. But when, on the very same hour of the very same day I came to sell my 5000 Utah Copper, the price broke five points. Please recall that I began buying both stocks at the same time and that I acted wisely in increasing my line of U. S. Steel from twenty thousand shares to seventy-two thousand, and equally wisely in not increasing my line of Utah from the original 5000 shares. The reason why I didn't sell out my Utah Copper before was that I was bullish on the copper trade and it was a bull market in stocks and I didn't think that Utah would hurt me much even if I didn't make a killing in it. But as for hunches, there weren't any.

The training of a stock trader is like a medical education. The physician has to spend long years learning anatomy, physiology, materia medica and collateral subjects by the dozen. He learns the theory and then proceeds to devote his life to the practice. He observes and classifies all sorts of pathological phenomena. He learns to diagnose. If his diagnosis is correct and that depends upon the accuracy of his observation he ought to do pretty well in his prognosis, always keeping in mind, of course, that human fallibility and the utterly unforeseen will keep him from scoring 100 per cent of bull's-eyes. And then, as he gains in experience, he learns not only to do the right thing but to do it instantly, so that many people will think he does it instinctively. It really isn't automatism. It is that he has diagnosed the case according to his observations of such cases during a period of many years; and, naturally, after he has diagnosed it, he can only treat it in the way that experience has taught him is the proper treatment. You can transmit knowledge that is, your particular collection of card-indexed facts but not your experience. A man may know what to do and lose money if he doesn't do it quickly enough.

Observation, experience, memory and mathematics these are what the successful trader must depend on. He must not only observe accurately but remember at all times what he has observed. He cannot bet on the unreasonable or on the unexpected, however strong his personal convictions may be about man's unreasonableness or however certain he may feel that the unexpected happens very frequently. He must bet always on probabilities that is, try to anticipate them. Years of practice at the game, of constant study, of always remembering, enable the trader to act on the instant when the unexpected happens as well as when the expected comes to pass.

A man can have great mathematical ability and an unusual power of accurate observation and yet fail in speculation unless he also possesses the experience and the memory. And then, like the physician who keeps up with the advances of science, the wise trader never ceases to study general conditions, to keep track of developments everywhere that are likely to affect or influence the course of the various markets. After years at the game it becomes a habit to keep posted. He acts almost automatically. He acquires the invaluable professional attitude and that enables him to beat the game at times! This difference between the professional and the amateur or occasional trader cannot be over emphasised. I find, for instance, that memory and mathematics help me very much. Wall Street makes its money on a mathematical basis. I mean, it makes its money by dealing with facts and figures.

When I said that a trader has to keep posted to the minute and that he must take a purely professional attitude toward all markets and all developments, I merely meant to emphasise again that hunches and the mysterious ticker-sense haven't so very much to do with success. Of course, it often happens that an experienced trader acts so quickly that he hasn't time to give all his reasons in advance but nevertheless they are good and sufficient reasons, because they are based on facts collected by him in his years of working and thinking and seeing things from the angle of the professional, to whom everything that comes to his mill is grist. Let me illustrate what I mean by the professional attitude.

I keep track of the commodities markets, always. It is a habit of years. As you know, the Government reports indicated a winter wheat crop about the same as last year and a bigger spring wheat crop than in 1921. The condition was much better and we probably would have an earlier harvest than usual. When I got the figures of condition and I saw what we might expect in the way of yield mathematics I also thought at once of the coal miners' strike and the railroad shopmen's strike. I couldn't help thinking of them because my mind always thinks of all developments that have a bearing on the markets. It instantly struck me that the strike which had already affected the movement of freight everywhere must affect wheat prices adversely. I figured this way: There was bound to be considerable delay in moving winter wheat to market by reason of the strike-crippled transportation facilities, and by the time those improved the Spring wheat crop would be ready to move. That means that when the railroads were able to move wheat in quantity they would be bringing in both crops together the delayed winter and the early spring wheat and that would mean a vast quantity of wheat pouring into the market at one fell swoop. Such being the facts of the case the obvious probabilities the traders, who would know and figure as I did, would not bull wheat for a while. They would not feel like buying it unless the price declined to such figures as made the purchase of wheat a good investment. With no buying power in the market, the price ought to go down. Thinking the way I did I must find whether I was right or not. As old Pat Hearne used to remark, "You can't tell till you bet." Between being bearish and selling there is no need to waste time.

Experience has taught me that the way a market behaves is

an excellent guide for an operator to follow. It is like taking a patient's temperature and pulse or noting the colour of the eyeballs and the coating of the tongue.

Now, ordinarily a man ought to be able to buy or sell a million bushels of wheat within a range of 1/4 cent. On this day when I sold the 250,000 bushels to test the market for timeliness, the price went down 1/4 cent. Then, since the reaction did not definitely tell me all I wished to know, I sold another quarter of a million bushels. I noticed that it was taken in driblets; that is, the buying was in lots of 10,000 or 15,000 bushels instead of being taken in two or three transactions which would have been the normal way. In addition to the homeopathic buying the price went down 1-1/4 cents on my selling. Now, I need not waste time pointing out that the way in which the market took my wheat and the disproportionate decline on my selling told me that there was no buying power there. Such being the case, what was the only thing to do? Of course, to sell a lot more. Following the dictates of experience may possibly fool you, now and then. But not following them invariably makes an ass of you. So I sold 2,000,000 bushels and the price went down some more. A few days later the market's behaviour practically compelled me to sell an additional 2,000,000 bushels and the price declined further still; a few days later wheat started to break badly and slumped off 6 cents a bushel. And it didn't stop there. It has been going down, with short-lived rallies.

Now, I didn't follow a hunch. Nobody gave me a tip. It was my habitual or professional mental attitude toward the commodities markets that gave me the profit and that attitude came from my years at this business. I study because my business is to trade. The moment the tape told me that I was on the right track my business duty was to increase my line. I did. That is all there is to it.

I have found that experience is apt to be steady dividend payer in this game and that observation gives you the best tips of all. The behaviour of a certain stock is all you need at times. You observe it. Then experience shows you how to profit by variations from the usual, that is, from the probable. For example, we know that all stocks do not move one way together but that all the stocks of a group will move up in a bull market and down in a bear market. This is a commonplace of speculation. It is the commonest of all self-given tips and the commission houses are well aware of it and pass it on to any customer who has not thought of it himself; I mean, the advice to trade in those stocks which have lagged behind other stocks of the same group. Thus, if U. S. Steel goes up, it is logically assumed that it is only a matter of time when Crucible or Republic or Bethlehem will follow suit. Trade conditions and prospects should work alike with all stocks of a group and the prosperity should be shared by all. On the theory, corroborated by experience times without number, that every dog has his day in the market, the public will buy A. B. Steel because it has not advanced while C. D. Steel and X. Y. Steel have gone up.

I never buy a stock even in a bull market, if it doesn't act as it ought to act in that kind of market. I have sometimes bought a stock during an undoubted bull market and found out that other stocks in the same group were not acting bullishly and I have sold out my stock. Why? Experience tells me that it is not wise to buck against what I may call the manifest group-tendency. I cannot expect to play certainties only. I must reckon on probabilities and anticipate them. An old broker once said to me: "If I am walking along a railroad track and I see a train coming toward me at sixty miles an hour, do I keep on walking on the ties? Friend, I sidestep. And I do not even pat myself on the back for being so wise and prudent."

Last year, after the general bull movement was well under way, I noticed that one stock in a certain group was not going with the rest of the group, though the group with that one exception was going with the rest of the market. I was long a very fair amount of Blackwood Motors. Everybody knew that the company was doing a very big business. The price was rising from one to three points a day and the public was coming in more and more. This naturally centered attention on the group and all the various motor stocks began to go up. One of them, however, persistently held back and that was Chester. It lagged behind the others so that it was not long before it made people talk. The low price of Chester and its apathy was contrasted with the strength and activity in Black-wood and other motor stocks and the public logically enough listened to the touts and tipsters and wiseacres and began to buy Chester on the theory that it must presently move up with the rest of the group.

Instead of going up on this moderate public buying, Chester actually declined. Now, it would have been no job to put it up in that bull market, considering that Blackwood, a stock of the same group, was one of the sensational leaders of the general advance and we were hearing nothing but the wonderful improvement in the demand for automobiles of all kinds and the record output.

It was thus plain that the inside clique in Chester were not doing any of the things that inside cliques invariably do in a bull market. For this failure to do the usual thing there might be two reasons. Perhaps the insiders did not put it up because they wished to accumulate more stock before advancing the price. But this was an untenable theory if you analysed the volume and character of the trading in Chester. The other reason was that they did not put it up because they were afraid of getting stock if they tried to.

When the men who ought to want a stock don't want it, why should I want it? I figured that no matter how prosperous other automobile companies might be, it was a cinch to sell Chester short. Experiences had taught me to beware of buying a stock that refuses to follow the group-leader.

I easily established the fact that not only there was no inside buying but that there was actually inside selling. There were other symptomatic warnings against buying Chester, though all I required was its inconsistent market behaviour. It was again the tape that tipped me off and that was why I sold Chester short. One day, not very long afterward, the stock broke wide open. Later on we learned officially, as it were that insiders had indeed been selling it, knowing full well that the condition of the company was not good. The reason, as usual, was disclosed after the break. But the warning came before the break. I don't look out for the breaks; I look out for the warnings. I didn't know what was the trouble with Chester; neither did I follow a hunch. I merely knew that something must be wrong.

Only the other day we had what the newspapers called a sensational movement in Guiana Gold. After selling on the Curb at 50 or close to it, it was listed on the Stock Exchange. It started there at around 35, began to go down and finally broke 20.

Now, I'd never have called that break sensational because it was fully to be expected. If you had asked you could have learned the history of the company. No end of people knew it. It was told to me as follows: A syndicate was formed consisting of a half dozen extremely well-known capitalists and a prominent banking-house. One of the members was the head of the Belle Isle Exploration Company, which advanced Guiana over $10,000,000 cash and received in return bonds and 250,000 shares out of a total of one million shares of the Guiana Gold Mining Company. The stock went on a dividend basis and it was mighty well advertised. The Belle Isle people thought it well to cash in and they gave a call on their 250,000 shares to the bankers, who arranged to try to market that stock and some of their own holdings as well. They thought of entrusting the market manipulation to a professional whose fee was to be one third of the profits from the sale of the 250,000 shares above 36. I understand that the agreement was drawn up and ready to be signed but at the last moment the bankers decided to undertake the marketing themselves and save the fee. So they organized an inside pool. The bankers had a call on the Belle Isle holdings of 250,000 at 36. They put this in at 41. That is, insiders paid their own banking colleagues a 5-point profit to start with. I don't know whether they knew it or not.

It is perfectly plain that to the bankers the operation had every semblance of a cinch. We had run into a bull market and the stocks of the group to which Guiana Gold belonged were among the market leaders. The company was making big profits and paying regular dividends. This together with the high character of the sponsors made the public regard Guiana almost as an investment stock. I was told that about 400,000 shares were sold to the public all the way up to 47.

The gold group was very strong. But presently Guiana began to sag. It declined ten points. That was all right if the pool was marketing stock. But pretty soon the Street began to hear that things were not altogether satisfactory and the property was not bearing out the high expectations of the promoters. Then, of course, the reason for the decline became plain. But before the reason was known I had the warning and had taken steps to test the market for Guiana. The stock was acting pretty much as Chester Motors did. I sold Guiana. The price went down. I sold more. The price went still lower. The stock was repeating the performance of Chester and of a dozen other stocks whose clinical history I remembered. The tape plainly told me that there was something wrong something that kept insiders from buying it insiders who knew exactly why they should not buy their own stock in a bull market. On the other hand, outsiders, who did not know, were now buying because having sold at 45 and higher the stock looked cheap at 35 and lower. The dividend was still being paid. The stock was a bargain.

Then the news came. It reached me, as important market news often does, before it reached the public. But the confirmation of the reports of striking barren rock instead of rich ore merely gave me the reason for the earlier inside selling. I myself didn't sell on the news. I had sold long before, on the stock's behaviour. My concern with it was not philosophical. I am a trader and therefore looked for one sign : Inside buying. There wasn't any. I didn't have to know why the insiders did not think enough of their own stock to buy it on the decline. It was enough that their market plans plainly did not include further manipulation for the rise. That made it a cinch to sell the stock short. The public had bought almost a half million shares and the only change in ownership possible was from one set of ignorant outsiders who would sell in the hope of stopping losses to another set of ignorant outsiders who might buy in the hope of making money.

I am not telling you this to moralise on the public's losses through their buying of Guiana or on my profit through my selling of it, but to emphasise how important the study of group-behaviourism is and how its lessons are disregarded by inadequately equipped traders, big and little. And it is not only in the stock market that the tape warns you. It blows the whistle quite as loudly in commodities.

I had an interesting experience in cotton. I was bearish on stocks and put out a moderate short line. At the same time I sold cotton short; 50,000 bales. My stock deal proved profitable and I neglected my cotton. The first thing I knew I had a loss of $250,000 on my 50,000 bales. As I said, my stock deal was so interesting and I was doing so well in it that I did not wish to take my mind off it. Whenever I thought of cotton I just said to myself: "I'll wait for a reaction and cover." The price would react a little but before I could decide to take my loss and cover the price would rally again, and go higher than ever. So I'd decide again to wait a little and I'd go back to my stock deal and confine my attention to that. Finally I closed out my stocks at a very handsome profit and went away to Hot Springs for a rest and a holiday.

That really was the first time that I had my mind free to deal with the problem of my losing deal in cotton. The trade had gone against me. There were times when it almost looked as if I might win out. I noticed that whenever anybody sold heavily there was a good reaction. But almost instantly the price would rally and make a new high for the move.

Finally, by the time I had been in Hot Springs a few days, I was a million to the bad and no let up in the rising tendency.

I thought over all I had done and had not done and I said to myself: "I must be wrong!" With me to feel that I am wrong and to decide to get out are practically one process. So I covered, at a loss of about one million.

The next morning I was playing golf and not thinking of anything else. I had made my play in cotton. I had been wrong. I had paid for being wrong and the receipted bill was in my pocket. I had no more concern with the cotton market than I have at this moment. When I went back to the hotel for luncheon I stopped at the broker's office and took a look at the quotations. I saw that cotton had gone off 50 points. That wasn't anything. But I also noticed that it had not rallied as it had been in the habit of doing for weeks, as soon as the pressure of the particular selling that had depressed it eased up. This had indicated that the line of least resistance was upward and it had cost me a million to shut my eyes to it.

Now, however, the reason that had made me cover at a big loss was no longer a good reason since there had not been the usual prompt and vigorous rally. So I sold 10,000 bales and waited. Pretty soon the market went off 50 points. I waited a little while longer. There was no rally. I had got pretty hungry by now, so I went into the dining- room and ordered my luncheon. Before the waiter could serve it, I jumped up, went to the broker's office, I saw that there had been no rally and so I sold 10,000 bales more. I waited a little and had the pleasure of seeing the price decline 40 points more. That showed me I was trading correctly so I returned to the dining-room, ate my luncheon and went back to the broker's. There was no rally in cotton that day. That very night I left Hot Springs.

It was all very well to play golf but I had been wrong in

cotton in selling when I did and in covering when I did. So I simply had to get back on the job and be where I could trade in comfort. The way the market took my first ten thousand bales made me sell the second ten thousand, and the way the market took the second made me certain the turn had come. It was the difference in behaviour.

Well, I reached Washington and went to my brokers' office there, which was in charge of my old friend Tucker. While I was there the market went down some more. I was more confident of being right now than I had been of being wrong before. So I sold 40,000 bales and the market went off 75 points. It showed that there was no support there. That night the market closed still lower. The old buying power was plainly gone. There was no telling at what level that power would again develop, but I felt confident of the wisdom of my position. The next morning I left Washington for New York by motor. There was no need to hurry.

When we got to Philadelphia I drove to a broker's office. I saw that there was the very dickens to pay in the cotton market. Prices had broken badly and there was a small-sized panic on. I didn't wait to get to New York. I called up my brokers on the long distance and I covered my shorts. As soon as I got my reports and found that I had practically made up my previous loss, I motored on to New York without having to stop en route to see any more quotations.

Some friends who were with me in Hot Springs talk to this day of the way I jumped up from the luncheon table to sell that second lot of 10,000 bales. But again that clearly was not a hunch. It was an impulse that came from the conviction that the time to sell cotton had now come, however great my previous mistake had been. I had to take advantage of it, It was my chance. The subconscious mind probably went on working, reaching conclusions for me. The decision to sell ir Washington was the result of my observation. My years of experience in trading told me that the line of least resistance had changed from up to down.

I bore the cotton market no grudge for taking a million dollars out of me and I did not hate myself for making a mistake of that calibre any more than I felt proud for covering in Philadelphia and making up my loss. My trading mind concerns itself with trading problems and I think I am justified in asserting that I made up my first loss because I had the experience and the memory.

Chapter XVIII

History repeats itself all the time in Wall Street. Do you remember a story I told you about covering my shorts at the time Stratton had corn cornered? Well, another time I used practically the same tactics in the stock market. The stock was Tropical Trading. I have made money bulling it and also bearing it. It always was an active stock and a favourite with adventurous traders. The inside coterie has been accused time and again by the newspapers of being more concerned over the fluctuations in the stock than with encouraging permanent investment in it. The other day one of the ablest brokers I know asserted that not even Daniel Drew in Erie or H. O. Havemeyer in Sugar developed so perfect a method for milking the market for a stock as President Mulligan and his friends have done in Tropical Trading. Many times they have encouraged the bears to sell TT short and then have proceeded to squeeze them with business-like thoroughness. There was no more vindictiveness about the process than is felt by a hydraulic press or no more squeamishness, either.

Of course, there have been people who have spoken about certain "unsavory incidents" in the market career of TT stock. But I dare say these critics were suffering from the squeezing. Why do the room traders, who have suffered so often from the loaded dice of the insiders, continue to go up against the game? Well, for one thing they like action and they certainly get it in Tropical Trading. No prolonged spells of dulness. No reasons asked or given. No time wasted. No patience strained by waiting for the tipped movement to begin. Always enough stock to go around except when the short interest is big enough to make the scarcity worth while. One born every minute!

It so happened some time ago that I was in Florida on my Usual winter vacation. I was fishing and enjoying myself without any thought of the markets excepting when we received a batch of newspapers. One morning when the semi-weekly mail came in I looked at the stock quotations and saw that Tropical Trading was selling at 155. The last time I'd seen a quotation in it, I think, was around 140. My opinion was that we were going into a bear market and I was biding my time before going short of stocks. But there was no mad rush. That was why I was fishing and out of hearing of the ticker. I knew that I'd be back home when the real call came. In the meanwhile nothing that I did or failed to do would hurry matters a bit.

The behaviour of Tropical Trading was the outstanding feature of the market, according to the newspapers I got that morning. It served to crystallise my general bearishness because I thought it particularly asinine for the insiders to run up the price of TT in the face of the heaviness of the general list. There are times when the milking process must be suspended. What is abnormal is seldom a desirable factor in a trader's calculations and it looked to me as if the marking up of that stock were a capital blunder. Nobody can make blunders of that magnitude with impunity; not in the stock market.

After I got through reading the newspapers I went back to my fishing but I kept thinking of what the insiders in Tropical Trading were trying to do. That they were bound to fail was as certain as that a man is bound to smash himself if he jumps from the roof of a twenty-story building without a parachute. I couldn't think of anything else and finally I gave up trying to fish and sent off a telegram to my brokers to sell 2000 shares of TT at the market. After that I was able to go back to my fishing. I did pretty well.

That afternoon I received the reply to my telegram by special courier. My brokers reported that they had sold the 2000 shares of Tropical Trading at 153. So far so good. I was selling short on a declining market, which was as it should be. But I could not fish any more. I was too far away from a quotation board. I discovered this after I began to think of all the reasons why Tropical Trading should go down with the rest of the market instead of going up on inside manipulation. I therefore left my fishing camp and returned to Palm Beach; or, rather, to the direct wire to New York.

The moment I got to Palm Beach and saw what the misguided insiders were still trying to do, I let them have a second lot of 2000 TT. Back came the report and I sold another 2000 shares. The market behaved excellently. That is, it declined on my selling. Everything being satisfactory I went out and had a chair ride. But I wasn't happy. The more I thought the unhappier it made me to think that I hadn't sold more. So back I went to the broker's office and sold another 2000 shares.

I was happy only when I was selling that stock. Presently I was short 10,000 shares.

Then I decided to return to New York. I had business to do now. My fishing I would do some other time.

When I arrived in New York I made it a point to get a line on the company's business, actual and prospective. What

I learned strengthened my conviction that the insiders had been worse than reckless in jacking up the price at a time when such an advance was not justified either by the tone of the general market or by the company's earnings.

The rise, illogical and ill-timed though it was, had developed some public following and this doubtless encouraged the insiders to pursue their unwise tactics. Therefore I sold more stock. The insiders ceased their folly. So I tested the market again and again, in accordance with my trading methods, until finally I was short 30,000 shares of the stock of the Tropical Trading Company. By then the price was 133.

I had been warned that the TT insiders knew the exact whereabouts of every stock certificate in the Street and the precise dimensions and identity of the short interest as well as other facts of tactical importance. They were able men and shrewd traders. Altogether it was a dangerous combination to go up against. But facts are facts and the strongest of all allies are conditions.

Of course, on the way down from 153 to 133 the short interest had grown and the public that buys on reactions began to argue as usual: That stock had been considered a good purchase at 153 and higher. Now 20 points lower, it was necessarily a much better purchase. Same stock; same dividend rate; same officers; same business. Great bargain!

The public's purchases reduced the floating supply and the insiders, knowing that a lot of room traders were short, thought the time propitious for a squeezing. The price was duly run up to 150. I daresay there was plenty of covering but I stayed pat. Why shouldn't I? The insiders might know that a short line of 30,000 shares had not been taken in but why should that frighten me? The reasons that had impelled me to begin selling at 153 and keep at it on the way down to 133, not only still existed but were stronger than ever. The insiders might desire to force me to cover but they adduced no convincing arguments. Fundamental conditions were fighting for me. It was not difficult to be both fearless and patient. A speculator must have faith in himself and in his judgment. The late Dickson G. Watts, ex-President of the New York Cotton Exchange and famous author of "Speculation as a Fine Art," says that courage in a speculator is merely confidence to act on the decision of his mind. With me, I cannot fear to be wrong because I never think I am wrong until I am proven wrong. In fact, I am uncomfortable unless I am capitalising my experience. The course of the market at a given time does not necessarily prove me wrong. It is the character of the advance or of the decline that determines for me the correctness or the fallacy of my market position. I can only rise by knowledge. If I fall it must be by my own blunders.

There was nothing in the character of the rally from 133 to 150 to frighten me into covering and presently the stock, as was to be expected, started down again. It broke 140 before the inside clique began to give it support. Their buying was coincident with a flood of bull rumors about the stock. The company, we heard, was making perfectly fabulous profits, and the earnings justified an increase in the regular dividend rate. Also, the short interest was said to be perfectly huge and the squeeze of the century was about to be inflicted on the bear party in general and in particular on a certain operator who was more than over-extended. I couldn't begin to tell you all I heard as they ran the price up ten points.

The manipulation did not seem particularly dangerous to me

but when the price touched 149 I decided that it was not wise to let the Street accept as true all the bull statements that were floating around. Of course, there was nothing that I or any other rank outsider could say that would carry conviction either to the frightened shorts or to those credulous customers of commission houses that trade on hearsay tips. The most effective retort courteous is that which the tape alone can print. People will believe that when they will not believe an affidavit from any living man, much less one from a chap who is short 30,000 shares. So I used the same tactics that I did at the time of the Stratton corner in corn, when I sold oats to make the traders bearish on corn. Experience and memory again.

When the insiders jacked up the price of Tropical Trading with a view to frightening the shorts I didn't try to check the rise by selling that stock. I was already short 30,000 shares of it which was as big a percentage of the floating supply as I thought wise to be short of. I did not propose to put my head into the noose so obligingly held open for me the second rally was really an urgent invitation. What I did when TT touched 149 was to sell about 10,000 shares of Equatorial Commercial Corporation. This company owned a large block of Tropical Trading.

Equatorial Commercial, which was not as active a stock as TT, broke badly on my selling, as I had foreseen; and, of course, my purpose was achieved. When the traders and the customers of the commission houses who had listened to the uncontradicted bull dope on TT saw that the rise in Tropical synchronised with heavy selling and a sharp break in Equatorial, they naturally concluded that the strength of TT was merely a smoke-screen a manipulated advance obviously designed to facilitate inside liquidation in Equatorial

Commercial, which was largest holder of TT stock. It must be both long stock and inside stock in Equatorial, because no outsider would dream of selling so much short stock at the very moment when Tropical Trading was so very strong. So they sold Tropical Trading and checked the rise in that stock, the insiders very properly not wishing to take all the stock that was pressed for sale. The moment the insiders took away their support the price of TT declined. The traders and principal commission houses now sold some Equatorial also and I took in my short line in that at a small profit. I hadn't sold it to make money out of the operation but to check the rise in TT.

Time and again the Tropical Trading insiders and their hard-working publicity man flooded the Street with all manner of bull items and tried to put up the price. And every time they did I sold Equatorial Commercial short and covered it with TT reacted and carried E C with it. It took the wind out of the manipulators' sails. The price of TT finally went down to 125 and the short interest really grew so big that the insiders were enabled to run it up 20 or 25 points. This time it was a legitimate enough drive against an over-extended short interest; but while I foresaw the rally I did not cover, not wishing to lose my position. Before Equatorial Commercial could advance in sympathy with the rise in TT I sold a raft of it short with the usual results. This gave the lie to the bull talk in TT which had got quite boisterous after the latest sensational rise.

By this time the general market had grown quite weak. As I told you, it was the conviction that we were in a bear market that started me selling TT short in the fishing- camp in Florida. I was short of quite a few other stocks but TT was my pet. Finally, general conditions proved too much for the inside clique to defy and TT hit the toboggan slide. It went below 120 for the first time in years; then below 110; below par; and still I did not cover. One day when the entire market was extremely weak Tropical Trading broke 90 and on the demoralisation I covered. Same old reason! I had the opportunity the big market and the weakness and the excess of sellers over buyers. I may tell you, even at the risk of appearing to be monotonously bragging of my cleverness, that I took in my 30,000 shares of TT at practically the lowest prices of the movement. But I wasn't thinking of covering at the bottom. I was intent on turning my paper profits into cash without losing much of the profit in the changing.

I stood pat throughout because I knew my position was sound. I wasn't bucking the trend of the market or going against basic conditions but the reverse, and that was what made me so sure of the failure of an over-confident inside clique. What they tried to do others had tried before and it had always failed. The frequent rallies, even when I knew as well as anybody that they were due, could not frighten me. I knew I'd do much better in the end by staying pat than by trying to cover to put out a new short line at a higher price. By sticking to the position that I felt was right I made over a million dollars. I was not indebted to hunches or to skilful tape reading or to stubborn courage. It was a dividend declared by my faith in my judgment and not by my cleverness or by my vanity. Knowledge is power and power need not fear lies not even when the tape prints them. The retraction follows pretty quickly.

A year later, TT was jacked up again to 150 and hung around there for a couple of weeks. The entire market was entitled to a good reaction for it had risen uninterruptedly and it did not bull any longer. I know because I tested it. Now, the group to which TT belonged had been suffering from very poor business and I couldn't see anything to bull those stocks on anyhow, even if the rest of the market were due for a rise, which it wasn't. So I began to sell Tropical Trading. I intended to put out 10,000 shares in all. The price broke on my selling. I couldn't see that there was any support whatever. Then suddenly, the character of the buying changed.

I am not trying to make myself out a wizard when I assure you that I could tell the moment support came in. It instantly struck me that if the insiders in that stock, who never felt a moral obligation to keep the price up, were now buying the stock in the face of a declining general market there must be a reason. They were not ignorant asses nor philanthropists nor yet bankers concerned with keeping the price up to sell more securities over the counter. The price rose notwithstanding my selling and the selling of others. At 153 I covered my 10,000 shares and at 156 I actually went long because by that time the tape told me the line of least resistance was upward. I was bearish on the general market but I was confronted by a trading condition in a certain stock and not by a speculative theory in general. The price went out of sight, above 200. It was the sensation of the year. I was flattered by reports spoken and printed that I had been squeezed out of eight or nine millions of dollars. As a matter of fact, instead of being short I was long of TT all the way up. In fact, I held on a little too long and let some of my paper profits get away. Do you wish to know why I did? Because I thought the TT insiders would naturally do what I would have done had I been in their place. But that, was something I had no business to think because my business is to trade that is, to stick to the facts before me and not to what I think other people ought to do.

Chapter XIX

I do not know when or by whom the word "manipulation" was first used in connection with what really are no more than common merchandising processes applied to the sale in bulk of securities on the Stock Exchange. Rigging the market to facilitate cheap purchases of a stock which it is desired to accumulate is also manipulation. But it is different. It may not be necessary to stoop to illegal practices, but it would be difficult to avoid doing what some would think illegitimate. How are you going to buy a big block of a stock in a bull market without putting up the price on yourself? That would be the problem. How can it be solved? It depends upon so many things that you can't give a general solution unless you say: possibly by means of very adroit manipulation. For instance? Well, it would depend upon conditions. You can't give any closer answer than that.

I am profoundly interested in all phases of my business, and of course I learn from the experience of others as well as from my own. But it is very difficult to learn how to manipulate stocks to-day from such yarns as are told of an afternoon in the brokers' offices after the close. Most of the tricks, devices and expedients of bygone days are obsolete and futile; or illegal and impracticable. Stock Exchange rules and conditions have changed, and the story even the accurately detailed story of what Daniel Drew or Jacob Little or Jay Gould could do fifty or seventy-five years ago is scarcely worth listening to. The manipulator to-day has no more need to consider what they did and how they did it than a cadet at West Point need study archery as practiced by the ancients in order to increase his working knowledge of ballistics.

On the other hand there is profit in studying the human factors the ease with which human beings believe what it pleases them to believe; and how they allow themselves - indeed, urge themselves -to be influenced by their cupidity or by the dollar-cost of the average man's carelessness. Fear and hope remain the same; therefore the study of the psychology of speculators is as valuable as it ever was. Weapons change, but strategy remains strategy, on the New York Stock Exchange as on the battlefield. I think the clearest summing up of the whole thing was expressed by Thomas F. Woodlock when he declared: "The principles of successful stock speculation are based on the supposition that people will continue in the future to make the mistakes that they have made in the past."

In booms, which is when the public is in the market in the greatest numbers, there is never any need of subtlety, so there is no sense of wasting time discussing either manipulation or speculation during such times; it would be like trying to find the difference in raindrops that are falling synchronously on the same roof across the street. The sucker has always tried to get something for nothing, and the appeal in all booms is always frankly to the gambling instinct aroused by cupidity and spurred by a pervasive prosperity. People who look for easy money invariably pay for the privilege of proving conclusively that it cannot be found on this sordid earth. At. first, when I listened to the accounts of old-time deals and devices I used to think that people were more gullible in the 1860's and '70's than in the 1900's. But I was sure to read in the newspapers that very day or the next something about the latest Ponzi or the bust-up of some bucketing broker and about the millions of sucker money gone to join the silent majority of vanished savings.

When I first came to New York there was a great fuss made about wash sales and matched orders, for all that such practices were forbidden by the Stock Exchange. At times the washing was too crude to deceive anyone. The brokers had no hesitation in saying that “the laundry was active” whenever anybody tried to wash up some stock or other, and, as I have said before, more than once they had what were frankly referred to as “bucket-shop drives,” when a stock was offered down two or three points in a jiffy just to establish the decline on the tape and wipe up the myriad shoe-string traders who were long of the stock in the bucket shops. As for matched orders, they were always used with some misgivings by reason of the difficulty of coordinating and synchronising operations by brokers, all such business being against Stock Exchange rules. A few years ago a famous operator canceled the selling but not the buying part of his matched orders, and the result was that an innocent broker ran up the price twenty-five points or so in a few minutes, only to see it break with equal celerity as soon as his buying ceased. The original intention was to create an appearance of activity. Bad business, playing with such unreliable weapons. You see, you can’t take your best brokers into your confidence not if you want them to remain members of the New York Stock Exchange. Then also, the taxes have made all practices involving fictitious transactions much more expensive than they used to be in the old times.

The dictionary definition of manipulation includes corners. Now, a corner might be the result of manipulation or it might be the result of competitive buying, as, for instance, the Northern Pacific corner on May 9, 1901, which certainly was not manipulation. The Stutz corner was expensive to everybody concerned, both in money and in prestige. And it was not a deliberately engineered corner, at that.

As a matter of fact very few of the great corners were profitable to the engineers of them. Both Commodore Vander-bilt's Harlem corners paid big, but the old chap deserved the millions he made out of a lot of short sports, crooked legislators and aldermen who tried to double-cross him. On the other hand, Jay Gould lost in his Northwestern corner. Deacon S. V. White made a million in his Lackawanna corner, but Jim Keene dropped a million in the Hannibal & St. Joe deal. The financial success of a corner of course depends upon the marketing of the accumulated holdings at higher than cost, and the short interest has to be of some magnitude for that to happen easily.

I used to wonder why corners were so popular among the big operators of a half-century ago. They were men of ability and experience, wide-awake and not prone to childlike trust in the philanthropy of their fellow traders. Yet they used to get stung with an astonishing frequency. A wise old broker told me that all the big operators of the '60's and '70's had one ambition, and that was to work a corner. In many cases this was the offspring of vanity; in others, of the desire for revenge. At all events, to be pointed out as the man who had successfully cornered this or the other stock was in reality recognition of brains, boldness and boodle. It gave the cornerer the right to be haughty. He accepted the plaudits of his fellows as fully earned. It was more than the prospective money profit that prompted the engineers of corners to do their damnedest. It was the vanity complex asserting itself among cold-blooded operators.

Dog certainly ate dog in those days with relish and ease. I think I told you before that I have managed to escape being squeezed more than once, not because of the possession of a mysterious ticker-sense but because I can generally tell the moment the character of the buying in the stock makes it imprudent for me to be short of it. This I do by common-sense tests, which must have been tried in the old times also. Old Daniel Drew used to squeeze the boys with some frequency and make them pay high prices for the Erie "sheers" they had sold short to him. He was himself squeezed by Commodore Vanderbilt in Erie, and when old Drew begged for mercy the Commodore grimly quoted the Great Bear's own deathless distich:

He that sells what isn't his'n Must buy it back or go to pris'n.

Wall Street remembers very little of an operator who for more than a generation was one of its Titans. His chief claim to immortality seems to be the phrase "watering stock."

Addison G. Jerome was the acknowledged king of the Public Board in the spring of 1863. His market tips, they tell me, were considered as good as cash in bank. From all accounts he was a great trader and made millions. He was liberal to the point of extravagance and had a great following in the Street until Henry Keep, known as William the Silent, squeezed him out of all his millions in the Old Southern corner. Keep, by the way, was the brother-in-law of Gov. Roswell P. Flower.

In most of the old corners the manipulation consisted chiefly of not letting the other man know that you were cornering the stock which he was variously invited to sell short. It therefore was aimed chiefly at fellow professionals, for the general public does not take kindly to the short side of the account. The reasons that prompted these wise professionals to put out short lines in such stocks were pretty much the same as prompts them to do the same thing to-day. Apart from the selling by faith-breaking politicians in the Harlem corner of the Commodore, I gather from the stories I have read that the professional traders sold the stock because it was too high. And the reason they thought it was too high was that it never before had sold so high; and that made it too high to buy; and if it was too high to buy it was just right to sell. That sounds pretty modern, doesn't it? They were thinking of the price, and the Commodore was thinking of the value! And so, for years afterwards, old-timers tell me that people used to say, "He went short of Harlem!" whenever they wished to describe abject poverty.

Many years ago I happened to be speaking to one of Jay Gould's old brokers. He assured me earnestly that Mr. Gould not only was a most unusual man it was of him that old Daniel Drew shiveringly remarked, "His touch is Death!" but that he was head and shoulders above all other manipulators past and present. He must have been a financial wizard indeed to have done what he did; there can be no question of that. Even at this distance I can see that he had an amazing knack for adapting himself to new conditions, and that is valu-able in a trader. He varied his methods of attack and defense without a pang because he was more concerned with the manipulation of properties than with stock speculation. He manipulated for investment rather than for a market turn. He early saw that the big money was in owning the railroads instead of rigging their securities on the floor of the Stock Exchange.

He utilised the stock market of course. But I suspect it was because that was the quickest and easiest way to quick and easy money and he needed many millions, just as old Collis P. Huntington was always hard up because he always needed twenty or thirty millions more than the bankers were willing to lend him. Vision without money means heartaches; with money, it means achievement; and that means power; and that means money; and that means achievement; and so on, over and over and over.

Of course manipulation was not confined to the great figures of those days. There were scores of minor manipulators. I remember a story an old broker told me about the manners and morals of the early '60's. He said:

"The earliest recollection I have of Wall Street is of my first visit to the financial district. My father had some business to attend to there and for some reason or other took me with him. We came down Broadway and I remember turning off at Wall Street. We walked down Wall and just as we came to Broad or, rather, Nassau Street, to the corner where the Bankers' Trust Company's building now stands, I saw a crowd following two men. The first was walking eastward, trying to look unconcerned. He was followed by the other, a red-faced man who was wildly waving his hat with one hand and shaking the other fist in the air. He was yelling to beat the band: 'Shylock! Shylock! What's the price of money? Shylock! Shylock!' I could see heads sticking out of windows. They didn't have skyscrapers in those days, but I was sure the second- and third-story rubbernecks would tumble out. My father asked what was the matter, and somebody answered something I didn't hear. I was too busy keeping a death clutch on my father's hand so that the jostling wouldn't separate us. The crowd was growing, as street crowds do, and I wasn't comfortable. Wild-eyed men came running down from Nassau Street and up from Broad as well as east and west on Wall Street. After we finally got out of the jam my father explained to me that the man who was shouting 'Shylock!' was So-and-So. I have forgotten the name, but he was the biggest operator in clique stocks in the city and was understood to have made and lost more money than any other man in Wall Street with the exception of Jacob Little. I remember Jacob Little's name because I thought it was a funny name for a man to have. The other man, the Shylock, was a notorious locker-up of money. His name has also gone from me. But I remember he was tall and thin and pale. In those days the cliques used to lock up money by borrowing it or, rather, by reducing the amount available to Stock Exchange borrowers. They would borrow it and get a certified check. They wouldn't actually take the money out and use it. Of course that was rigging. It was a form of manipulation, I think."

I agree with the old chap. It was a phase of manipulation that we don't have nowadays.

I myself never spoke to any of the great stock manipulators that the Street still talks about. I don't mean leaders; I mean manipulators. They were all before my time, although when I first came to New York, James R. Keene, greatest of them all, was in his prime. But I was a mere youngster then, exclusively concerned with duplicating, in a reputable broker's office, the success I had enjoyed in the bucket shops of my native city. And, then, too, at the time Keene was busy with the U. S. Steel stocks -his manipulative masterpiece -I had no experience with manipulation, no real knowledge of it or of its value or meaning, and, for that matter, no great need of such knowledge. If I thought about it at all I suppose I must have regarded it as a well-dressed form of thimble-rigging, of which the lowbrow form was such tricks as had been tried on me in the bucket shops. Such talk as I since have heard on the subject has consisted in great part of surmises and suspicions; of guesses rather than intelligent analyses.

More than one man who knew him well has told me that

Keene was the boldest and most brilliant operator that ever worked in Wall Street. That is saying a great deal, for there have been some great traders. Their names are now all but forgotten, but nevertheless they were kings in their day for a day! They were pulled up out of obscurity into the sunlight of financial fame by the ticker tape and the little paper ribbon didn't prove strong enough to keep them suspended there long enough for them to become historical fixtures. At all events Keene was by all odds the best manipulator of his day and it was a long and exciting day.

He capitalized his knowledge of the game, his experience as an operator and his talents when he sold his services to the Havemeyer brothers, who wanted him to develop a market for the Sugar stocks. He was broke at the time or he would have continued to trade on his own hook; and he was some plunger! He was successful with Sugar; made the shares trading favourites, and that made them easily vendible. After that, he was asked time and again to take charge of pools. I am told that in these pool operations he never asked or accepted a fee, but paid for his share like the other members of the pool. The market conduct of the stock, of course, was exclusively in his charge. Often there was talk of treachery on both sides. His feud with the Whitney-Ryan clique arose from such accusations. It is not difficult for a manipulator to be misunderstood by his associates. They don't see his needs as he himself does. I know this from my own experience.

It is a matter of regret that Keene did not leave an accurate record of his greatest exploit the successful manipulation of the U. S. Steel shares in the spring of 1901. As I understand it, Keene never had an interview with J. P. Morgan about it. Morgan's firm dealt with or through Talbot J. Taylor & Co., at whose office Keene made his headquarters. Talbot Taylor was Keene's son-in-law. I am assured that Keene's fee for his work consisted of the pleasure he derived from the work. That he made millions trading in the market he helped to put up that spring is well known. He told a friend of mine that in the course of a few weeks he sold in the open market for the underwriters' syndicate more than seven hundred and fifty thousand shares. Not bad when you consider two things: That they were new and untried stocks of a corporation whose capitalization was greater than the entire debt of the United States at that time; and second, that men like D. G. Reid, W. B. Leeds, the Moore brothers, Henry Phipps, H. C. Frick and the other Steel magnates also sold hundreds of thousands of shares to the public at the same time in the same market that Keene helped to create.

Of course, general conditions favoured him. Not only actual business but sentiment and his unlimited financial backing made possible his success. What we had was not merely a big bull market but a boom and a state of mind not likely to be seen again. The undigested-securities panic came later, when Steel common, which Keene had marked up to 55 in 1901, sold at 10 in 1903 and at 8-7/8 in 1904.

We can't analyse Keene's manipulative campaigns. His books are not available; the adequately detailed record is nonexistent. For example, it would be interesting to see how he worked in Amalgamated Copper. H. H. Rogers and William Rockefeller had tried to dispose of their surplus stock in the market and had failed. Finally they asked Keene to market their line, and he agreed. Bear in mind that H. H. Rogers was one of the ablest business men of his day in Wall Street and that William Rockefeller was the boldest speculator of the entire Standard Oil coterie. They had practically unlimited resources and vast prestige as well as years of experience in the stock-market game. And yet they had to go to Keene. I mention this to show you that there are some tasks which it requires a specialist to perform. Here was a widely touted stock, sponsored by America's greatest capitalists, that could not be sold except at a great sacrifice of money and prestige. Rogers and Rockefeller were intelligent enough to decide that Keene alone might help them.

Keene began to work at once. He had a bull market to work in and sold two hundred and twenty thousand shares of Amalgamated at around par. After he disposed of the insiders' line the public kept on buying and the price went ten points higher. Indeed the insiders got bullish on the stock they had sold when they saw how eagerly the public was taking it. There was a story that Rogers actually advised Keene to go long of Amalgamated. It is scarcely credible that Rogers meant to unload on Keene. He was too shrewd a man not to know that Keene was no bleating lamb. Keene worked as he always did that is, doing his big selling on the way down after the big rise. Of course his tactical moves were directed by his needs and by the minor currents that changed from day to day. In the stock market, as in warfare, it is well to keep in mind the difference between strategy and tactics.

One of Keene's confidential men he is the best fly fisherman I know told me only the other day that during the Amalgamated campaign Keene would find himself almost out of stock one day that is, out of the stock he had been forced to take in marking up the price; and on the next day he would buy back thousands of shares. On the day after that, he would sell on balance. Then he would leave the market absolutely alone, to see how it would take care of itself and also to accustom it to do so. When it came to the actual marketing of the line he did what I told you: he sold it on the way down. The trading public is always looking for a rally, and, besides, there is the covering by the shorts.

The man who was closest to Keene during that deal told me that after Keene sold the Rogers-Rockefeller line for something like twenty or twenty-five million dollars in cash Rogers sent him a check for two hundred thousand. This reminds you of the millionaire's wife who gave the Metropolitan Opera House scrub-woman fifty cents reward for finding the one-hundred-thousand-dollar pearl necklace. Keene sent the check back with a polite note saying he was not a stock broker and that he was glad to have been of some service to them. They kept the check and wrote him that they would be glad to work with him again. Shortly after that it was that H. H. Rogers gave Keene the friendly tip to buy Amalgamated at around 130!

A brilliant operator, James R. Keene! His private secretary told me that when the market was going his way Mr. Keene was irascible; and those who knew him say his irascibility was expressed in sardonic phrases that lingered long in the memory of his hearers. But when he was losing he was in the best of humour, a polished man of the world, agreeable, epigrammatic, interesting.

He had in superlative degree the qualities of mind that are associated with successful speculators anywhere. That he did not argue with the tape is plain. He was utterly fearless but never reckless. He could and did turn in a twinkling, if he found he was wrong.

Since his day there have been so many changes in Stock Exchange rules and so much more rigorous enforcement of old rules, so many new taxes on stock sales and profits, and so on, that the game seems different. Devices that Keene could use with skill and profit can no longer be utilised. Also, we are assured, the business morality of Wall Street is on a higher plane. Nevertheless it is fair to say that in any period of our financial history Keene would have been a great manipulator because he was a great stock operator and knew the game of speculation from the ground tip. He achieved what he did because conditions at the time permitted him to do so. He would have been as successful in his undertakings in 1922 as he was in 1901 or in 1876, when he first came to New York from California and made nine million dollars in two years. There are men whose gait is far quicker than the mob's. They are bound to lead no matter how much the mob changes.

As a matter of fact, the change is by no means as radical as you'd imagine. The rewards are not so great, for it is no longer pioneer work and therefore it is not pioneer's pay. But in certain respects manipulation is easier than it was; in other ways much harder than in Keene's day.

There is no question that advertising is an art, and manipulation is the art of advertising through the medium of the tape. The tape should tell the story the manipulator wishes its readers to see. The truer the story the more convincing it is bound to be, and the more convincing it is the better the advertising is. A manipulator to-day, for instance, has not only to make a stock look strong but also to make it be strong. Manipulation therefore must be based on sound trading principles. That is what made Keene such a marvellous manipulator; he was a consummate trader to begin with.

Chapter XX

The word "manipulation" has come to have an ugly sound, It needs an alias. I do not think there is anything so very mysterious or crooked about the process itself when it has for an object the selling of a stock in bulk, provided, of course, that such operations are not accompanied by misrepresentation. There is little question that a manipulator necessarily seeks his buyers among speculators. He turns to men who are looking for big returns on their capital and are therefore willing to run a greater than normal business risk. I can't have much sympathy for the man who, knowing this, nevertheless blames others for his own failure to make easy money. He is a devil of a clever fellow when he wins. But when he loses money the other fellow was a crook; a manipulator! In such moments and from such lips the word connotes the use of marked cards. But this is not so.

Usually the object of manipulation is to develop marketability that is, the ability to dispose of fair-sized blocks at some price at any time. Of course a pool, by reason of a reversal of general market conditions, may find itself unable to sell except at a sacrifice too great to be pleasing. They then may decide to employ a professional, believing that his skill and experience will enable him to conduct an orderly retreat instead of suffering an appalling rout.

You will notice that I do not speak of manipulation designed to permit considerable accumulation of a stock as cheaply as possible, as, for instance, in buying for control, because this does not happen often nowadays.

When Jay Gould wished to cinch his control of Western Union

and decided to buy a big block of the stock, Washington E. Connor, who had not been seen on the. floor of the Stock Exchange for years, suddenly showed up in person at the Western Union post. He began to bid for Western Union. The traders to a man laughed at his stupidity in thinking them so simple and they cheerfully sold him all the stock he wanted to buy. It was too raw a trick, to think he could put up the price by acting as though Mr. Gould wanted to buy Western Union. Was that manipulation? I think I can only answer that by saying "No; and yes!"

In the majority of cases the object of manipulation is, as I said, to sell stock to the public at the best possible price. It is not alone a question of selling but of distributing. It is obviously better in every way for a stock to be held by a thousand people than by one man better for the market in it. So it is not alone the sale at a good price but the character of the distribution that a manipulator must consider.

There is no sense in marking up the price to a very high level if you cannot induce the public to take it off your hands later. Whenever inexperienced manipulators try to unload at the top and fail, old-timers look mighty wise and tell you that you can lead a horse to water but you cannot make him drink. Original devils! As a matter of fact, it is well to remember a rule of manipulation, a rule that Keene and his able predecessors well knew. It is this: Stocks are manipulated to the highest point possible and then sold to the public on the way down.

Let me begin at the beginning. Assume that there is some one -an underwriting syndicate or a pool or an individual -that has a block of stock which it is desired to sell at the best price possible. It is a stock duly listed on the New York Stock

Exchange. The best place for selling it ought to be the open market, and the best buyer ought to be the general public. The negotiations for the sale are in charge of a man. He or some present or former associate has tried to sell the stock on the Stock Exchange and has not succeeded. He is or soon becomes sufficiently familiar with stock-market operations to realise that more experience and greater aptitude for the work are needed than he possesses. He knows personally or by hearsay several men who have been successful in their handling of similar deals, and he decides to avail himself of their professional skill. He seeks one of them as he would seek a physician if he were ill or an engineer if he needed that kind of expert.

Suppose he has heard of me as a man who knows the game. Well, I take it that he tries to find out all he can about me. He then arranges for an interview, and in due time calls at my office.

Of course, the chances are that I know about the stock and what it represents. It is my business to know.

That is how I make my living. My visitor tells me what he and his associates wish to do, and asks me to undertake the deal.

It is then my turn to talk. I ask for whatever information I deem necessary to give me a clear understanding of what I am asked to undertake. I determine the value and estimate the market possibilities of that stock. That and my reading of current conditions in turn help me to gauge the likelihood of success for the proposed operation.

If my information inclines me to a favourable view I accept the proposition and tell him then and there what my terms will be for my services. If he in turn accepts my terms the honorarium and the conditions I begin my work at once.

I generally ask and receive calls on a block of stock. I insist upon graduated calls as the fairest to all concerned. The price of the call begins at a little below the prevailing market price and goes up; say, for example, that I get calls on one hundred thousand shares and the stock is quoted at 40. I begin with a call for some thousands of shares at 35, another at 37, another at 40, and at 45 and 50, and so on up to 75 or 80.

If as the result of my professional work my manipulation the price goes up, and if at the highest level there is a good demand for the stock so that I can sell fair-sized blocks of it I of course call the stock. I am making money; but so are my clients making money. This is as it should be. If my skill is what they are paying for they ought to get value. Of course, there are times when a pool may be wound up at a woss, but that is seldom, for I do not undertake the work unless * see my way clear to a profit. This year I was not so fortunate in one or two deals, and I did not make a profit. There are reasons, but that is another story, to be told later perhaps.

The first step in a bull movement in a stock is to advertise the fact that there is a bull movement on. Sounds silly, doesn't it? Well, think a moment. It isn't as silly as it sounded, is it? The most effective way to advertise what, in effect, are your honourable intentions is to make the stock active and strong. After all is said and done, the greatest publicity agent in the wide world is the ticker, and by far the best advertising medium is the tape. I do not need to put out any literature for my clients. I do not have to inform the daily press as to the value of the stock or to work the financial reviews for notices about the company's prospects. Neither do I have to get a following. I accomplish all these highly desirable things by merely making the stock active. When there is activity there is a synchronous demand for explanations; and that means, of course, that the necessary reasons for publication supply themselves without the slightest aid from me.

Activity is all that the floor traders ask. They will buy or sell any stock at any level if only there is a free market for it. They will deal in thousands of shares wherever they see activity, and their aggregate capacity is considerable. It necessarily happens that they constitute the manipulator's first crop of buyers. They will follow you ail the way up and they thus are a great help at all the stages of the operation. I understand that James R. Keene used habitually to employ the most active of the room traders, both to conceal the source of the manipulation and also because he knew that they were by far the best business-spreaders and tip-distributors. He often gave calls to them verbal calls above the market, so that they might do some helpful work before they could cash in. He made them earn their profit. To get a professional following I myself have never had to do more than to make a stock active. Traders don't ask for more. It is well, of course, to remember that these professionals on the floor of the Exchange buy stocks with the intention of selling them at a profit. They do not insist on its being a big profit; but it must be a quick profit.

I make the stock active in order to draw the attention of speculators to it, for the reasons I have given. I buy it and I sell it and the traders follow suit. The selling pressure is not apt to be strong where a man has as much speculatively held stock sewed up in calls as I insist on having. The buying, therefore, prevails over the selling, and the public follows the lead not so much of the manipulator as of the room traders. It comes in as a buyer. This highly desirable demand I fill that is, I sell stock on balance. If the demand is what it ought to be it will absorb more than the amount of stock I was compelled to accumulate in the earlier stages of the manipulation; and when this happens I sell the stock short that is, technically. In other words, I sell more stock than I actually hold. It is perfectly safe for me to do so since I am really selling against my calls. Of course, when the demand from the public slackens, the stock ceases to advance. Then I wait.

Say, then, that the stock has ceased to advance. There comes a weak day. The entire market may develop a reactionary tendency or some sharp-eyed trader my perceive that there are no buying orders to speak of in my stock, and he sells it, and his fellows follow. Whatever the reason may be, my stock starts to go down. Well, I begin to buy it. I give it the support that a stock ought to have if it is in good odour with its own sponsors. And more: I am able to support it without accumulating it that is, without increasing the amount I shall have to sell later on. Observe that I do this without decreasing my financial resources. Of course what I am really doing is covering stock I sold short at higher prices when the demand from the public or from the traders or from both enabled me to do it. It is always well to make it plain to the traders and to the public, also that there is a demand for the stock on the way down. That tends to check both reckless short selling by the professionals and liquidation by frightened holders which is the selling you usually see when a stock gets weaker and weaker, which in turn is what a stock does when it is not supported. These covering purchases of mine constitute what I call the stabilising process.

As the market broadens I of course sell stock on the way

up, but never enough to check the rise. This is in strict accordance with my stabilising plans. It is obvious that the more stock I sell on a reasonable and orderly advance the more I encourage the conservative speculators, who are more numerous than the reckless room traders; and in addition the more support I shall be able to give to the stock on the inevitable weak days. By always being short I always am in a position to support the stock without danger to myself. As a rule I begin my selling at a price that will show me a profit. But I often sell without having a profit, simply to create or to increase what I may call my riskless buying power. My business is not alone to put up the price or to sell a big block of stock for a client but to make money for myself. That is why I do not ask any clients to finance my operations. My fee is contingent upon my success.

Of course what I have described is not my invariable practice. I neither have nor adhere to an inflexible system. I modify my terms and conditions according to circumstances.

A stock which it is desired to distribute should be manipulated to the highest possible point and then sold. I repeat this both because it is fundamental and because the public apparently believes that the selling is all done at the top. Sometimes a stock gets waterlogged, as it were; it doesn't go up. That is the time to sell. The price naturally will go down on your selling rather further than you wish, bur you can generally nurse it back. As long as a stock that I am manipulating goes up on my buying I know I am all hunky, and if need be I buy it with confidence and use my own money without fear precisely as I would any other stock that acts the same way. It is the line of least resistance. You remember my trading theories about that line, don't you? Well, when the price line of least resistance is established I follow it, not because I am manipulating that particular stock at that particular moment but because I am a stock operator at all times.

When my buying does not put the stock up I stop buying and then proceed to sell it down; and that also is exactly what I would do with that same stock if I did not happen to be manipulating it. The principal marketing of the stock, as you know, is done on the way down. It is perfectly astonishing how much stock a man can get rid of on a decline.

I repeat that at no time during the manipulation do I forget to be a stock trader. My problems as a manipulator, after all, are the same that confront me as an operator. All manipulation comes to an end when the manipulator cannot make a stock do what he wants it to do. When the stock you are manipulating doesn't act as it should, quit. Don't argue with the tape. Do not seek to lure the profit back. Quit while the quitting is good and cheap.

Chapter XXI

I am well aware that all these generalities do not sound especially impressive. Generalities seldom do. Possibly I may succeed better if I give a concrete example. I'll tell you how I marked up the price of a stock 30 points, and in so doing accumulated only seven thousand shares and developed a market that would absorb almost any amount of stock.

It was Imperial Steel. The stock had been brought out by reputable people and it had been fairly well tipped as a property of value. About 30 per cent of the capital stock was placed with the general public through various Wall Street houses, but there had been no significant activity in the shares after they were listed. From time to time somebody would ask about it and one or another insider members of the original underwriting syndicate would say that the company's earnings were better than expected and the prospects more than encouraging. This was true enough and very good as far as it went, but not exactly thrilling. The speculative appeal was absent, and from the investor's point of view the price stability and dividend permanency of the stock were not yet demonstrated. It was a stock that never behaved sensationally. It was so gentlemanly that no corroborative rise ever followed the insiders' eminently truthful reports. On the other hand, neither did the price decline.

Imperial Steel remained unhonoured and unsung and un-tipped, content to be one of those stocks that don't go down because nobody sells and that nobody sells because nobody likes to go short of a stock that is not well distributed; the seller is too much at the mercy of the loaded-up inside clique. Similarly, there is no inducement to buy such a stock. To the investor Imperial Steel therefore remained a speculation. To the speculator it was a dead one the kind that makes an investor of you against your will by the simple expedient of falling into a trance the moment you go long of it. The chap who is compelled to lug a corpse a year or two always loses more than the original cost of the deceased; he is sure to find himself tied up with it when some really good things come his way.

One day the foremost member of the Imperial Steel syndicate, acting for himself and associates, came to see me. They wished to create a market for the stock, of which they controlled the undistributed 70 per cent. They wanted me to dispose of their holdings at better prices than they thought they would obtain if they tried to sell in the open market. They wanted to know on what terms I would undertake the job.

I told him that I would let him know in a few days. Then I looked into the property. I had experts go over the various departments of the company industrial, commercial and financial. They made reports to me which were unbiased. I wasn't looking for the good or the bad points, but for the facts, such as they were.

The reports showed that it was a valuable property. The prospects justified purchases of the stock at the prevailing market price if the investor were willing to wait a little. Under the circumstances an advance in the price would in reality be the commonest and most legitimate of all market movements to wit, the process of discounting the future. There was therefore no reason that I could see why I should not conscientiously and confidently undertake the bull manipulation of Imperial Steel.

I let my man know my mind and he called at my office to talk the deal over in detail. I told him what my terms were. For my services I asked no cash, but calls on one hundred thousand shares of the Imperial Steel stock. The price of the calls ran up from 70 to 100. That may seem like a big fee to some. But they should consider that the insiders were certain they themselves could not sell one hundred thousand shares, or even fifty thousand shares, at 70. There was no market for the stock. All the talk about wonderful earnings and excellent prospects had not brought in buyers, not to any great extent. In addition, I could not get my fee in cash without my clients first making some millions of dollars. What I stood to make was not an exorbitant selling commission. It was a fair contingent fee.

Knowing that the stock had real value and that general market conditions were bullish and therefore favourable for an advance in all good stocks, I figured that I ought to do pretty well. My clients were encouraged by the opinions I expressed, agreed to my terms at once, and the deal began with pleasant feelings all around.

I proceeded to protect myself as thoroughly as I could. The syndicate owned or controlled about 70 per cent of the outstanding stock. I had them deposit their 70 per cent under a trust agreement. I didn't propose to be used as a dumping ground for the big holders. With the majority holdings thus securely tied up, I still had 30 per cent of scattered holdings to consider, but that was a risk I had to take. Experienced speculators do not expect ever to engage in utterly riskless ventures. As a matter of fact, it was not much more likely that all the untrusteed stock would be thrown on the market at one fell swoop than that all the policyholders of a life-insurance company would die at the same hour, the same day. There are unprinted actuarial tables of stock-market risks as well as of human mortality.

Having protected myself from some of the avoidable dangers of a stock-market deal of that sort, I was ready to begin my campaign. Its objective was to make my calls valuable. To do this I must put up the price and develop a market in which I could sell one hundred thousand shares the stock in which I held options.

The first thing I did was to find out how much stock was likely to come on the market on an advance. This was easily done through my brokers, who had no trouble in ascertaining what stock was for sale at or a little above the market. I don't know whether the specialists told them what orders they had on their books or not. The price was nominally 70, but I could not have sold one thousand shares at that price. I had no evidence of even a moderate demand at that figure or even a few points lower. I had to go by what my brokers found out. But it was enough to show me how much stock there was for sale and how little was wanted.

As soon as I had a line on these points I quietly took all the stock that was for sale at 70 and higher. When I say "I" you will understand that I mean my brokers. The sales were for account of some of the minority holders because my clients naturally had cancelled whatever selling orders they might have given out before they tied up their stock.

I didn't have to buy very much stock. Moreover, I knew that the right kind of advance would bring in other buying orders and, of course, selling orders also.

I didn't give bull tips on Imperial Steel to anybody. I didn't have to. My job was to seek directly to influence sentiment by the best possible kind of publicity. I do not say that there should never be bull propaganda. It is as legitimate and indeed as desirable to advertise the value of a new stock as to advertise the value of woolens or shoes or automobiles. Accurate and reliable information should be given by the public. But what I meant was that the tape did all that was needed for my purpose. As I said before, the reputable newspapers always try to print explanations for market movements. It is news. Their readers demand to know not only what happens in the stock market but why it happens. Therefore without the manipulator lifting a finger the financial writers will print all the available information and gossip, and also analyse the reports of earnings, trade condition and outlook; in short, whatever may throw light on the advance. Whenever a newspaperman or an acquaintance asks my opinion of a stock and I have one I do not hesitate to express it. I do not volunteer advice and I never give tips, but I have nothing to gain in my operations from secrecy. At the same time I realise that the best of all tipsters, the most persuasive of all salesmen, is the tape.

When I had absorbed all the stock that was for sale at 70 and a little higher I relieved the market of that pressure, and naturally that made clear for trading purposes the line of least resistance in Imperial Steel. It was manifestly upward. The moment that fact was perceived by the observant traders on the floor they logically assumed that the stock was in for an advance the extent of which they could not know; but they knew enough to begin buying. Their demand for Imperial Steel, created exclusively by the obviousness of the stock's rising tendency the tape's infallible bull tip! I promptly filled. I sold to the traders the stock that I had bought from the tired-out holders at the beginning. Of course this selling was judiciously done; I contented myself with supplying the demand. I was not forcing my stock on the market and I did not want too rapid an advance. It wouldn't have been good business to sell out the half of my one hundred thousand shares at that stage of the proceedings. My job was to make a market on which I might sell my entire line.

But even though I sold only as much as the traders were anxious to buy, the market was temporarily deprived of my own buying power, which I had hitherto exerted steadily. In due course the traders' purchases ceased and the price stopped rising. As soon as that happened there began the selling by disappointed bulls or by those traders whose reasons for buying disappeared the instant the rising tendency was checked. But I was ready for this selling, and on the way down I bought back the stock I had sold to the traders a couple of points higher. This buying of stock I knew was bound to be sold in turn checked the downward course; and when the price stopped going down the selling orders stopped coming in.

I then began all over again. I took all the stock that was for sale on the way up it wasn't very much and the price began to rise a second time; from a higher starting point than
70. Don't forget that on the way down there are many holders who wish to heaven they had sold theirs but won't do it three or four points from the top. Such speculators always vow they will surely sell out if there is a rally. They put in their orders to sell on the way up, and then they change their minds with the change in the stock's price-trend. Of course there is always profit taking from safe-playing quick runners

to whom a profit is always a profit to be taken.

All I had to do after that was to repeat the process; alternately buying and selling; but always working higher.

Sometimes, after you have taken all the stock that is for sale, it pays to rush up the price sharply, to have what might be called little bull flurries in the stock you are manipulating. It is excellent advertising, because it makes talk and also brings in both the professional traders and that portion of the speculating public that likes action. It is, I think, a large portion. I did that in Imperial Steel, and whatever demand was created by those spurts I supplied. My selling always kept the upward movement within bounds both as to extent and as to speed. In buying on the way down and selling on the way up I was doing more than marking up the price: I was developing the marketability of Imperial Steel.

After I began my operations in it there never was a time when a man could not buy or sell the stock freely; I mean by this, buy or sell a reasonable amount without causing over-violent fluctuations in the price. The fear of being left high and dry if he bought, or squeezed to death if he sold, was gone. The gradual spread among the professionals and the public of a belief in the permanence of the market for Imperial Steel had much to do with creating confidence in the movement; and, of course, the activity also put an end to a lot of other objections. The result was that after buying and selling a good many thousands of shares I succeeded in making the stocks sell at par. At one hundred dollars a share everybody wanted to buy Imperial Steel. Why not? Everybody now knew that it was a good stock; that it had been and still was a bargain. The proof was the rise. A stock that could go thirty points from 70 could go up thirty more from par. That is the way a good many argued.

In the course of marking up the price those thirty points I accumulated only seven thousand shares. The price on this line averaged me almost exactly 85. That meant a profit of fifteen points on it; but, of course, my entire profit, still on paper, was much more. It was a safe enough profit, for I had a market for all I wanted to sell. The stock would sell higher on judicious manipulation and I had graduated calls on one hundred thousand shares beginning at 70 and ending at 100.

Circumstances prevented me from carrying out certain plans of mine for converting my paper profits into good hard cash. It had been, if I do say so myself, a beautiful piece of manipulation, strictly legitimate and deservedly successful. The property of the company was valuable and the stock was not dear at the higher price. One of the members of the original syndicate developed a desire to secure the control of the property a prominent banking house with ample resources. The control of a prosperous and growing concern like the Imperial Steel Corporation is possibly more valuable to a banking firm than to individual investors. At all events, this firm made me an offer for all my options on the stock. It meant an enormous profit for me, and I instantly took it. I am always willing to sell out when I can do so in a lump at a good profit. I was quite content with what I made out of it.

Before I disposed of my calls on the hundred thousand shares I learned that these bankers had employed more experts to make a still more thorough examination of the property. Their reports showed enough to bring me in the offer I got. I kept several thousand shares of the stock for investment. I believe in it.

There wasn't anything about my manipulation of Imperial

Steel that wasn't normal and sound. As long as the price went up on my buying I knew I was O.K. The stock never got waterlogged, as a stock sometimes does. When you find that it fails to respond adequately to your buying you don't need any better tip to sell. You know that if there is any value to a stock and general market conditions are right you can always nurse it back after a decline, no matter if it's twenty points. But I never had to do anything like that in Imperial Steel.

In my manipulation of stocks I never lose sight of basic trading principles. Perhaps you wonder why I repeat this or why I keep on harping on the fact that I never argue with the tape or lose my temper at the market because of its behaviour. You would think wouldn't you? that shrewd men who have made millions in their own business and in addition have successfully operated in Wall Street at times would realise the wisdom of playing the game dispassionately. Well, you would be surprised at the frequency with which some of our most successful promoters behave like peevish women because the market does not act the way they wish it to act. They seem to take it as a personal slight, and they proceed to lose money by first losing their temper.

There has been much gossip about a disagreement between John Prentiss and myself. People have been led to expect a dramatic narrative of a stock-market deal that went wrong or some double-crossing that cost me or him millions; or something of that sort. Well, it wasn't.

Prentiss and I had been friendly for years. He had given me at various times information that I was able to utilise profitably, and I had given him advice which he may or may not have followed. If he did he saved money.

He was largely instrumental in the organisation and promotion of the Petroleum Products Company. After a more or less successful market debut general conditions changed for the worse and the new stock did not fare as well as Prentiss and his associates had hoped. When basic conditions took a turn for the better Prentiss formed a pool and began operations in Pete Products.

I cannot tell you anything about his technique. He didn't tell me how he worked and I didn't ask him. But it was plain that notwithstanding his Wall Street experience and his undoubted cleverness, whatever it was he did proved of little value and it didn't take the pool long to find out that they couldn't get rid of much stock. He must have tried everything he knew, because a pool manager does not ask to be superseded by an outsider unless he feels unequal to the task and that is the last thing the average man likes to admit. At all events he came to me and after some friendly preliminaries he said he wanted me to take charge of the market for Pete Products and dispose of the pool's holdings, which amounted to a little over one hundred thousand shares. The stock was selling at 102 to 103.

The thing looked dubious to me and I declined his proposition with thanks. But he insisted that I accept. He put it on personal grounds, so that in the end I consented. I constitutionally dislike to identify myself with enterprises in the success of which I cannot feel confidence, but I also think a man owes something to his friends and acquaintances. I said I would do my best, but I told him I did not feel very cocky about it and I enumerated the adverse factors that I would have to contend with. But all Prentiss said to that was that he wasn't asking me to guarantee millions in profits to the pool. He was sure that if I took hold I'd make out well enough to satisfy any reasonable being.

Well, there I was, engaged in doing something against my own judgment. I found, as I feared, a pretty tough state of affairs, due in great measure to Prentiss' own mistakes while he was manipulating the stock for account of the pool. But the chief factor against me was time. I was convinced that we were rapidly approaching the end of a bull swing and therefore that the improvement in the market, which had so encouraged Prentiss, would prove to be merely a short-lived rally. I feared that the market would turn definitely bearish before I could accomplish much with Pete Products. However, I had given my promise and I decided to work as hard as I knew how.

I started to put up the price. I had moderate success. I think I ran it up to 107 or thereabouts, which was pretty fair, and I was even able to sell a little stock on balance. It wasn't much, but I was glad not to have increased the pool's holdings. There were a lot of people not in the pool who were just waiting for a small rise to dump their stock, and I was a godsend to them. Had general conditions been better I also would have done better. It was too bad that I wasn't called in earlier. All I could do now, I felt, was to get out with as little loss as possible to the pool.

I sent for Prentiss and told him my views. But he started to object. I then explained to him why I took the position I did. I said: "Prentiss, I can feel very plainly the pulse of the market. There is no follow-up in your stock. It is no trick to see just what the public's reaction is to my manipulation. Listen: When Pete Products is made as attractive to traders as possible and you give it all the support needed at all times and notwithstanding all that you find that the public leaves it alone you may be sure that there is something wrong, not with the stock but with the market. There is absolutely no use in trying to force matters. You are bound to lose if you do. A pool manager should be willing to buy his own stock when he has company. But when he is the only buyer in the market he'd be an ass to buy it. For every five thousand shares I buy the public ought to be willing or able to buy five thousand more. But I certainly am not going to do all the buying. If I did, all I would succeed in doing would be to get soaked with a lot of long stock that I don't want. There is only one thing to do, and that is to sell. And the only way to sell is to sell."

"You mean, sell for what you can get?" asked Prentiss.

"Right!" I said. I could see he was getting ready to object. "If I am to sell the pool's stock at all you can make up your mind that the price is going to break through par and "

"Oh, no! Never!" he yelled. You'd have imagined I was asking him to join a suicide club.

"Prentiss," I said to him, "it is a cardinal principle of stock manipulation to put up a stock in order to sell it. But you don't sell in bulk on the advance. You can't. The big selling is done on the way down from the top. I cannot put up your stock to 125 or 130. I'd like to, but it can't be done. So you will have to begin your selling from this level. In my opinion all stocks are going down, and Petroleum Products isn't going to be the one exception. It is better for it to go down now on the pool's selling than for it to break next month on selling by some one else. It will go down anyhow."

I can't see that I said anything harrowing, but you could have heard his howls in China. He simply wouldn't listen to such a thing. It would never do. It would play the dickens with the stock's record, to say nothing of inconvenient possibilities at the banks where the stock was held as collateral on loans, and so on.

I told him again that in my judgment nothing in the world could prevent Pete Products from breaking fifteen or twenty points, because the entire market was headed that way, and I once more said it was absurd to expect his stock to be a dazzling exception. But again my talk went for nothing. He insisted that I support the stock.

Here was a shrewd business man, one of the most successful promoters of the day, who had made millions in Wall Street deals and knew much more than the average man about the game of speculation, actually insisting on supporting a stock in an incipient bear market. It was his stock, to be sure, but it was nevertheless bad business. So much so that it went against the grain and I again began to argue with him. But it was no use. He insisted on putting in supporting orders.

Of course when the general market got weak and the decline began in earnest Pete Products went with the rest. Instead of selling I actually bought stock for the insiders' pool by Prentiss' orders.

The only explanation is that Prentiss did not believe the bear market was right on top of us. I myself was confident that the bull market was over. I had verified my first surmise by tests not alone in Pete Products but in other stocks as well. I didn't wait for the bear market to announce its safe arrival before I started selling. Of course I didn't sell a share of Pete Products, though I was short of other stocks.

The Pete Products pool, as I expected, was hung up with

all they held to begin with and with all they had to take in their futile effort to hold up the price. In the end they did liquidate; but at much lower figures than they would have got if Prentiss had let me sell when and as I wished. It could not be otherwise. But Prentiss still thinks he was right or says he does. I understand he says the reason I gave him the advice I did was that I was short of other stocks and the general market was going up. It implies, of course, that the break in Pete Products that would have resulted from selling out the pool's holdings at any price would have helped my bear position in other stocks.

That is all tommyrot. I was not bearish because I was short of stocks. I was bearish because that was the way I sized up the situation, and I sold stocks short only after I turned bearish. There never is much money in doing things wrong end to; not in the stock market. My plan for selling the pool's stock was based on what the experience of twenty years told me alone was feasible and therefore wise. Prentiss ought to have been enough of a trader to see it as plainly as I did. It was too late to try to do anything else.

I suppose Prentiss shares the delusion of thousands of outsiders who think a manipulator can do anything. He can't. The biggest thing Keene did was his manipulation of U. S. Steel common and preferred in the spring of 1901. He succeeded not because he was clever and resourceful and not because he had a syndicate of the richest men in the country back of him. He succeeded partly because of those reasons but chiefly because the general market was right and the public's state of mind was right.

It isn't good business for a man to act against the teachings of experience and against common sense. But the suckers in

Wall Street are not all outsiders. Prentiss' grievance against me is what I have just told you. He feels sore because I did my manipulation not as I wanted to but as he asked me to.

There isn't anything mysterious or underhanded or crooked about manipulation designed to sell a stock in bulk provided such operations are not accompanied by deliberate misrepresentations. Sound manipulation must be based on sound trading principles. People lay great stress on old-time practices, such as wash sales. But I can assure you that the mere mechanics of deception count for very little. The difference between stock-market manipulation and the over-the-counter sale of stocks and bonds is in the character of the clientele rather than in the character of the appeal. J. P. Morgan & Co. sell an issue of bonds to the public that is, to investors. A manipulator disposes of a block of stock to the public that is, to speculators. An investor looks for safety, for permanence of the interest return on the capital he invests. The speculator looks for a quick profit.

The manipulator necessarily finds his primary market among speculators who are willing to run a greater than normal business risk so long as they have a reasonable chance to get a big return on their capital. I myself never have believed in blind gambling. I may plunge or I may buy one hundred shares. But in either case I must have a reason for what I do.

I distinctly remember how I got into the game of manipulation that is, in the marketing of stocks for others. It gives me pleasure to recall it because it shows so beautifully the professional Wall Street attitude toward stock-market operations. It happened after I had "come back" that is, after my Bethlehem Steel trade in 1915 started me on the road to financial recovery.

I traded pretty steadily and had very good luck. I have never sought newspaper publicity, but neither have I gone out of my way to hide myself. At the same time, you know that professional Wall Street exaggerates both the successes and the failures of whichever operator happens to be active; and, of course, the newspapers hear about him and print rumors. I have been broke so many times, according to the gossips, or have made so many millions, according to the same authorities, that my only reaction to such reports is to wonder how and where they are born. And how they grow! I have had broker friend after broker friend bring the same story to me, a little changed each time, improved, more circumstantial.

All this preface is to tell you how I first came to undertake the manipulation of a stock for someone else. The stories the newspapers printed of how I had paid back in full the millions I owed did the trick. My plungings and my winnings were so magnified by the newspapers that I was talked about in Wall Street. The day was past when an operator swinging a line of two hundred thousand shares of stock could dominate the market. But, as you know, the public always desires to find successors to the old leaders. It was Mr. Keene's reputation as a skilful stock operator, a winner of millions on his own hook,that made promoters and banking houses apply to him for selling large blocks of securities. In short, his services as manipulator were in demand because of the stories the Street had heard about his previous successes as a trader.

But Keene was gone passed on to that heaven where he once said he wouldn't stay a moment unless he found Sysonby there waiting for him. Two or three other men who made stock-market history for a few months had relapsed into the obscurity of prolonged inactivity. I refer particularly to certain of those plunging Westerners who came to Wall Street in 1901 and after making many millions out of their Steel holdings remained in Wall Street. They were in reality superpromoters rather than operators of the Keene type. But they were extremely able, extremely rich and extremely successful in the securities of the companies which they and their friends controlled. They were not really great manipulators, like Keene or Governor Flower. Still, the Street found in them plenty to gossip about and they certainly had a following among the professionals and the sportier commission houses. After they ceased to trade actively the Street found itself without manipulators; at least, it couldn't read about them in the newspapers.

You remember the big bull market that began when the Stock Exchange resumed business in 1915. As the market broadened and the Allies' purchases in this country mounted into billions we ran into a boom. As far as manipulation went, it wasn't necessary for anybody to lift a finger to create an unlimited market for a war bride. Scores of men made millions by capitalizing contracts or even promises of contracts. They became successful promoters, either with the aid of friendly bankers or by bringing out their companies on the Curb market. The public bought anything that was adequately touted.

When the bloom wore off the boom, some of these promoters found themselves in need of help from experts in stock salesmanship. When the public is hung up with all kinds of securities, some of them purchased at higher prices, it is not an easy task to dispose of untried stocks. After a boom the public is positive that nothing is going up. It isn't that buyers become more discriminating, but that the blind buying is over. It is the state of mind that has changed. Prices don't even have to go down to make people pessimistic. It is enough if the market gets dull and stays dull for a time. In every boom companies are formed primarily if not exclusively to take advantage of the public's appetite for all kinds of stocks. Also there are belated promotions. The

reason why promoters make that mistake is that being human they are unwilling to see the end of the boom. Moreover, it is good business to take chances when the possible profit is big enough. The top is never in sight when the vision is vitiated by hope. The average man sees a stock that nobody wanted at twelve dollars or fourteen dollars a share suddenly advance to thirty which surely is the top until it rises to fifty. That is absolutely the end of the rise. Then it goes to sixty; to seventy; to seventy-five. It then becomes a certainty that this stock, which a few weeks ago was selling for less than fifteen, can't go any higher. But it goes to eighty; and to eighty-five. Whereupon the average man, who never thinks of values but of prices, and is not governed in his actions by conditions but by fears, takes the easiest way he stops thinking that there must be a limit to the advances. That is why those outsiders who are wise enough not to buy at the top make up for it by not taking profits. The big money in booms is always made first by the public on paper. And it remains on paper.

Chapter XXII

One day Jim Barnes, who not only was one of my principal brokers but an intimate friend as well, called on me. He said he wanted me to do him a great favour. He never before had talked that way, and so I asked him to tell me what the favour was, hoping it was something I could do, for I certainly wished to oblige him. He then told me that his firm was interested in a certain stock; in fact, they had been the principal promoters of the company and had placed the greater part of the stock. Circumstances had arisen that made it imperative for them to market a rather large block. Jim wanted me to undertake to do the marketing for him. The stock was Consolidated Stove.

I did not wish to have anything to do with it for various reasons. But Barnes, to whom I was under some obligations, insisted on the personal-favour phase of the matter, which alone could overcome my objections. He was a good fellow, a friend, and his firm, I gathered, was pretty heavily involved, so in the end I consented to do what I could.

It has always seemed to me that the most picturesque point of difference between the war boom and other booms was the part that was played by a type new in stock-market affairs the boy banker.

The boom was stupendous and its origins and causes were plainly to be grasped by all. But at the same time the greatest banks and trust companies in the country certainly did all they could to help make millionaires overnight of all sorts and conditions of promoters and munition makers. It got so that all a man had to do was to say that he had a friend who was a friend of a member of one of the Allied commissions and he would be offered all the capital needed to carry out the contracts he had not yet secured. I used to hear incredible stories of clerks becoming presidents of companies doing a business of millions of dollars on money borrowed from trusting trust companies, and of contracts that left a trail of profits as they passed from man to man. A flood of gold was pouring into this country from Europe and the banks had to find ways of impounding it.

The way business was done might have been regarded with misgivings by the old, but there didn't seem to be so many of them about. The fashion for gray-haired presidents of banks was all very well in tranquil times, but youth was the chief qualification in these strenuous times. The banks certainly did make enormous profits.

Jim Barnes and his associates, enjoying the friendship and confidence of the youthful president of the Marshall National Bank, decided to consolidate three well-known stove companies and sell the stock of the new company to the public that for months had been buying any old thing in the way of engraved stock certificates.

One trouble was that the stove business was so prosperous that all three companies were actually earning dividends on their common stock for the first time in their history. Their principal stockholders did not wish to part with the control. There was a good market for their stocks on the Curb; and they had sold as much as they cared to part with and they were content with things as they were. Their individual capitalisation was too small to justify big market movements, and that is where Jim Barnes' firm came in. It pointed out that the consolidated company must be big enough to list on the Stock Exchange, where the new shares could be made more valuable than the old ones. It is an old device in Wall Street to change the colour of the certificates in order to make them more valuable. Say a stock ceases to be easily vendible at par. Well, sometimes by quadrupling the stock you may make the new shares sell at 30 or 35. This is equivalent to 120 or 140 for the old stock a figure it never could have reached.

It seems that Barnes and his associates succeeded in inducing some of their friends who held speculatively some blocks of Gray Stove Company a large concern to come into the consolidation on the basis of four shares of Consolidated for each share of Gray. Then the Midland and the Western followed their big sister and came in on the basis of share for share. Theirs had been quoted on the Curb at around 25 to 30, and the Gray, which was better known and paid dividends, hung around 125.

In order to raise the money to buy out those holders who insisted upon selling for cash, and also to provide additional working capital for improvements and promotion expenses, it became necessary to raise a few millions. So Barnes saw the president of his bank, who kindly lent his syndicate three million five hundred thousand dollars. The collateral was one hundred thousand shares of the newly organised corporation. The syndicate assured the president, or so I was told, that the price would not go below 50. It would be a very profitable deal as there was big value there.

The promoters' first mistake was in the matter of timeliness. The saturation point for new stock issues had been reached by the market, and they should have seen it. But even then they might have made a fair profit after all if they had not tried to duplicate the unreasonable killings which other promoters had made at the very height of the boom.

Now you must not run away with the notion that Jim Barnes and his associates were fools or inexperienced kids. They were shrewd men. All of them were familiar with Wall Street methods and some of them were exceptionally successful stock traders. But they did rather more than merely overestimate the public's buying capacity. After all, that capacity was something that they could determine only by actual tests. Where they erred more expensively was in expecting the bull market to last longer than it did. I suppose the reason was that these same men had met with such great and particularly with such quick success that they didn't doubt they'd be all through with the deal before the bull market turned. They were all well known and had a considerable following among the professional traders and the wire houses.

The deal was extremely well advertised. The newspapers certainly were generous with their space. The older concerns were identified with the stove industry of America and their product was known the world over. It was a patriotic amalgamation and there was a heap of literature in the daily papers about the world conquests. The markets of Asia, Africa and South America were as good as cinched.

The directors of the company were all men whose names were familiar to all readers of the financial pages. The publicity work was so well handled and the promises of unnamed insiders as to what the price was going to do were so definite and convincing that a great demand for the new stock was created. The result was that when the books were closed it was found that the stock which was offered to the public at fifty dollars a share had been oversubscribed by 25 per cent.

Think of it! The best the promoters should have expected was to succeed in selling the new stock at that price after weeks of work and after putting up the price to 75 or higher in order to average 50. At that, it meant an advance of about 100 per cent in the old prices of the stocks of the constituent companies. That was the crisis and they did not meet it as it should have been met. It shows you that every business has its own needs.

General wisdom is less valuable than specific savvy. The promoters, delighted by the unexpected oversubscription, concluded that the public was ready to pay any price for any quantity of that stock. And they actually were stupid enough to underallot the stock. After the promoters made up their minds to be hoggish they should have tried to be intelligently hoggish.

What they should have done, of course, was to allot the stock in full. That would have made them short to the extent of 25 per cent of the total amount offered for subscription to the public, and that, of course, would have enabled them to support the stock when necessary and at no cost to themselves. Without any effort on their part they would have been in the strong strategic position that I always try to find myself in when I am manipulating a stock. They could have kept the price from sagging, thereby inspiring confidence in the new stock's price stability and in the underwriting syndicate back of it. They should have remembered that their work was not over when they sold the stock offered to the public. That was only a part of what they had to market.

They thought they had been very successful, but it was not

long before the consequences of their two capital blunders became apparent. The public did not buy any more of the new stock, because the entire market developed reactionary tendencies. The insiders got cold feet and did not support Consolidated Stove; and if insiders don't buy their own stock on recessions, who should? The absence of inside support is generally accepted as a pretty good bear tip.

There is no need to go into statistical details. The price of Consolidated Stove fluctuated with the rest of the market, but it never went above the initial market quotations, which were only a fraction above 50. Barnes and his friends in the end had to come in as buyers in order to keep it above 40. Not to have supported that stock at the outset of its market career was regrettable. But not to have sold all the stock the public subscribed for was much worse.

At all events, the stock was duly listed on the New York Stock Exchange and the price of it duly kept sagging until it nominally stood at 37. And it stood there because Jim Barnes and his associates had to keep it there because then bank had loaned them thirty- five dollars a share on one hundred thousand shares. If the bank ever tried to liquidate that loan there was no telling what the price would break to. The public that had been eager to buy it at 50, now didn't care for it at 37, and probably wouldn't want it at 27.

As time went on the banks' excesses in the matter of extensions of credits made people think. The day of the boy banker was over. The banking business appeared to be on the ragged edge of suddenly relapsing into conservatism. Intimate friends were now asked to pay off loans, for all the world as though they had never played golf with the president.

There was no need to threaten on the lender's part or to plead for more time on the borrower's. The situation was highly uncomfortable for both. The bank, for example, with which my friend Jim Barnes did business, was still kindly disposed. But it was a case of "For heaven's sake take up that loan or we'll all be in a dickens of a mess!"

The character of the mess and its explosive possibilities were enough to make Jim Barnes come to me to ask me to sell the one hundred thousand shares for enough to pay off the bank's three-million-five-hundred-thousand-dollar loan. Jim did not now expect to make a profit on that stock. If the syndicate only made a small loss on it they would be more than grateful.

It seemed a hopeless task. The general market was neither active nor strong, though at times there were rallies, when everybody perked up and tried to believe the bull swing was about to resume.

The answer I gave Barnes was that I'd look into the matter and let him know under what conditions I'd undertake the work. Well, I did look into it. I didn't analyse the company's last annual report. My studies were confined to the stock-market phases of the problem. I was not going to tout the stock for a rise on its earnings or its prospects, but to dispose of that block in the open market. All I considered was what should, could or might help or hinder me in that task.

I discovered for one thing that there was too much stock held by too few people that is, too much for safety and far too much for comfort. Clifton P. Kane & Co., bankers and brokers, members of the New York Stock Exchange, were carrying seventy thousand shares. They were intimate friends of Barnes and had been influential in effecting the consolidation, as they had made a specialty of stove stocks for years. Their customers had been let into the good thing. Ex-Senator Samuel Gordon, who was the special partner in his nephews' firm, Gordon Bros., was the owner of a second block of seventy thousand shares; and the famous Joshua Wolff had sixty thousand shares. This made a total of two hundred thousand shares of Consolidated Stove held by this handful of veteran Wall Street professionals. They did not need any kind person to tell them when to sell their stock. If I did anything in the manipulating line calculated to bring in public buying that is to say, if I made the stock strong and active I could see Kane and Gordon and Wolff unloading, and not in homeopathic doses either. The vision of their two hundred thousand shares Niagaraing into the market was not exactly entrancing. Don't forget that the cream was off the bull movement and that no overwhelming demand was going to be manufactured by my operations, however skilfully conducted they might be. Jim Barnes had no illusions about the job he was modestly sidestepping in my favour. He had given me a waterlogged stock to sell on a bull market that was about to breathe its last. Of course there was no talk in the newspapers about the ending of the bull market, but I knew it, and Jim Barnes knew it, and you bet the bank knew it.

Still, I had given Jim my word, so I sent for Kane, Gordon and Wolff. Their two hundred thousand shares was the sword of Damocles. I thought I'd like to substitute a steel chain for the hair. The easiest way, it seemed to me, was by some sort of reciprocity agreement. If they helped me passively by holding off while I sold the bank's one hundred thousand shares, I would help them actively by trying to make a market: for all of us to unload on. As things were, they couldn't sell one-tenth of their holdings without having Consolidated Stove break wide open, and they knew it so well that they had never dreamed of trying. All I asked of them was judgment in timing the selling and an intelligent unselfishness in order not to be unintelligently selfish. It never pays to be a dog in the manger in Wall Street or anywhere else. I desired to convince them that premature or ill-considered unloading would prevent complete unloading. Time urged.

I hoped my proposition would appeal to them because they were experienced Wall Street men and had no illusions about the actual demand for Consolidated Stove. Clifton P. Kane was the head of a prosperous commission house with branches in eleven cities and customers by the hundreds. His firm had acted as managers for more than one pool in the past.

Senator Gordon, who held seventy thousand shares, was an exceedingly wealthy man. His name was as familiar to the readers of the metropolitan press as though he had been sued for breach of promise by a sixteen-year-old manicurist possessing a five-thousand- dollar mink coat and one hundred and thirty-two letters from the defendant. He had started his nephews in business as brokers and he was a special partner in their firm. He had been in dozens of pools. He had inherited a large interest in the Midland Stove Company and he got one hundred thousand shares of Consolidated Stove for it. He had been carrying enough to disregard Jim Barnes' wild bull tips and had cashed in on thirty thousand shares before the market petered out on him. He told a friend later that he would have sold more only the other big holders, who were old and intimate friends, pleaded with him not to sell any more, and out of regard for them he stopped. Besides which, as I said, he had no market to unload on.

The third man was Joshua Wolff. He was probably the best known of all the traders. For twenty years everybody had known him as one of the plungers on the floor. In bidding up stocks or offering them down he had few equals, for ten or twenty thousand shares meant no more to him than two or three hundred. Before I came to New York I had heard of him as a plunger. He was then trailing with a sporting coterie that played a no limit game, whether on the race track or in the stock market.

They used to accuse him of being nothing but a gambler, but he had real ability and a strongly developed aptitude for the speculative game. At the same time his reputed indifference to highbrow pursuits made him the hero of numberless anecdotes. One of the most widely circulated of the yarns was that Joshua was a guest at what he called a swell dinner and by some oversight of the hostess several of the other guests began to discuss literature before they could be stopped. A girl who sat next to Josh and had not heard him use his mouth except for masticating purposes, turned to him and looking anxious to hear the great financier's opinion asked him, "Oh, Mr. Wolff, what do you think of Balzac?"

Josh politely ceased to masticate, swallowed and answered, "I never trade in them Curb stocks!"

Such were the three largest individual holders of Consolidated Stove. When they came over to see me I told them that if they formed a syndicate to put up some cash and gave me a call on their stock at a little above the market I would do what I could to make a market. They promptly asked me how much money would be required.

I answered, "You've had that stock a long time and you can't do a thing with it. Between the three of you you've got two hundred thousand shares, and you know very well that you haven't the slightest chance of getting rid of it unless you make a market for it. It's got to be some market to absorb what you've got to give it, and it will be wise to have enough cash to pay for whatever stock it may be necessary to buy at first. It's no use to begin and then have to stop because there isn't enough money. I suggest that you form a syndicate and raise six millions in cash. Then give the syndicate a call on your two hundred thousand shares at 40 and put all your stock in escrow. If everything goes well you chaps will get rid of your dead pet and the syndicate will make some money."

As I told you before, there had been all sorts of rumours about my stock-market winnings. I suppose that helped, for nothing succeeds like success. At all events, I didn't have to do much explaining to these chaps. They knew exactly how far they'd get if they tried to play a lone hand. They thought mine was a good plan. When they went away they said they would form the syndicate at once.

They didn't have much trouble in inducing a lot of their friends to join them. I suppose they spoke with more assurance than I had of the syndicate's profits. From all I heard they really believed it, so theirs were no conscienceless tips. At all events the syndicate was formed in a couple of days. Kane, Gordon and Wolff gave calls on the two hundred thousand shares at 40 and I saw to it that the stock itself was put in escrow, so that none of it would come out on the market if I should put up the price. I had to protect myself. More than one promising deal has failed to pan out as expected because the members of the pool or clique failed to keep faith with one another. Dog has no foolish prejudices against eating dog in Wall Street. At the time the second American Steel and Wire Company was brought out the insiders accused one another of breach of faith and trying to unload. There had been a gentlemen's agreement between John W. Gates and his pals and the Seligmans and their banking associates. Well, I heard somebody in a broker's office reciting this quatrain, which was said to have been composed by John W. Gates:

The tarantula jumped on the centipede's back And chortled with ghoulish glee: "I'll poison this murderous son of a gun. If I don't he'll poison me!"

Mind you, I do not mean for one moment to imply that any of my friends in Wall Street would even dream of double-crossing me in a stock deal. But on general principles it is just as well to provide for any and all contingencies. It's plain sense.

After Wolff and Kane and Gordon told me that they had formed their syndicate to put up six millions in cash there was nothing for me to do but wait for the money to come in. I had urged the vital need of haste. Nevertheless the money came in driblets. I think it took four or five installments. I don't know what the reason was, but I remember that I had to send out an S O S call to Wolff and Kane and Gordon.

That afternoon I got some big checks that brought the cash in my possession to about four million dollars and the promise of the rest in a day or two. It began at last to look as though the syndicate might do something before the bull market passed away. At best it would be no cinch, and the sooner I began work the better. The public had not been particularly keen about new market movements in inactive stocks. But a man could do a great deal to arouse interest in any stock with four millions in cash. It was enough to absorb all the probable offerings. If time urged, as I had said, there was no sense in waiting for the other two millions. The sooner the stock got up to 50 the better for the syndicate. That was obvious.

The next morning at the opening I was surprised to see that there were unusually heavy dealings in Consolidated Stove. As I told you before, the stock had been waterlogged for months. The price had been pegged at 37, Jim Barnes taking good care not to let it go any lower on account of the big bank loan at 35. But as for going any higher, he'd as soon expect to see the Rock of Gibraltar shimmying across the Strait as to see Consolidated Stove do any climbing on the tape.

Well, sir, this morning there was quite a demand for the stock, and the price went up to 39. In the first hour of the trading the transactions were heavier than for the whole previous half year. It was the sensation of the day and affected bullishly the entire market. I heard afterwards that nothing else was talked about in the customers' rooms of the commission houses.

I didn't know what it meant, but it didn't hurt my feelings any to see Consolidated Stove perk up. As a rule I do not have to ask about any unusual movement in any stock because my friends on the floor brokers who do business for me, as well as personal friends among the room traders keep me posted. They assume I'd like to know and they telephone me any news or gossip they pick up. On this day all I heard was that there was unmistakable inside buying in Consolidated Stove. There wasn't any washing. It was all genuine. The purchasers took all the offerings from 37 to 39 and when importuned for reasons or begged for a tip, flatly refused to give any. This made the wily and watchful traders conclude that there was something doing; something big. When a stock goes up on buying by insiders who refuse to encourage the world at large to follow suit the ticker hounds begin to wonder aloud when the official notice will be given out.

I didn't do anything myself. I watched and wondered and kept track of the transactions.

But on the next day the buying was not only greater in volume but more aggressive in character. The selling orders that had been on the specialists' books for months at above the pegged price of 37 were absorbed without any trouble, and not enough new selling orders came in to check the rise. Naturally, up went the price. It crossed 40. Presently it touched 42.

The moment it touched that figure I felt that I was justified in starting to sell the stock the bank held as collateral. Of course I figured that the price would go down on my selling, but if my average on the entire line was 37 I'd have no fault to find. I knew what the stock was worth and I had gathered some idea of the vendibility from the months of inactivity. Well, sir, I let them have stock carefully until I had got rid of thirty thousand shares. And the advance was not checked!

That afternoon I was told the reason for that opportune but mystifying rise. It seems that the floor traders had been tipped off after the close the night before and also the next morning before the opening, that I was bullish as blazes on Consolidated Stove and was going to rush the price right up fifteen or twenty points without a reaction, as was my custom that is, my custom according to people who never kept my books. The tipster in chief was no less a personage than Joshua Wolff. It was his own inside buying that started the rise of the day before. His cronies among the floor traders were only too willing to follow his tip, for he knew too much to give wrong steers to his fellows.

As a matter of fact, there was not so much stock pressing on the market as had been feared. Consider that I had tied up three hundred thousand shares and you will realise that the old fears had been well founded. It now proved less of a job than I had anticipated to put up the stock. After all, Governor Flower was right. Whenever he was accused of manipulating his firm's specialties, like Chicago Gas, Federal Steel or B. R. T., he used to say: "The only way I know of making a stock go up is to buy it." That also was the floor traders' only way, and the price responded.

On the next day, before breakfast, I read in the morning papers what was read by thousands and what undoubtedly was sent over the wires to hundreds of branches and out-of-town offices, and that was that Larry Livingston was about to begin active bull operations in Consolidated Stove. The additional details differed. One version had it that I had formed an insiders' pool and was going to punish the overextended short interest. Another hinted at dividend announcements in the near future. Another reminded the world that what I usually did to a stock I was bullish on was something to remember. Still another accused the company of concealing its assets in order to permit accumulation by insiders. And all of them agreed that the rise hadn't fairly started.

By the time I reached my office and read my mail before the market opened I was made aware that the Street was flooded with red-hot tips to buy Consolidated Stove at once. My telephone bell kept ringing and the clerk who answered the calls heard the same question asked in one form or another a hundred times that morning: Was it true that Consolidated Stove was going up? I must say that Joshua Wolff and Kane and Gordon and possibly Jim Barnes handled that little tipping job mighty well.

I had no idea that I had such a following. Why, that morning the buying orders came in from all over the country orders to buy thousands of shares of a stock that nobody wanted at any price three days before. And don't forget that, as a matter of fact, all that the public had to go by was my newspaper reputation as a successful plunger; something for which I had to thank an imaginative reporter or two.

Well, sir, on that, the third day of the rise, I sold Consolidated Stove; and on the fourth day and the fifth; and the first thing I knew I had sold for Jim Barnes the one hundred thousand shares of stock which the Marshall National Bank held as collateral on the three-million-five-hundred-thousand-dollar loan that needed paying off. If the most successful manipulation consists of that in which the desired end is gained at the least possible cost to the manipulator, the Consolidated Stove deal is by all means the most successful of my Wall Street career. Why, at no time did I have to take any stock. I didn't have to buy first in order to sell the more easily later on. I did not put up the price to the highest possible point and then begin my real selling. I didn't even do my principal selling on the way down, but on the way up. It was like a dream of Paradise to find an adequate buying power created for you without your stirring a finger to bring it about, particularly when you were in a hurry. I once heard a friend of Governor Flower's say that in one of the great bull-leader's operations for the account of a pool in B. R. T. the pool sold fifty thousand shares of the stock at a profit, but Flower & Co. got commissions on more than two hundred and fifty thousand shares and W. P. Hamilton says that to distribute two hundred and twenty thousand shares of Amalgamated Copper, James R. Keene must have traded in at least seven hundred thousand shares of the stock during the necessary manipulation. Some commission bill! Think of that and then consider that the only commissions that I had to pay were the commissions on the one hundred thousand shares I actually sold for Jim Barnes. I call that some saving.

Having sold what I had engaged to sell for my friend Jim, and all the money the syndicate had agreed to raise not having been sent in, and feeling no desire to buy back any of the stock I had sold, I rather think I went away somewhere for a short vacation. I do not remember exactly. But I do remember very well that I let the stock alone and that it was not long before the price began to sag. One day, when the entire market was weak, some disappointed bull wanted to get rid of his Consolidated Stove in a hurry, and on his offerings the stock broke below the call price, which was 40. Nobody seemed to want any of it. As I told you before, I wasn't bullish on the general situation and that made me more grateful than ever for the miracle that had enabled me to dispose of the one hundred thousand shares without having to put the price up twenty or thirty points in a week, as the kindly tipsters had prophesied.

Finding no support, the price developed a habit of declining regularly until one day it broke rather badly and touched 32. That was the lowest that had ever been recorded for it, for, as you will remember, Jim Barnes and the original syndicate had pegged it at 37 in order not to have their one hundred thousand shares dumped on the market by the bank.

I was in my office that day peacefully studying the tape when Joshua Wolff was announced. I said I would see him. He rushed in. He is not a very large man, but he certainly seemed all swelled up with anger, as I instantly discovered.

He ran to where I stood by the ticker and yelled, "Hey? What the devil's the matter?"

"Have a chair, Mr. Wolff," I said politely and sat down myself to encourage him to talk calmly.

"I don't want any chair! I want to know what it means!" he cried at the top of his voice. "What does what mean?"

"What in hell are you doing to it?" "What am I doing to what?"

"That stock! That stock!"

"What stock?" I asked him.

But that only made him see red, for he shouted, "Consolidated Stove! What are you doing to it?"

"Nothing! Absolutely nothing. What's wrong?" I said.

He stared at me fully five seconds before he exploded: "Look at the price! Look at it!" He certainly was angry. So I got up and looked at the tape.

I said, "The price of it is now 31-1/4."

"Yeh! Thirty-one and a quarter, and I've got a raft of it."

"I know you have sixty thousand shares. You have had it a long time, because when you originally bought your Gray Stove "

But he didn't let me finish. He said, "But I bought a lot more. Some of it cost me as high as 40! And I've got it yet!"

He was glaring at me so hostilely that I said, "I didn't tell you to buy it." "You didn't what?"

"I didn't tell you to load up with it."

"I didn't say you did. But you were going to put it up"

"Why was I?" I interrupted. He looked at me, unable to speak for anger. When he found his voice again, he said, "You were going to put it up. You had the money to buy it."

"Yes. But I didn't buy a share," I told him. That was the last straw.

"You didn't buy a share, and you had over four millions in cash to buy with? You didn't buy any?"

"Not a share!" I repeated.

He was so mad by now that he couldn't talk plainly. Finally he managed to say, "What kind of a game do you call that?"

He was inwardly accusing me of all sorts of unspeakable crimes. I sure could see a long list of them in his eyes. It made me say to him: "What you really mean to ask me,

Wolff, is, why I didn't buy from you above 50 the stock you bought below 40. Isn't that it?"

"No, it isn't. You had a call at 40 and four millions in cash to put up the price with."

"Yes, but I didn't touch the money and the syndicate has not lost a cent by my operations."

"Look here, Livingston " he began. But I didn't let him say any more.

"You listen to me, Wolff. You knew that the two hundred thousand shares you and Gordon and Kane held were tied up, and that there wouldn't be an awful lot of floating stock to come on the market if I put up the price, as I'd have to do for two reasons: The first to make a market for the stock; and the second to make a profit out of the call at 40. But you weren't satisfied to get 40 for the sixty thousand shares you'd been lugging for months or with your share of the syndicate profits, if any; so you decided to take on a lot of stock under 40 to unload on me when I put the price up with the syndicate's money, as you were sure I meant to do. You'd buy before I did and you'd unload before I did; in all probability I'd be the one to unload on. I suspect you figured on my having to put the price up to 60. It was such a cinch that you probably bought ten thousand shares strictly for unloading purposes, and to make sure somebody held the bag if I didn't, you tipped off everybody in the United States, Canada and Mexico without thinking of my added difficulties. All your friends knew what I was supposed to do. Between their buying and mine you were going to be all hunky. Well, your intimate friends to whom you gave the tip passed it on to their friends after they had bought their lines, and the third stratum of tip-takers planned to supply the fourth, fifth and possibly sixth strata of suckers, so that when I finally came to do some selling I'd find myself anticipated by a few thousands of wise speculators. It was a friendly thought, that notion of yours, Wolff. You can't imagine how surprised I was when Consolidated Stove began to go up before I even thought of buying a single share; or how grateful, either, when the underwriting syndicate sold one hundred thousand shares around 40 to the people who were going to sell those same shares to me at 50 or 60. I sure was a sucker not to use the four millions to make money for them, wasn't I? The cash was supplied to buy stock with, but only if I thought it necessary to do so. Well,I didn't."

Joshua had been in Wall Street long enough not to let anger interfere with business. He cooled off as he heard me, and when I was through talking he said in a friendly tone of voice, "Look here, Larry, old chap, what shall we do?"

"Do whatever you please."

"Aw, be a sport. What would you do if you were in our place?"

"If I were in your place," I said solemnly, "do you know what I'd do?" "What?"

"I'd sell out!" I told him.

He looked at me a moment, and without another word turned on his heel and walked out of my office. He's never been in it since.

Not long after that, Senator Gordon also called. He, too, was quite peevish and blamed me for their troubles. Then Kane joined the anvil chorus. They forgot that their stock had been unsalable in bulk when they formed the syndicate. All they could remember was that I didn't sell their holdings when I had the syndicate's millions and the stock was active at 44, and that now it was 30 and dull as dishwater. To their way of thinking I should have sold out at a good fat profit.

Of course they also cooled down in due time. The syndicate wasn't out a cent and the main problem remained unchanged: to sell their stock. A day or two later they came back and asked me to help them out. Gordon was particularly insistent, and in the end I made them put in their pooled stock at My fee for my services was to be one-half of whatever I got above that figure. The last sale had been at about 30.

There I was with their stock to liquidate. Given general market conditions and specifically the behaviour of Consolidated Stove, there was only one way to do it, and that was, of course, to sell on the way down and without first trying to put up the price, and I certainly would have got stock by the ream on the way up. But on the way down I could reach those buyers who always argue that a stock is cheap when it sells fifteen or twenty points below the top of the movement, particularly when that top is a matter of recent history. A rally is due, in their opinion. After seeing Consolidated Stove sell up to close to 44 it sure looked like a good thing below 30.

It worked out as always. Bargain hunters bought it in sufficient volume to enable me to liquidate the pool's holdings. But do you think that Gordon or Wolff or Kane felt any gratitude? Not a bit of it. They are still sore at me, or so their friends tell me. They often tell people how I did them. They cannot forgive me for not putting up the price on myself, as they expected.

As a matter of fact I never would have been able to sell the bank's hundred thousand shares if Wolff and the rest had not passed around those red-hot bull tips of theirs. If I had worked as I usually do that is, in a logical natural way I would have had to take whatever price I could get. I told you we ran into a declining market. The only way to sell on such a market is to sell not necessarily recklessly but really regardless of price. No other way was possible, but I suppose they do not believe this. They are still angry. I am not. Getting angry doesn't get a man anywhere. More than once it has been borne in on me that a speculator who loses his temper is a goner. In this case there was no aftermath to the grouches. But I'll tell you something curious. One day Mrs. Livingston went to a dressmaker who had been warmly recommended to her. The woman was competent and obliging and had a very pleasing personality. At the third or fourth visit, when the dressmaker felt less like a stranger, she said to Mrs. Livingston: "I hope Air. Livingston puts up Consolidated Stove soon. We have some that we bought because we were told he was going to put it up, and we'd always heard that he was very successful in all his deals."

I tell you it isn't pleasant to think that innocent people may have lost money following a tip of that sort. Perhaps you understand why I never give any myself. That dressmaker made me feel that in the matter of grievances I had a real one against Wolff.

Chapter XXIII

Speculation in stocks will never disappear. It isn't desirable that it should. It cannot be checked by warnings as to its dangers. You cannot prevent people from guessing wrong no matter how able or how experienced they may be. Carefully laid plans will miscarry because the unexpected and even the unexpectable will happen. Disaster may come from a convulsion of nature or from the weather, from your own greed or from some man's vanity; from fear or from uncontrolled hope. But apart from what one might call his natural foes, a speculator in stocks has to contend with certain practices or abuses that are indefensible morally as well as commercially.

As I look back and consider what were the common practices twenty-five years ago when I first came to Wall Street, I have to admit that there have been many changes for the better. The old-fashioned bucket shops are gone, though bucketeering "brokerage" houses still prosper at the expense of men and women who persist in playing the game of getting rich quick. The Stock Exchange is doing excellent work not only in getting after these out-and-out swindlers but in insisting upon strict adherence to its rules by its own members. Many wholesome regulations and restrictions are now strictly enforced but there is still room for improvement. The ingrained conservatism of Wall Street rather than ethical callousness is to blame for the persistence of certain abuses.

Difficult as profitable stock speculation always has been it is becoming even more difficult every day. It was not so long ago when a real trader could have a good working knowledge of practically every stock on the list. In 1901, when J. P. Morgan brought out the United States Steel Corporation, which was merely a consolidation of lesser consolidations most of which were less than two years old, the Stock Exchange had 275 stocks on its list and about 100 in its "unlisted department" ; and this included a lot that a chap didn't have to know anything about because they were small issues, or inactive by reason of being minority or guaranteed stocks and therefore lacking in speculative attractions. In fact, an overwhelming majority were stocks in which there had not been a sale in years. Today there are about 900 stocks on the regular list and in our recent active markets about 600 separate issues were traded in. Moreover, the old groups or classes of stocks were easier to keep track of. They not only were fewer but the capitalization was smaller and the news a trader had to be on the lookout for did not cover so wide a field. But today, a man is trading in everything; almost every industry in the world is represented. It requires more time and more work to keep posted and to that extent stock speculation has become much more difficult for those who operate intelligently.

There are many thousands of people who buy and sell stocks speculatively but the number of those who speculate profitably is small. As the public always is "in" the market to some extent, it follows that there are losses by the public all the time. The speculator's deadly enemies are: Ignorance, greed, fear and hope. All the statute books in the world and all the rules of all the Exchanges on earth cannot eliminate these from the human animal. Accidents which knock carefully conceived plans skyhigh also are beyond regulation by bodies of coldblooded economists or warm-hearted philanthropists. There remains another source of loss and that is, deliberate misinformation as distinguished from straight tips. And because it is apt to come to a stock trader variously disguised and camouflaged, it is the more insidious and dangerous.

The average outsider, of course, trades either on tips or on rumours, spoken or printed, direct or implied. Against ordinary tips you cannot guard. For instance, a lifelong friend sincerely desires to make you rich by telling you what he has done, that is, to buy or sell some stock. His intent is good. If the tip goes wrong what can you do? Also against the professional or crooked tipster the public is protected to about the same extent that he is against gold-bricks or wood-alcohol.

But against the typical Wall Street rumours, the speculating public has neither protection nor redress. Wholesale dealers in securities, manipulators, pools and individuals resort to various devices to aid them in disposing of their surplus holdings at the best possible prices. The circulation of bullish items by the newspapers and the tickers is the most pernicious of all.

Get the slips of the financial news-agencies any day and it will surprise you to see how many statements of an implied semi-official nature they print. The authority is some "leading insider" or "a prominent director" or "a high official" or someone "in authority" who presumably knows what he is talking about. Here are today's slips. I pick an item at random. Listen to this: "A leading banker says it is too early yet to expect a declining market."

Did a leading banker really say that and if he said it why did he say it? Why does he not allow his name to be printed? Is he afraid that people will believe him if he does?

Here is another one about a company the stock of which has been active this week. This time the man who makes the statement is a "prominent director." Now which if any of the company's dozen directors is doing the talking? It is plain that by remaining anonymous nobody can be blamed for any damage that may be done by the statement.

Quite apart from the intelligent study of speculation everywhere the trader in stocks must consider certain facts in connection with the game in Wall Street. In addition to trying to determine how to make money one must also try to keep from losing money. It is almost as important to know what not to do as to know what should be done. It is therefore well to remember that manipulation of some sort enters into practically all advances in individual stocks and that such advances are engineered by insiders with one object in view and one only and that is to sell at the best profit possible. However, the average broker's customer believes himself to be a business man from Missouri if he insists upon being told why a certain stock goes up. Naturally, the manipulators "explain" the advance in a way calculated to facilitate distribution. I am firmly convinced that the public's losses would be greatly reduced if no anonymous statements of a bullish nature were allowed to be printed. I mean statements calculated to make the public buy or hold stocks.

The overwhelming majority of the bullish articles printed on the authority of unnamed directors or insiders convey unreliable and misleading impressions to the public. The public loses many millions of dollars every year by accepting such statements as semi- official and therefore trustworthy.

Say for example that a company has gone through a period of depression in its particular line of business. The stock is inactive. The quotation represents the general and presumably accurate belief of its actual value. If the stock were too cheap at that level somebody would know it and buy it and it would advance. If too dear somebody would know enough to sell it and the price would decline. As nothing happens one way or another nobody talks about it or does anything.

The turn comes in the line of business the company is engaged in. Who are the first to know it, the insiders or the public? You can bet it isn't the public. What happens next? Why, if the improvement continues the earnings will increase and the company will be in position to resume dividends on the stock; or, if dividends were not discontinued, to pay a higher tate. That is, the value of the stock will increase.

Say that the improvement keeps up. Does the management make public that glad fact? Does the president tell the stockholders? Does a philanthropic director come out with a signed statement for the benefit of that part of the public that reads the financial page in the newspapers and the slips of the news agencies? Does some modest insider pursuing his usual policy of anonymity come out with an unsigned statement to the effect that the company's future is most promising? Not this time. Not a word is said by anyone and no statement whatever is printed by newspapers or tickers.

The value-making information is carefully kept from the public while the now taciturn "prominent insiders" go into the market and buy all the cheap stock they can lay their hands on. As this well-informed but unostentatious buying keeps on, the stock rises. The financial reporters, knowing that the insiders ought to know the reason for the rise, ask questions. The unanimously anonymous insiders unanimously declare that they have no news to give out. They do not know that there is any warrant for the rise. Sometimes they even state that they are not particularly concerned with the vagaries of the stock market or the actions of stock speculators.

The rise continues and there comes a happy day when those who know have all the stock they want or can carry. The Street at once begins to hear all kinds of bullish rumours. The tickers tell the traders "on good authority" that the company has definitely turned the corner. The same modest director who did not wish his name used when he said he knew no warrant for the rise in the stock is now quoted of course not by name as saying that the stockholders have every reason to feel greatly encouraged over the outlook.

Urged by the deluge of bullish news items the public begins to buy the stock. These purchases help to put the price still higher. In due course the predictions of the uniformly unnamed directors come true and the company resumes dividend payments; or increases the rate, as the case may be. With that the bullish items multiply. They not only are more numerous than ever but much more enthusiastic. A "leading director," asked point blank for a statement of conditions, informs the world that the improvement is more than keeping up. A "prominent insider," after much coaxing, is finally induced by a news- agency to confess that the earnings are nothing short of phenomenal. A "well-known banker," who is affiliated in a business way with the company, is made to say that the expansion in the volume of sales is simply unprecedented in the history of the trade. If not another order came in the company would run night and day for heaven knows how many months. A "member of the finance committee," in a double-leaded manifesto, expresses his astonishment at the public's astonishment over the stock's rise. The only astonishing thing is the stock's moderation in the climbing line. Anybody who will analyse the forthcoming annual report can easily figure how much more than the market-price the book-value of the stock is.

But in no instance is the name of the communicative philanthropist given.

As long as the earnings continue good and the insiders do not discern any sign of a let up in the company's prosperity they sit on the stock they bought at the low prices. There is nothing to put the price down, so why should they sell? But the moment there is a turn for the worse in the company's business, what happens? Do they come out with statements or warnings or the faintest of hints? Not much. The trend is now downward. Just as they bought without any flourish of trumpets when the company's business turned for the better, they now silently sell. On this inside selling the stock naturally declines. Then the public begins to get the familiar "explanations." A "leading insider" asserts that everything is O.K. and the decline is merely the result of selling by bears who are trying to affect the general market. If on one fine day, after the stock has been declining for some time, there should be a sharp break, the demand for "reasons" or "explanations" becomes clamorous. Unless somebody says something the public will fear the worst. So the news- tickers now print something like this: "When we asked a prominent director of the company to explain the weakness in the stock, he replied that the only conclusion he could arrive at was that the decline today was caused by a bear drive. Underlying conditions are unchanged. The business of the company was never better than at present and the probabilities are that unless something entirely unforeseen happens in the meanwhile, there will be an increase in the rate at the next dividend meeting. The bear party in the market has become aggressive and the weakness in the stock was clearly a raid intended to dislodge weakly held stock." The news-tickers, wishing to give good measure, as likely as not will go on to state that they are "reliably informed" that most of the stock bought on the day's decline was taken by inside interests and that the bears will find that they have sold themselves into a trap. There will be a day of reckoning.

In addition to the losses sustained by the public through believing bullish statements and buying stocks, there are the losses that come through being dissuaded from selling out. The next best thing to having people buy the stock the "prominent insider" wishes to sell is to prevent people from selling the same stock when he does not wish to support or accumulate it. What is the public to believe after reading the statement of the "prominent director"? What can the average outsider think? Of course, that the stock should never have gone down; that it was forced down by bear-selling and that as soon as the bears stop the insiders will engineer a punitive advance during which the shorts will be driven to cover at high prices. The public properly believes this because it is exactly what would happen if the decline had in truth been caused by a bear raid.

The stock in question, notwithstanding all the threats or promises of a tremendous squeeze of the overextended short interest, does not rally. It keeps on going down. It can't help it. There has been too much stock fed to the market from the inside to be digested.

And this inside stock that has been sold by the "prominent directors" and "leading insiders" becomes a football among the professional traders. It keeps on going down. There seems to be no bottom for it. The insiders knowing that trade conditions will adversely affect the company's future earnings do not dare to support that stock until the next turn for the better in the company's business. Then there will be inside buying and inside silence.

I have done my share of trading and have kept fairly well posted on the stock market for many years and I can say that I do not recall an instance when a bear raid caused a stock to decline extensively. What was called bear raiding was nothing but selling based on accurate knowledge of real conditions. But it would not do to say that the stock declined on inside selling or on inside non-buying. Everybody would hasten to sell and when everybody sells and nobody buys there is the dickens to pay.

The public ought to grasp firmly this one point: That the real reason for a protracted decline is never bear raiding. When a stock keeps on going down you can bet there is something wrong with it, either with the market for it or with the company. If the decline were unjustified the stock would soon sell below its real value and that would bring in buying that would check the decline. As a matter of fact, the only time a bear can make big money selling a stock is when that stock is too high. And you can gamble your last cent on the certainty that insiders will not proclaim that fact to the world.

Of course, the classic example is the New Haven. Everybody knows today what only a few knew at the time. The stock sold at 255 in 1902 and was the premier railroad investment of New England. A man in that part of the country measured his respectability and standing in the community by his holdings of it. If somebody had said that the company •was on the road to insolvency he would not have been sent to jail for saying it. They would have clapped him in an insane asylum with other lunatics. But when a new and aggressive president was placed in charge by Mr. Morgan and the debacle began, it was not clear from the first that the new policies would land the road where it did. But as property after property began to be saddled in the Consolidated Road at inflated prices, a few clear sighted observers began to doubt the wisdom of the Mellen policies. A trolley system was bought for two million and sold to the New Haven for $10,000,000; whereupon a reckless man or two committed lese majeste by saying that the management was acting recklessly. Hinting that not even the New Haven could stand such extravagance was like impugning the strength of Gibraltar.

Of course, the first to see breakers ahead were the insiders. They became aware of the real condition of the company and they reduced their holdings of the stock. On their selling as well as on their nonsupport, the price of New England's gilt-edged railroad stock began to yield. Questions were asked, and explanations were demanded as usual; and the usual explanations were promptly forthcoming. "Prominent insiders" declared that there was nothing wrong that they knew of and that the decline was due to reckless bear selling. So the "investors" of New England kept their holdings of New York, New Haven & Hartford Stock. Why shouldn't they? Didn't insiders say there was nothing wrong and cry bear selling? Didn't dividends continue to be declared and paid?

In the meantime the promised squeeze of the bears did not come but new low records did. The insider selling became more urgent and less disguised. Nevertheless public spirited men in Boston were denounced as stock-jobbers and demagogues for demanding a genuine explanation for the stock's deplorable decline that meant appalling losses to everybody in New England who had wanted a safe investment and a steady dividend payer.

That historic break from $255 to $12 a share never was and never could have been a bear drive. It was not started and it was not kept up by bear operations. The insiders sold right along and always at higher prices than they could have done if they had told the truth or allowed the truth to be told. It did not matter whether the price was 250 or 200 or 150 or 100 or 50 or 25, it still was too high for that stock, and the insiders knew it and the public did not. The public might profitably consider the disadvantages under which it labours when it tries to make money buying and selling the stock of a company concerning whose affairs only a few men are in position to know the whole truth.

The stocks which have had the worst breaks in the past 20 years did not decline on bear raiding. But the easy acceptance of that form of explanation has been responsible for losses by the public amounting to millions upon millions of dollars. It has kept people from selling who did not like the way his stock was acting and would have liquidated if they had not expected the price to go right back after the bears stopped their raiding. I used to hear Keene blamed in the old days. Before him they used to accuse Charley Woerishoffer or Addison Cammack. Later on I became the stock excuse.

I recall the case of Intervale Oil. There was a pool in it that put the stock up and found some buyers on the advance. The manipulators ran the price to 50. There the pool sold and there was a quick break. The usual demand for explanations followed. Why was Intervale so weak? Enough people asked this question to make the answer important news. One of the financial news tickers called up the brokers who knew the most about Intervale Oil's advance and ought to be equally well posted as to the decline. What did these brokers, members of the bull pool, say when the news agency asked them for a reason that could be printed and sent broadcast over the country? Why, that Larry Livingston was raiding the market! And that wasn't enough. They added that they were going to "get" him. But of course, the Intervale pool continued to sell. The stock only stood then about $12 a share and they could sell it down to 10 or lower and their average selling price would still be above cost.

It was wise and proper for insiders to sell on the decline. But for outsiders who had paid 35 or 40, it was a different matter. Reading what the tickers printed there outsiders held on and waited for Larry Livingston to get what was coming to him at the hands of the indignant inside pool.

In a bull market and particularly in booms the public at first makes money which it later loses simply by overstaying the bull market. This talk of "bear raids" helps them to overstay. The public should beware of explanations that explain only what unnamed insiders wish the public to believe.

Chapter XXIV

The public always wants to be told. That is what makes tip-giving and tip-taking universal practices. It is proper that brokers should give their customers trading advice through the medium of their market letters as well as by word of mouth. But brokers should not dwell too strongly on actual conditions because the course of the market is always from six to nine months ahead of actual conditions. Today's earnings do not justify brokers in advising their customers to buy stocks unless there is some assurance that six or nine months from today the business outlook will warrant the belief that the same rate of earnings will be maintained. If on looking that far ahead you can see, reasonably clearly, that conditions are developing which will change the present actual power, the argument about stocks being cheap today will disappear. The trader must look far ahead, but the broker is concerned with getting commissions now; hence the inescapable fallacy of the average market letter. Brokers make their living out of commissions from the public and yet they will try to induce the public through their market letters or by word of mouth to buy the same stocks in which they have received selling orders from insiders or manipulators.

It often happens that an insider goes to the head of a brokerage concern and says: "I wish you'd make a market in which to dispose of 50,000 shares of my stock."

The broker asks for further details. Let us say that the quoted price of that stock is 50. The insider tells him: "I will give you calls on 5000 shares at 45 and 5000 shares every point up for the entire fifty thousand shares. I also will give you a put on 50,000 shares at the market."

Now, this is pretty easy money for the broker, if he has a large following and of course this is precisely the kind of broker the insider seeks. A house with direct wires to branches and connections in various parts of the country can usually get a large following in a deal of that kind. Remember that in any event the broker is playing absolutely safe by reason of the put. If he can get his public to follow he will be able to dispose of his entire line at a big profit in addition to his regular commissions.

I have in mind the exploits of an "insider" who is well-known in Wall Street.

He will call up the head customers' man of a large brokerage house. At times he goes even further and calls up one of the junior partners of the firm. He will say something like this:

"Say, old man, I want to show you that I appreciate what you have done for me at various times. I am going to give you a chance to make some real money. We are forming a new company to absorb the assets of one of our companies and we'll take over that stock at a big advance over present quotations. I'm going to send in to you 500 shares of Bantam Shops at $65. The stock is now quoted at 72."

The grateful insider tells the thing to a dozen of the headmen in various big brokerage houses. Now since these recipients of the insider's bounty are in Wall Street what are they going to do when they get that stock that already shows them a profit? Of course, advise every man and woman they can reach to buy that stock. The kind donor knew this. They will help to create a market in which the kind insider can sell his good things at high prices to the poor public.

There are other devices of stock-selling promoters that should be barred. The Exchanges should not allow trading in listed stocks that are offered outside to the public on the partial payment plan. To have the price officially quoted gives a sort of sanction to any stock. Moreover, the official evidence of a free market, and at times the difference in prices, is all the inducement needed.

Another common selling device that costs the unthinking public many millions of dollars and sends nobody to jail because it is perfectly legal, is that of increasing the capital stock exclusively by reason of market exigencies. The process does not really amount to much more than changing the color of the stock certificates.

The juggling whereby 2 or 4 or even 10 shares of new stock are given in exchange for one of the old, is usually prompted by a desire to make the old merchandise more easily vendible. The old price was $1 per pound package and hard to move. At 25 cents for a quarter-pound box it might go better; and perhaps at 27 or 30 cents.

Why does not the public ask why the stock is made easy to buy? It is a case of the Wall Street philanthropist operating again, but the wise trader bewares of the Greeks bearing gifts. It is all the warning needed. The public disregards it and loses millions of dollars annually.

The law punishes whoever originates or circulates rumors calculated to affect adversely the credit or business of individuals or corporations, that is, that tend to depress the values of securities by influencing the public to sell. Originally, the chief intention may have been to reduce the danger of panic by punishing anyone who doubted aloud the solvency of banks in times of stress. But of course, it serves also to protect the public against selling stocks below their real value. In other words the law of the land punishes the disseminator of bearish items of that nature.

How is the public protected against the danger of buying stocks above their real value? Who punishes the distributor of unjustified bullish news items? Nobody; and yet, the public loses more money buying stocks on anonymous inside advice when they are too high than it does selling out stocks below their value as a consequence of bearish advice during so-called "raids."

If a law were passed that would punish bull liars as the law now punishes bear liars, I believe the public would save millions.

Naturally, promoters, manipulators and other beneficiaries of anonymous optimism will tell you that anyone who trades on rumors and unsigned statements has only himself to blame for his losses. One might as well argue that any one who is silly enough to be a drug addict is not entitled to protection.

The Stock Exchange should help. It is vitally interested in protecting the public against unfair practices. If a man in position to know wishes to make the public accept his statements of fact or even his opinions, let him sign his name. Signing bullish items would not necessarily make them true. But it would make the "insiders" and "directors" more careful.

The public ought always to keep in mind the elementals

of stock trading. When a stock is going up no elaborate explanation is needed as to why it is going up. It takes continuous buying to make a stock keep on going up. As long as it does so, with only small and natural reactions from time to time, it is a pretty safe proposition to trail along with it. But if after a long steady rise a stock turns and gradually begins to go down, with only occasional small rallies, it is obvious that the line of least resistance has changed from upward to downward. Such being the case why should any one ask for explanations? There are probably very good reasons why it should go down, but these reasons are known only to a few people who either keep those reasons to themselves, or else actually tell the public that the stock is cheap. The nature of the game as it is played is such that the public should realise that the truth cannot be told by the few who know.

Many of the so-called statements attributed to "insiders" or officials have no basis in fact. Sometimes the insiders are not even asked to make a statement, anonymous or signed. These stories are invented by somebody or other who has a large interest in the market. At a certain stage of an advance in the market-price of a security the big insiders are not averse to getting the help of the professional element to trade in that stock. But while the insider might tell the big plunger the right time to buy, you can bet he will never tell when is the time to sell. That puts the big professional in the same position as the public, only he has to have a market big enough for him to get out on. Then is when you get the most misleading "information." Of course, there are certain insiders who cannot be trusted at any stage of the game. As a rule the men who are at the head of big corporations may act in the market upon their inside knowledge, but they don't actually tell lies. They merely say nothing, for they have discovered that there are times when silence is golden.

I have said many times and cannot say it too often that the experience of years as a stock operator has convinced me that no man can consistently and continuously beat the stock market though he may make money in individual stocks on certain occasions. No matter how experienced a trader is the possibility of his making losing plays is always present because speculation cannot be made 100 per cent safe. Wall Street professionals know that acting on "inside" tips will break a man more quickly than famine, pestilence, crop failures, political readjustments or what might be called normal accidents. There is no asphalt boulevard to success in Wall Street or anywhere else. Why additionally block traffic?

-THE END-

www.ingramcontent.com/pod-product-compliance
Lightning Source LLC
Chambersburg PA
CBHW051359240926
51852CB00002B/65
* 9 7 8 9 3 4 8 5 8 4 7 2 4 *